# THE RISE OF
# EUROPEAN
# LIBERALISM

# HAROLD J. LASKI

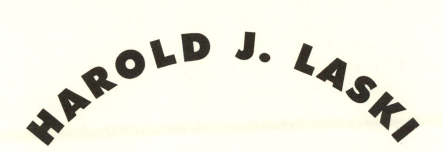

# THE RISE OF
# EUROPEAN LIBERALISM

### with a new introduction by
### JOHN L. STANLEY

**TRANSACTION PUBLISHERS**
New Brunswick (U.S.A.) and London (U.K.)

Library of Congress Catalog Number: 96-20337
ISBN: 1-56000-845-8
Printed in the United States of America

Library of Congress Cataloging-in-Publication Data

Laski, Harold Joseph, 1893–1950.
    The rise of European liberalism / Harold J. Laski ; with a new introduction by John L. Stanley.
        p.  cm.
    Originally published: London : George Allen & Unwin, 1936.
    Includes bibliographical references and index.
    ISBN 1-56000-845-8 (pbk. : alk. paper)
    1. Liberalism—Europe, Western—History.  I. Title.
JC574.2.E85L37   1996
320.5'1'094—dc20                                        96-20337
                                                            CIP

# INTRODUCTION TO THE
# TRANSACTION EDITION

PERHAPS the most remarkable aspect of the career and writings of Harold Laski is that while there are at least fourteen books devoted to his life and thought, practically none of Laski's own vast work remains in print today. Even this book, Laski's exciting and provocative account of the rise of liberalism and one of the few of his works to be found in recommended readings in political theory, has for the last generation been found mainly in university libraries.

Laski's decline in popularity can be explained by his persistent left-wing positions in a postwar society whose political moderation and conservatism contrasts markedly with the radical times in which this book was written; and even the radicals of the 1960s were contemptuous of the historical perspective on which Laski's own work rests. Indeed as an exponent of the historical method in political theory, Laski's fame is both derived from and is victimized by the truths which that method illuminates.

Laski's brilliant first work depicted the anti-statism in Victorian religious thought as if these ideas were of lasting relevance. Yet as Laski became increasingly attracted to Marxist methods, he became all the more strongly convinced that this same historical method demonstrates that political ideas, including anti-statism, cannot transcend the circumstances that give birth to them. When Laski's scholarship became tied to his own increasingly statist political program, he at first became immensely popular at a time in which statist ideas were the order of the day. With the decline of their popularity, the more his later efforts became as dated as his political agenda. At certain crucial moments, he overlooked both the possibility of a trans-historical anti-centralism as well as the truths of his own historicism applied to his own ideas.

Yet, at other moments, despite his growing conviction that ideas vanish with their times, Laski remained haunted by remnants of his former viewpoint that ideas can endure beyond their times. Nowhere is that tension between temporality and permanence better shown than in the present work. We see depicted here some of the principles of liberal thought that are still very much with us and with which Laski was always in great sympathy. But this depiction is made against a backdrop of a Marxist methodology that regards liberalism as being tied to bourgeois class structures that are destined to disappear. Indeed, the very tension between Laski's recognition of the lasting testament of liberalism and his Marxist historicism which predicted liberalism's disappearance lends this book its drama. Furthermore, and somewhat ironically, even Laski's historical perspective strengthened the historical tradition in political thought which is regnant today.

Laski's life-long commitment to certain liberal principles is seen in the many accounts of his colorful career, most recently depicted with great brilliance by Isaac Kramnick and Barry Sheerman.[1] By all these accounts, Laski was a meteor; he sky-rocketed to political and academic prominence at a very young age. Writing some twenty-five books and thousands of essays, often in a single uncorrected draft and referring to sources culled from an astonishing memory and an equally astonishing erudition, he was no less effective as a teacher. His lectures drew packed classrooms, and to hear his former students tell it, they were highly entertaining. He learned and remembered the names of his students and influenced a wide array of future scholars and world leaders including Joseph and John Kennedy and J. Krishna Mennon, India's future foreign minister. He was no less dazzling as a dinner companion and story teller. He adored recounting stories of his friends in high places, some of which were reputedly invented or highly exaggerated. In any case, by the 1930s, he had become a shining light of both liberalism and socialism on three continents.[2] Yet soon after his untimely death in 1950 at the age of 57 most of his political writings fell into oblivion.

Born in June 1893 to a politically influential Jewish family in Manchester, the frail, often bed-ridden boy found refuge in books. Yet since his father, Nathan Laski, the untitled "king" of Manchester Jewry, was heavily involved in Liberal politics, the young Laski was exposed to political life at an early age. One of his earliest memories was of the young, then-Liberal Winston Churchill practicing speeches in front of a bedroom mirror in his father's house. At Oxford, what Kramnick and Sheerman call "Laski's combative and self-confident personality" allowed this grammar school outsider to shine in Oxford Union debates.

But even his success at persuasion didn't prevent Laski from being attracted to less verbal politics. Not only was he drawn to feminism, with which he had become closely identified in Union debates, but to syndicalism and its concept of direct action. Indeed, he remained sympathetic to the anti-statist position of the syndicalists until 1920.[3] After graduation from Oxford in 1914, Laski went to work as an anti-war editorialist for the *Daily Herald*. Even so, he tried to enlist in the army, but was rejected for his weak heart. He may have predicted this rejection because of his own frail health, for it seems that there was little feeling of guilt when he and his wife Frida, whom he had married in 1911, sailed for Montreal to take up a position as lecturer in history at McGill University.

It was at McGill that Laski met Felix Frankfurter, who was to remain a life-long friend even after Laski's turn to Marxism in the 1930s. It was through the Frankfurter connection that Laski was able to move to Harvard. There he dazzled students and colleagues and began to build an extensive network of admirers among some of the luminaries of the newly emerging American political establishment, including Pound, Brandeis, and Herbert Croly, the editor of the *New Republic*, with which Laski became closely involved. Later he would befriend Franklin and Eleanor Roosevelt, Edward R. Murrow, and Max Lerner among many others. Then of course there was Oliver Wendell Holmes, whose correspondence with Laski has proven to be among the most enduring of Laski's works.[4]

Despite his friendship with the statist Croly, the young Harvard instructor was still an anti-centralist, and these views were reflected in his first books, *Studies in the Problem of Sovereignty* and *Authority in the Modern State,* published by Yale University Press in 1917 and 1919. Conceived as a part of a larger theory of the state, the first of these works focussed on the anti-statist component of Victorian religious controversies while the second was a study of the political theory of the Catholic reaction in France. Both had as their stated purpose to demonstrate that the idea of absolute sovereignty is a myth, because virtually all social orders which feign unity must rely on the consent of a plurality of men. The ideologues of the "state" (by which Laski means central political authority), whether ancient, medieval or modern, have failed to realize that there is "no epoch in social history where organized resistance to state-decision has not its root in some deep grievance honestly conceived. It was so in 1381...and in 1789."[5]

To be sure, these accounts were historical narratives, and Laski predicted that the specifically modern doctrine of sovereignty was as sure to disappear as the doctrine of the divine right of kings. But this disappearance was based on other transcendent principles, principles couched in terms of a pragmatic pluralism (supposedly originating in Aristotle) which denies that the part can only be defined in connection to the whole: the State "is only one of the associations to which a man's personality attracts him."

Both of these early works staunchly defended liberal principles of freedom of speech and individual expression against state authority, and the second book was written against the backdrop of an intense flurry of controversy provoked by Laski's support of the Boston Police strike and his criticism of the "Red Scare" of 1919. Despite his popularity, Laski made numerous enemies by his positions on these questions, and it did not help that he was often guilty of a conceitedness which was hardly mitigated by his tendency to exaggerate the extent of his network of friends.[6] Still, the self-centeredness that had so alienated certain acquaintances was of course not very surprising in light of the very real impression he made on people. When Laski returned to England in 1920, his politics leaving the Harvard faculty and Board of Overseers in turmoil, he had published three university press books, several important scholarly essays and numerous reviews and essays in magazines. He was twenty-seven years old.[7]

Many of Laski's connections were genuine enough,[8] and his friendships gained him a post at the London School of Economics and Political Science, where he was to remain for the rest of his life. Laski was at first nominally aligned with the Liberals, the party of his family, but his increasing dislike of Lloyd George's opportunism and the close ties he made with Sidney and Beatrice Webb soon encouraged his move away from an anti-statist liberalism, toward Fabianism and the Labour party. By 1921, Laski had immersed himself in Fabian committee work and tirelessly ground out Fabian tracts, the most important of which was *Karl Marx: An Essay* (1923), an appreciative work, but far more critical of Marx's economic determinism than is the present volume. He also devoted considerable time to worker education, giving countless lectures to workers groups around Britain, and he helped Haldane found the British Institute for Adult Education. The influence of this institute was astonishing. By the late 1930s, according to Kramnick and Sheerman, 87 percent of all British laborers had done some studies in their working career.[9]

Labour politics was reflected more directly in Laski's next work, *A Grammar of Politics* (1925), where the state is depicted much more positively as a means of controlling capitalist power and making equal opportunity realizable. Here he sees the welfare state and nationalization of some industry as means toward those ends, though he also envisions decision-making by teams of laborers on the factory floor. Furthermore Laski continued his liberal defense of freedom of expression and conscience against the power of the state, once again against a background of a "red scare" and prosecution of Communist party leaders—this time in Britain.

In the wake of the 1926 General Strike, Laski was appointed an arbitrator on the Industrial Court, an agency established for the resolution of industrial disputes, on which he was to serve for the rest of his life. He also wrote the immensely popular *Communism*, a work that was highly critical of the sectarianism of the communists and which advised against alliances with them. The book was widely praised (except of course by the communists) and solidified Laski's already extensive connections with the Labour party establishment. Several times Laski had been asked to stand for Labour as a Parliamentary candidate; while he always refused, he campaigned in over thirty constituencies during the general election of 1929 which brought Labour to power. The following year he became an immensely popular weekly columnist for the revitalized *Daily Herald,* the first paper in the world to sell 2 million copies a day.[10]

While Laski became gradually more identified with the Labour party left during this period—if only at first in contrast to a leadership that, in his view, was largely devoid of any political theory—it did not mean that he abandoned the staunchly liberal defense of free expression which he reiterated in *Liberty in the Modern State* (1930). Yet after the Great MacDonald Betrayal in September 1931 which brought down the Labour government and ushered in a "National" coalition still led by MacDonald, Laski became more solidly identified with the Left. It was during this "pink decade" of the 1930s, one which Max Beloff dubbed "the age of Laski," that Laski became the premier spokesman of the Left in both England and America.[11] Laski's attacks on MacDonald, who was even expelled from his own local party, attracted great controversy. The "betrayal," which he regarded as a "palace coup" in which George V unconstitutionally manipulated events, seems to have solidified Laski's conviction that when the capitalist class is truly endangered, it will resort to any methods—even unconstitutional ones—to retain its power.[12]

But in light of these views, how could Labour defend itself against communist ridicule of parliamentary politics? Laski's response to this dilemma, which involved him even more deeply in Labour politics, was characteristic of his two-fold allegiance to socialism as well as to liberal constitutional principles. Laski's hope was, in his biographers' words, "to try to craft parliamentary solutions to lay to rest the potential for extra-parliamentary sabotage by the forces of capitalism."[13] This proved at times to be a difficult balancing act. Hoping that the 1931 debacle would purge the party of centrists and liberals, Laski, with Stafford Cripps, formed the Socialist League and proclaimed its goal of a party in which every member was a socialist.

In 1933 he published *Democracy in Crisis,* which, though his most "centralist" book yet—one that rejected pluralism, federalism, and guild socialism—nonetheless continued to demonstrate Laski's sometimes conflicting inner voices of liberalism and socialism. On the one hand, he argued that the ruling powers would not sit idly by during the socialist revolution (a theme repeated in the present volume)[14] and even suggested that a new socialist government might resort to emergency powers or constitutional dictatorship. On the other hand, he assumed that the British ruling classes would consent to peaceful revolution, and he affirmed his commitment to liberal parliamentary institutions.

The backlash in the party against the former viewpoint was predictable. The moderates in the party mobilized to counteract what they saw as the embarrassment that Laski had caused the party: Labour's program remained Keynesian and moderate. While Laski was a popular figure in the Labour ranks, he had yet to win enough support to win a place on the party's National Executive Council. It appeared that

Laski was headed for even further marginalization when in 1935 he wrote *The State in Theory and Practice* in which he openly adopted a Marxist viewpoint—albeit a noncommunist one—and became virtually the first prominent British academic to do so.[15] Once again he stated his firm commitment to civil liberties and the faith that the ruling classes in Britain would listen to reason and adhere to British traditions; but once again, only now in fully Marxist terms, he asserted that the class struggle dominated public life.

A year later, in 1936, Laski attempted to confront on a more theoretical level the dilemma that had permeated his previous left-wing works, addressing the relationship between socialism and the liberal tradition. *The Rise of European Liberalism* is a historical survey of the development of liberal thought, from its earliest whispers in Protestant thought to its significance for the "Red Decade" of the 1930s. Yet while the work is astonishing in its breadth and insight, its subtitle, *An Essay in Interpretation,* is certainly fitting. This is not a textbook or a work whose judgments were meant to go unchallenged. Indeed, its significance for the English-speaking world is that it became the standard Marxist interpretation of liberal thought, a viewpoint later dubbed by C.B. MacPherson, one of Laski's many admiring students, as the political theory of "possessive individualism."

Laski argues here that liberalism is a philosophy that came into existence with the rise of capitalism and thus functions primarily as an ideological defense of private property in a business civilization. A socialist revolution overthrowing the rule of property will overthrow liberalism. That is, in standard Marxian fashion, Laski claims that liberalism contains in its property-defending birth "the conditions of its own destruction."[16] Laski depicts a tendency in liberalism that has often been at odds with its bourgeois defense of property, a progressive or social action tendency that would regulate property in order to strengthen other liberal values; but, he says, most liberals cannot radicalize themselves to the point where their ideology would become compatible with regulation. Liberalism's progressive or "social" side is doomed to defeat, because throughout its history the "bourgeois" side of the ideology has always prevailed; and Laski predicts that this will continue to be the case.

Yet Laski was still committed to liberty and to many democratic institutions that were inspired by the very liberalism that was supposedly destined to be swept away by the socialist tide. Indeed, despite its brevity, the present work offers so many rich examples of the social action side of liberalism that we might well ask if Laski undermines his own case for its eventual defeat. Despite its brilliance, then, the present work continues the ambiguities of Laski's own thought in regard to liberalism's supposed incompatibility with socialism.

The inability to clear up many of these ambiguities in the course of the four chapters of this work raises four corresponding interrelated methodological problems with Laski's Marxist historical approach. This approach, as outlined in Chapter I, downplays (even if it does not efface) the independence of ideas while stressing their dependence on economic and class relationships, and emphasizes the causal importance of material historical forces upon ideas rather more than the reciprocal influence of ideas and concrete action. First, if, on this general basis, Laski can go on to claim that liberalism "like all social philosophies...could not transcend the [historical] medium in which it was born,"[17] how can he attribute trans-historical characteristics to liberalism and extol the permanent contributions of liberal ideas as he does?

Second, if, as Laski says in Chapter II, at the time of the "birth" of liberalism in the seventeenth century, the predominant strand of liberalism was Lockean and if Lockeanism was the ideology of the propertied classes, how do we account for the quite radical expressions of liberalism—depicted by Laski himself—that were made by the Levellers who preceded Locke and by the later reformers who were influenced by him?

Third, in Chapter III Laski depicts the political victory of liberalism's conservative defense of property over the "leftist" or social current in the eighteenth century. In so doing has he excessively minimized the degree to which the latter current was still alive as an expression of protest or of possible victories in future times? That is, does he link too closely the fate of political theories with the fate of parties espousing them?

Finally, from what we now know, how valid is the thesis of Laski's concluding chapter that the social revolution must be inspired by theoretical constructions that are external to liberalism because social

xvi

action is incompatible with liberalism's essentially bourgeois nature?

Has Laski either committed a genetic fallacy by overestimating the lasting influence of the circumstances which provided the original grounding of liberalism or has he misinterpreted those historical circumstances? Or has he misinterpreted the liberal texts themselves? Has he done all of these things?

Despite these possible shortcomings of "Marxist" historiography, the wealth of knowledge that Laski displays in this book, the abundant information it provides, certainly makes it more than a *livre de circonstance* of the "red decade." Furthermore, the four interrelated problems that emerge in the course of Laski's presentation illuminate the book's valuable lasting qualities precisely because of the questions it raises—questions that are very much alive today in scholarly debates—rather than for the answers it provides. It is to the first of these questions relating to the lasting qualities of ideas in general that we should now turn.

I

Laski begins his introductory chapter by giving a general definition of liberalism as promoting secularism, minority rights, and of course freedom of thought and inquiry. These are the aspects of liberalism that apply "as a rule, though by no means universally" and which Laski embraces wholeheartedly. But, he goes on to say that because it "always serves the ends"[18] of men of property, liberalism "has always taken a negative attitude to social action...always preferred to bless individual innovation than to sanction the uniformities sought by political power" and "always tended to make an antithesis between liberty and equality." These negative characteristics of liberalism are what Laski condemns.

In subsequent chapters, Laski will admit to a social action side of liberalism, one which arises in response to changing historical conditions. Here, in saying that liberalism has "always" been negative toward social action, he is imputing a trans-historical character to liberalism, an imputation which contradicts his own emphasis on the historicity of ideas. But while attributing a universal character to liberalism's opposition to social action, Laski seems anxious to assert that the principles of tolerance and liberty to which he so enthusiastically subscribes "had no title to universality."[19]

Laski asserts that the history of liberalism is not a "conscious and persistent search" for these good libertarian ends. Instead, he suggests that these good ends were the unintended, unconscious by-products that served the consciously intended ends of safeguarding private property. Consequently, when liberalism seeks to make conscious universal claims beyond its original narrow, propertied scope, it cannot succeed in doing so because somehow its very historical origins act as a fatal check to those claims.

Rather than address the possible counterclaim that liberals were conscious of all of their goals and that this consciousness extended its reach beyond its original scope, Laski seems to say that the crude ideological dimension of liberalism, its defense of property,

xviii

was consciously held because that is the aspect of liberalism that has been historically realized. Its less conscious dimension, the universalist defense of liberty, is its unfulfilled or "utopian" aspect. But of course a civil libertarian like Laski cannot question the validity or the appeal of the defense of liberty simply because that defense has been unfulfilled. What he must show is that the universalist claims of liberalism in particular and of ideas in general have had less historical impact than have the material interests behind them; and he begins his demonstration of this point by criticizing Max Weber's famous account of the relationship between the rise of the Protestant work ethic and the rise of liberal capitalism.

Protestantism, in Laski's view, aided the development of liberalism and of capitalism as an unintended consequence rather than (as he says Weber contends) an intended one: thus, Weber and his disciples have committed a grave anachronism by projecting a capitalist work ethic back onto a theology that was, if taken in its actual historical context, "in full accord with the later view of the medieval canonists."[20] In particular, the Calvinist idea of the "calling," which Weber says gives such force to the work ethic, was actually at the time of its origins not too far from St. Thomas Aquinas. The specifically Protestant idea of the calling was a century and a half old when it became, in Laski's terms, "infected with the capitalist spirit... and by that time, it had at least as fundamentally influenced the Catholic attitude as the Puritan."[21] (Indeed even the Puritans "were not men to compromise with Mammon.")[22]

Protestantism, then, did not act as a causal force of capitalism as much as it "synchronized with, and, in part, was caused by, the great economic dislocations of the time."[23] Thus, it was only later that a new attitude develops which begins to equate failure with the absence of grace. A sense that private advantage makes for public good comes later to permeate the outlook of Puritanism. But if Laski can say that Protestantism was taken up only later by capitalist classes, that is, can adapt to new circumstances and alter the meaning of its doctrines according to new historically shaped class interests, why couldn't other ideas exhibit a similar staying power and be accepted by classes other than those who originally adhered to them? In any case, is Laski right in ascribing a narrow class base to liberalism in general and even to Lockean liberalism in particular?

II

In his second chapter, devoted to the seventeenth century, Laski turns to the concrete development of liberalism. In the course of his account there emerge, more fully, two currents in liberalism: one bourgeois, property-oriented, individualistic, and devoted to the limited state; the other radical, experimental, utopian, universalistic, statist, and not "always" hostile to social action. While here depicting this second, radical current more openly than he did in the previous chapter, Laski maintains that it lies "outside the mainstream" and hence beyond the thought of John Locke whom he appropriately describes as having "defined the essential outlines of liberal doctrine for the next two centuries."[24] "Leftist" or social liberalism was marginalized because it was politically vanquished by Locke's cautious, property-defending theory, whose historical roots were more firmly planted in the time.

Laski argues that since the original purpose of the Lockean doctrine was the protection of property owners, it was quite different from the more radical current of thought in the revolutionary period of the generations preceding the Second Treatise. Hence, Laski wishes to dissociate Locke from the broader, more egalitarian demands of the failed social revolution of the left wing of the English Levellers whose generous proposals of poor relief by a positive state "intimate the emergence of a proletarian ideology" more suited to the nineteenth century than the seventeenth.[25] Instead, Locke is most representative of what Laski calls the "mood" of the men of the time: "rationalism, toleration, constitutional government, without excess in any."[26] Locke's defense of life, liberty, and property, his theory of limited government to protect those rights, his individualistic view of man and his obligation to labor, were stated "in such a way as to offer the rising middle class exactly the ideas they were seeking"; thus, unlike the more radical Leveller programs, Locke's defense did not apply to propertyless laborers.[27]

However, if liberalism is the ideology of the propertied classes and as such a historically rooted reality, how can Laski also say that Lockeanism "was a conception fantastically untrue when Locke made it"?[28] Such a "utopian" presentation of liberalism entails a higher degree of independence from the historical forces of its birth—especially when the theoretical baby grows and matures. In fact Laski's view of Locke's political theory as one that benefits landowners, farmers, merchants, and shopkeepers is supplemented by what he calls the "loose ends" of Locke's philosophy. As he notes, Locke's theories led to Berkeley's idealism, Hume's skepticism, Kant's categories as well as leftist currents "outside the mainstream": Marx's labor theory, Godwin's anarchism, and the thought of various radicals, utopians, and reformers who were not "conscious exponents" of liberalism.[29] This is not a bad performance for one whose political theory Laski depicted previously as "nothing so much as a contract between a group of businessmen who form a limited liability company whose memorandum of association forbids to the directors all those practices of which the Stuarts had...been guilty."[30]

Whatever the ambiguities of Laski's account, it has, as we have noted, helped to stimulate a wide degree of subsequent debate. Since Laski outlines two directions for liberal thought in general (even if he hesitates to give enough credit to one of them), he has thus helped to open the possibility for future scholars to see more radical directions for Lockean thought in particular. On the one hand, Laski's own "limited liability company" interpretation of Locke was made more precise a decade after Laski's death by his student C.B. MacPherson who penned what became the standard Marxist interpretation of Locke, *The Political Theory of Possessive Individualism*—a book

whose views were affirmed by Neal Wood a generation later. Indeed MacPherson stressed the property-
owning ideology of the Levellers much more than
Laski did.[31]

On the other hand, more recent scholarship has
claimed a far stronger connection between Locke and
the programs of the radical Levellers than Laski
would admit. The most prominent critic of the Laski-
Wood-MacPherson thesis of the bourgeois Locke is
Richard Ashcraft, also a Marxist and a strong proponent of the historical school in political theory.
Ashcraft's work, *Revolutionary Politics and Locke's Two
Treatises of Government,*[32] agrees with Laski that
Locke's theory is an ideological reflection of historically specific interests. He also argues with Laski and
against MacPherson that the radical Levellers were
social and egalitarian; yet he differs from both in regard to Locke's radicalism. By virtue of Locke's close
ties to Shaftsbury and to former Levellers, some of
whom had demanded suffrage for day laborers,
Ashcraft depicts Locke's Second Treatise as a radical moral egalitarian manifesto upholding the Leveller claims to the right of all to subsistence rather than
as a bourgeois defense of property.[33]

David Wootton has recently challenged Ashcraft
and argued for a more conservative Locke.[34] Indeed
Ashcraft does admit to Locke's conservative defense
of social and economic inequality, and this admission is at least a step in the direction of Laski's view
of the contradiction between liberalism's defense of
political equality and its justification for economic
inequality. Certainly, Locke justifies enclosure of land

from the common. In any case, while Ashcraft's book seems to be part of a larger project that, as opposed to Laski, attempts to reconcile the liberal and socialist traditions, Laski's own book is also rich in examples of a visible "leftist" current of liberalism in Locke's time and in the century following Locke.

III

In his chapter on the Enlightenment, Laski says that France was the creative center of liberalism during the eighteenth century. In England theoretical construction was little more than a mopping up operation on behalf of property-defending liberalism and was devoid of originality. For only in Britain had the middle classes and capitalism already been firmly launched.[35] According to Laski's rich and complex account of the eighteenth century, British liberal thought achieves its highest expression in Adam Smith's defense of free trade and ironically in Edmund Burke's conservative defense of property.

Laski devotes as much space to Smith as he does to any other figure including Locke. In this light it is interesting that rather than stress Smith's originality, Laski depicts him as the "representative man" of the eighteenth century whose ideas are "a summary of a doctrine being beaten out of the needs of his time."[36] In Smith the doctrines of liberalism that began fully in the previous century are now completed; inheriting Locke's individualism and defense of property, Smith drove the ideas of the Second Treatise to their logical conclusion: if Locke sees the need for minimal state interference in property, Smith sees little need for it at all; if Locke implied the maxims of business enterprise, Smith elevated these maxims to the status of theology.

It is interesting that Laski takes care to observe in Smith "an uneasy sense that the limits of state interference were less easy to define in concrete than in abstract terms." He notes too, the radical dimension of Smith's thought: a dislike of the silent shareholder, an affection for the workingman, the indiscreet confession that the function of the state was to allow the rich to sleep soundly.[37] But Laski is clear that Smith's texts criticizing capitalism are overwhelmed by the texts promoting laissez-faire. It is through the triumph of this dimension of Smith, one that solidifies liberalism's connections with the established order, that Laski connects the most prominent British liberal of the eighteenth century to the founder of conservatism, Edmund Burke, who had arrived independently at a laissez-faire standpoint similar to Smith's.

It is clear that Laski has the highest respect for Burke, whose criticism of the French Revolution is "in substance still the soundest we have," and whom he had dubbed "the greatest man since Milton."[38] Indeed what is vital in Burke's outlook, according to Laski, "is as living to-day as when he first uttered it." For Laski it was the Whig-liberal Burke who "more than any other thinker...gave the metaphysical outline of Locke's theory of the state that substantial content it has possessed down to our time."[39] It was the conservative Burke who solidified the Lockean view of property rights by placing it within a long

British tradition.[40] For Laski, property rights were "the inarticulated major premise of Burke's thinking," one which implied a minimal economic role for the state, labor as the source of wealth, an autonomous labor market, an implied labor contract and the common interest of classes and competitors.[41]

All this is part of Laski's larger case for the inherently conservative character of the liberal defense of property and for the diminutive role played by "leftist" or social liberalism. He goes to great lengths to stress that Burke's articulation of Lockean doctrine and his separation of that tradition from the French Revolution completed the dissociation of the thinking of the general company of English liberals from any social content. Instead they were concerned with superficial political forms. "Nothing they said indicated any realization of the relation between property and power."[42] Such interest in the social question that was shown was grudging and more in the interest of disciplining the working classes than of emancipating them.

While attributing greater creativity to French liberals in this period, Laski still tries to minimize their treatment of the social question. He admits that in France in the eighteenth century undoubtedly "there is immense pre-occupation with social problems"; that on the problem of poverty alone, there is a vast inventive literature even among the clergy; that there are a number of highly detailed plans for national workshops; that Mably even defends a communist framework of social organization; that Linguet predicts revolution and social catastrophe arising from

xxvi

injustice. Yet all of this is minimized as mostly utopian or as an exercise in futility or because, Mably aside, it fails to attack the principle of private property and free enterprise. Laski again implies that the social current in liberalism is less significant because it is speculative and not specifically Marxian.

Yet such speculation cannot be dismissed as idle utopianism when the French Revolution actually brought the power of property into political speculation, as Laski notes. Certainly he observes that the thinkers who contributed to that event, Linguet, Meslier, Mably, and of course Rousseau, addressed the social question. Laski does not deny a liberal dimension to Rousseau and takes care to note the "special genius" and even a "proletarian nuance" to "Rousseau's assault upon the adequacy of social foundations."[43] Yet the inspirer of Marat, Robespierre, Savigny, and of the great Kant receives far less attention than Voltaire, "the most characteristic representative" of the period in France.

Laski compares Voltaire's contempt for "the rabble" and for "popular enlightenment" to that of Burke.[44] But if Laski can say that "there is nothing [in Voltaire] of that passionate indignation against an unjust social order which is the clue to all of Rousseau's thinking," why does he emphasize this relatively superficial thinker against Rousseau, who certainly had immense historical influence? Furthermore, Laski says that Diderot "seems to outdistance" even Rousseau in his attack on the "foundation of civilized society" in advocating progressive taxation, a more equitable distribution of wealth, tenderness for the poor, and attention to education.[45] However, because Diderot's ideas had a weak social basis, since they were what Mannheim would later call "utopian," they are dismissed as little more than pious hopes or as if none of his ideas were later realized by liberal regimes. As Laski had said in an earlier pamphlet, even the explicitly socialistic pamphlets of 1789 were mere declamatory denunciations, not definite programs, while the one clear socialist program was dictatorial and anti-liberal.[46]

Yet while the social activism of the time is obviously not all socialist, Laski could have stressed the anti-liberal and even totalitarian elements in the Jacobin stage of the Revolution, the one in which universal suffrage was most closely achieved. However, he does not take this path. Indeed the tone of his account suggests the view that, despite the nonliberal political currents at the time, there was also a liberal dimension in the quite pronounced demands for the alleviation of misery. As he had earlier noted, "all parties in the state agreed upon the undesirability of excessive differences in fortune," and there was widespread sentiment for a progressive income tax.[47] Even though the Revolution is considered by many historians, Laski included, to be the bourgeois revolution par excellence, in the course of that upheaval, we find leftist and working-class claims that are voiced openly in liberal language— that "the fruits of the earth belong to the poor by natural right" for example.[48]

Laski suggests quite correctly that the demands for universal suffrage achieved little actual significance;

that the Revolution was oligarchic and bourgeois, not democratic. Certainly there was a de facto restriction of suffrage even during the brief height of the Revolution. But while Laski is right to say that the bourgeois strand in liberalism triumphed during the revolution and in the century after, this does not mean the stifling of any liberal voice protesting that success. While he notes that there was no other revolutionary player than the bourgeoisie, and "no evidence of working class meetings" among the electoral assemblies, he does admit to "working class organizations."[49]

Laski says that French liberalism did in fact "formulate the demands of the new [bourgeois] claimant to human rights without seeing that when [the demands] had been satisfied, they would merely set the conditions for the new conflict." On these grounds, Laski tends to doubt the ability of liberalism to satisfy these new conditions, those of the industrial revolution that liberalism helped to justify if not create. "Left" liberalism, even if succeeding to power, would prove to be inadequate to the needs of survival and adaptation to new circumstances. Instead he tends to envision the great social changes of modern times as transformations that would occur from forces external to the liberal tradition. Liberalism cannot be restored or renewed from within.

## IV

Everyone agrees that many liberals in the nineteenth century were concerned with the social question, and in his concluding chapter Laski pays considerable attention to progressive European and American thought. Nevertheless, he repeats the attempt to drive home the view that because it leaves untouched the idea of private ownership, "political democracy, and the liberal ideology which expressed its inner purposes, could no more pass beyond the framework within which it was confined than feudal society could pass beyond its own constitutive principle." Hence, the "more generous minds" of liberalism who did address social questions—Mill, Hobhouse, and T.H. Green are examples—had a minimal influence on "the evolution of the doctrine as a whole."[50] In today's terminology, Laski sees the private property paradigm of liberalism as fundamentally incompatible with the socialist alternative.

It is understandable that Laski could take this either-or position in the 1930s, especially in light of the then strong influence of European socialism and of Marx. If we examine this leftist tradition, he says, we see that starting in the nineteenth century the continental socialists rejected liberal ideas as "simply one more particular of history masquerading as a universal," as a mere "fitful and temporary phase in man's endless struggle."[51] But where, after all, does the "democracy" in social democracy come from? By Laski's own account in the present work, the evidence is hardly convincing for his position that liberal ideas should be wholly replaced by socialism or that liberalism and socialism are mutually exclusive.

For one thing, Laski notes that by the nineteenth century, even within liberal opinion there was a high degree of sentiment that was both democratic and statist. Indeed to the great consternation of conservative liberals such as Tocqueville "the people had been schooled by their nineteenth century experience to see in the state an organ from which, under sufficient pressure, they might expect a continuous flow of material benefit."[52] Laski further notes that while conservative liberals looked upon state regulation as an enemy, associating it with the regulations of the old regime, the most important of the "advanced liberals," J.S. Mill, flirted with socialist thought. Indeed if Laski can say that the typical English socialist was not Marxian but Fabian, "a body of doctrine upon which the emphasis of John Stuart Mill's ideas was far more profound than that of Marx,"[53] then, at the very least, his account suggests a rapprochement between liberalism and socialism.

However, Laski dismisses Mill's abandonment of free market convictions on the grounds that it took place only in his last years.[54] He criticizes the Fabians for their failure to see clearly that their beliefs were dependent on two of liberalism's most important principles: since they wished to continue parliamentary institutions, they had to rely on a consensus concerning the liberal political postulates of electoral government in which losers concede power without a sense of outrage; and since they wished to depend on taxing the profits of private enterprise, they continued their reliance on the economic postulates of liberal capitalism.[55]

Yet Laski for the most part accepted the democratic etiquette governing the behavior of losers, and followed it repeatedly in his trials and tribulations within the Labour party. Indeed, if for Laski, as for most British socialists, socialism was essentially democratic, and if liberalism is the core idea of modern democracy, as Laski says it is, then a divorce of liberalism and socialism is not only undesirable but conceptually impossible. Laski has said, however, that a democratic etiquette depends on capitalism. While in this volume he does not envisage any specifically new socialist institutions, he later would say that we must accept the idea that political democracy must operate in the economic field. Yet as late as 1949 he could complain that "we have not yet found the proper forms through which to associate trade unions with the management of nationalized industry in a way that makes their relation democratically effective."[56]

Laski argues that the integration of Fabianism and of liberalism was, like liberalism itself, "dependent upon a conjuncture of economic circumstances which alone could guarantee their effective functioning."[57] However, for Laski all political ideas—including true ones—are historically dependent on such conjunctures, which are always unique in one way or another. Laski's own position at the time of writing this book during the extraordinary crises of the 1930s depended in no small measure on his reading of the special circumstances that would supposedly lead to the ultimate defeat of left or social liberalism in the twentieth century. But other unique conditions might lead to opposite conclusions, and Laski notes the "exceptional circumstances" which produced the liberal consensus in the United States. Such a consensus, he says "may not illegitimately be regarded as the fulfillment of the liberal ideal."[58] While that fulfillment is expressed in what Laski calls America's "worldwide empire," he does not envision that the worldwide imperial "exception" might become the universal rule, the cosmopolitan intent of later modern society.

The circumstantial reasons Laski gives for his reluctance to envision such a possibility included the U.S. Supreme Court's then continual refusal to sanction the various projects of economic regulation and market interference of "The Roosevelt Experiment," which Laski praised. Because this book was written prior to the famous "switch" in which the Court legitimated the New Deal, Laski depicts the American liberal tradition as unable to come to grips with New Deal regulation of private property. At this point, in Laski's view, liberalism is at a cross-roads. Either class relations must change in America, he says, or the present ruling classes will be compelled to change the democratic form of government in order to realize their fundamental objective of profit.

However, in an address delivered in 1940, after New Deal regulation had prevailed, Laski modified his position. He then noted the vociferous attacks on Roosevelt as a result of these triumphs. But to prevent such attacks from creating the ugliest reaction, he also suggests the possibility, indeed the imperative, that "America must revitalize the concepts of liberalism speedily enough to provide a new philosophy for its new world."[59] At least America might find a way to overcome the "inability in a given creed to transcend the circumstances of its origin," which, even at the beginning of this same 1940 address, Laski repeated was "always" the case.[60] The struggle over the soul of liberalism might now be resolved within the bosom of the liberal tradition itself.

The bad political news of the 1930s had led Laski, along with many socialists of the time, to conclude that the resolution lay in a choice between two ideologies outside liberalism: either the emancipating socialism of the proletariat or the repressive fascism of the bourgeoisie. It was yet to happen that the Anglophone liberal countries were to defeat fascism and at the same time embrace the "social-democratic" or mixed economy that combines private property liberalism and the "social" regulation of property.

The bad news for Laski's political heirs in our time is of course the defensive position in which this mixed economy finds itself. Once the threats of working-class insurgence from the inside and of Marxism-Leninism from the outside have receded, are Western liberals no longer in need of the stabilizing devices of the welfare state or of a need to demonstrate their social concerns? Will Laski's heirs have the last word if or when liberalism reveals its "true" colors by proclaiming the triumph of market principles over all else?

Whether or not the twenty-first century will find all social institutions turned finally and triumphantly into businesses, it is likely that in the realm of ideas, liberalism will continue the debate between its classical and social forms. Laski could not have predicted that in the late decades of this century the Philosophy Department of his old Harvard would see a debate between the explicitly Lockean minimal state liberalism of Robert Nozick and the "welfare state liberalism" that the neo-Kantian John Rawls is seen to justify.[61] Whatever the outcome of that intra-liberal debate—if it should ever have an outcome—both currents of liberal thought have shown a remarkable ability to survive until now.

During the years of the Second World War, Laski seemed generally pessimistic about the possibility of a revived American liberalism. At one point he angered Roosevelt when he suggested that the New Deal had been captured by big business, and his relations with Felix Frankfurter became tense. Laski's militant socialism often strained his old friendships including those in the Labour party. Even after he had finally been elected to the National Executive Committee of the Labour party in 1937, Laski's relations with the party and with the NEC were rarely easy. At one point, they considered expelling him for making public criticisms of the party that would more properly be raised behind the closed doors of the NEC.[62] Furthermore, the Labour party members of the wartime coalition government were focussed almost entirely on the immediate tasks at hand, and, in Laski's view, softened by power. Laski, on the other hand, wanted clear socialist goals in wartime, and became progressively disillusioned as his socialism became increasingly marginalized in the party.

By the 1945 general election near the end of the war, Laski, by now chairman of the NEC by rotation, became for some Conservatives more the focus of opposition than Clement Attlee, the Labour leader who was soon to be prime minister. Laski himself seemed to invite these attacks when he asserted the right of the NEC to give orders to Attlee. His controversial and combative speeches on various topics to European audiences sufficiently embarrassed the party to provoke Attlee to suggest in a famous letter to Laski that "a period of silence on your part would be welcome."[63]

It is not without some irony that at the time of Laski's death in 1950 at age 57, the great number of friends that he had established in America, the capital of the "worldwide liberal empire," uttered some of the strongest eulogies. Such was his reputation among numerous broadcasters and statesmen, as well as the many editors of liberal journals for whom Laski had written so much, that Felix Frankfurter could extol him as the figure who "probably influenced political thought and political action in the west more than any other individual."[64] Such plaudits from many, including those who differed strongly with him, strengthen the impression that Laski was as powerful in provoking political thought as he was in depicting it. In that respect, his books were like his teaching. He loved to argue with students and relished their disagreements with him; and they loved him in turn. The present volume is invaluable to students for the questions and arguments it raises: whether about the basis of textual interpretation, about the sociology of knowledge, about Marxian historical analysis, or about the very essence of liberalism itself. These questions are still very much with us today. Laski's book, whatever its inconsistencies, is a touchstone for the examination not only of liberalism, but of political ideas in general.

# NOTES

1. Isaac Kramnick and Barry Sheerman, *Harold Laski: A Life on the Left* (New York and Harmondsworth: Allen Lane/The Penguin Press, 1993). I have relied primarily on this work for Laski's biographical information. Previous studies include: Herbert Deane, *The Political Ideas of Harold Laski* (New York: Columbia University Press, 1955); Granville Eastwood, *Harold Laski* (London: Mowbrays, 1977); Kingsley Martin, *Harold Laski, 1893–1950* (London: Gollancz, 1953); Michael Newman, *Harold Laski: A Political Biography* (Basingstoke: Macmillan, 1993); Bernard Zylstra, *From Pluralism to Collectivism: The Development of Harold Laski's Political Thought* (Assen: Van Gorcum, 1968).

2. Laski was not only influential in Britain and America, but his close contacts with Krishna Mennon and later with Jawaharlal Nehru testify to his influence in India. At least five books devoted to Laski have been published there: Ram Chandra Gupta, *Harold Laski, A Critical Analysis of His Political Ideas* (Agra: Asia Press, 1966); G. N. Sarma, *The Political Thought of Harold J. Laski*, 2d ed. (New Delhi: Sterling, 1984); G. L. Mehta, *Harold Laski Revisited* (Ahmedabad: Harold Laski Institute for Political Science, 1960); Yaakov Morris, *Laski's Concept of Socialism and Israel* (Ahmedabad: Harold Laski Institute, 1970); G. N. Singh, *Laski—the Teacher and the Political Scientist* (Ahmedabad: Harold Laski Institute, 1957). There are also one Mexican and two Japanese studies.

3. See Herbert Deane, *The Political Ideas of Harold Laski*, pp. 55–68 for an analysis of Laski's early syndicalism.

4. Mark DeWolfe Howe, ed., *Holmes-Laski Letters* (Cambridge: Harvard University Press, 1953).

5. Laski, *Authority in the Modern State*, p. 387.

6. One informant reported a claim of friendship with President Wilson according to Kramnick and Sheerman, *Harold Laski*, p. 149.

7. Ibid., p. 149.

8. Kramnick and Sheerman observe that "even if we apply Rebecca West's more rigorous rule of roughly 50 per cent accuracy in Laski's claims as insider and power-broker instead of Saville's more generous 85–90 per cent, it is likely that at least some of Laski's claims are true, since two of the most powerful people to whom [Labour leader Ramsay] MacDonald had to pay some attention were strong Patrons of Laski, Sidney Webb and...Lord Haldane," in *Harold Laski*, p. 212.

9. Ibid., p. 181.

10. Ibid., p. 287.

11. Ibid., p. 291.

12. The charge has been ardently denied by many historians of the period, including Reginald Bassett, *Nineteen Thirty-One: Political Crisis* (London: Macmillan, 1958); and Kramnick and Sheerman, *Harold Laski*, pp. 299–300.

13. Kramnick and Sheerman, *Harold Laski*, p. 301. A similar judgment is made by Herbert A. Deane, *The Political Ideas of Harold Laski*, chapter 5.

14. See below, pp. 247–48.

15. Kramnick and Sheerman, *Harold Laski*, pp. 360–61.

16. See below, p. 17. The first American edition of this work was entitled, *The Rise of European Liberalism: The Philosophy of a Business Civilization* (New York: Harper, 1936); the first British edition was published by Allen and Unwin in 1936, and reprinted in 1947, 1958, and 1962.

17. See below, p. 17. Laski repeats this view in *The Decline of Liberalism* (Oxford: Oxford University Press, 1940), p. 5.

18. See below, p. 18.

19. See below, p. 15.

20. See below, p. 33.

21. See below, p. 34.

22. See below, p. 93.

23. See below, p. 35.

24. See below, pp. 104–105.

25. See below, pp. 103, 114.

26. See below, p. 115.

27. See below, p. 118; cf. p. 103.

28. See below, p. 198.

29. See below, pp. 117, 125. See also Herbert Deane, *The Political Ideas of Harold Laski*, pp. 180–81 for a brief critique of Laski's treatment of Locke.

30. See below, p. 116. In 1920, before his Marxist period, Laski also says Locke's state is a limited liability company; but this mention was then only a way of expressing the Lockean notion of a minimal state. At the time however there is virtually no mention of Locke as a bourgeois philosopher or a defender of capitalism. See *Political Thought in England: From Tyndale to Hooker* (London: Oxford University Press, 1920, 1961), p. 44. But compare pages 34 and 50 where Locke is depicted as a democrat and where Dean Tucker is quoted as depicting Locke, anachronistically, as "the idol of the Levellers."

31. C. B. Macpherson, *The Political Theory of Possessive Individualism: Hobbes to Locke* (Oxford: Oxford University Press, 1962); Neal Wood, *John Locke and Agrarian Capitalism* (Berkeley: University of California

Press, 1984); and *The Politics of Locke's Philosophy: A Study of An Essay Concerning Human Understanding* (Berkeley: University of California Press, 1983).

32. Richard Ashcraft, *Revolutionary Politics and Locke's Two Treatises of Government* (Princeton: Princeton University Press, 1986); for a similar view of Locke as activist, see Maurice Cranston, *John Locke* (New York: Macmillan, 1957).

33. See Locke, *Second Treatise*, para. 25.

34. See David Wootton, "John Locke and Richard Ashcraft's Revolutionary Politics," in *Political Studies* 40, no. 1 (March 1992): 79–98, and Ashcraft's reply, "Simple Objections and Complex Reality: Theorizing Political Radicalism in Seventeenth-Century England," in ibid., pp. 99–115. Wootton sees Locke as a Socinian, or Christian rationalist in "John Locke: Socinian or Natural Law Theorist?" in *Religion, Secularization, and Political Thought: Thomas Hobbes to J.S. Mill*, ed. J. E. Crimmins (New York: Routledge, 1989), pp. 39–67. For another perspective on Locke's religious motives, see John Dunn, *The Political Thought of John Locke: An Historical Account of the Argument of the Two Treatises of Government* (Cambridge: Cambridge University Press, 1969).

35. See below, pp. 161 and 210. Laski ignores the Netherlands here.

36. See below, p. 182.

37. See below, p. 181. For more modern revisionary views of Smith, see Donald Winch, *Adam Smith's Politics* (Cambridge: Cambridge University Press, 1978) and William Letwin, "Was Adam Smith a Liberal?" in Knud Haakonssen, ed., *Traditions of Liberalism* (St. Leonards: Centre for Independent Studies, 1988).

38. See Kramnick and Sheerman, *Harold Laski*, pp. 184 and 287.

39. See below pp. 196–97.

40. See below, p. 198. This modifies the bold claim made earlier that liberalism has "always regarded tradition as on the defensive" (p. 16). Burke of course thought otherwise.

41. See below, pp. 200–201.

42. See below, p. 205.

43. See below, pp. 210 and 219.

44. See below, pp. 214–15.

45. See below, pp. 217–18.

46. Laski, *The Socialist Tradition in the French Revolution* (London: Fabian Society/Allen Unwin, 1930), p. 9. Thus, Gracchus Babeuf's ideas resulted in "the one genuine socialist movement in this epoch" by virtue of "a definite program and an equally definite method of moving towards its realization" (p. 7). Cf. pp. 32–33 where Laski compares Babeuf's dictatorial program to that of Marxism-Leninism whose anti-liberal views he had criticized three years earlier in Communism.

47. Ibid, p. 15.

48. Ibid., p. 23. Laski here speaks of the demands of Boissel, a maverick Jacobin of the extreme left, in his *Le Catechisme du genre humaine.*

49. See below, p. 224. Cf. p. 225 below and Laski's *The Socialist Tradition in the French Revolution,* p. 27, which speaks of "meetings in the workmen's clubs."

50. See below, pp. 243 and 259.

51. See below, p. 240.

52. See below, p. 244; cf. pp. 245 and 254.

53. See below, p. 241. Leaving the utilitarian Fabians aside, Richard Ashcraft has detailed many cases in which the theoretical expression of nineteenth-century English working-class organizations was often in the liberal language of natural rights. "Liberal Political Theory and Working Class Radicalism in Nineteenth Century England," *Political Theory* 21, no. 2 (May 1993): 249.

54. See below, p. 256. See also John Stuart Mill, *On Socialism,* ed. Lewis S. Feuer (Buffalo: Prometheus Books, 1987). For the continuity in the utilitarian tradition that extends from Mill to the Webbs, see Shirley Letwin, *The Pursuit of Certainty* (Cambridge: Cambridge University Press, 1961).

55. See below, p. 242.

56. Laski, *Trade Unions and the New Society* (New York: Viking, 1949), p. 156. He adds that "no serious observer could accept the demand of some trade unions to [be] the main director of a nationalized industry."

57. See below, p. 242.

58. See below, 238.

59. Laski, *The Decline of Liberalism* (Oxford: Oxford University Press). The Hobhouse Memorial Trust Lecture delivered on 24 May 1940, pp. 20–21.

60. Ibid., p. 5. Cf. below, p. 17. Thus, Laski was not terribly optimistic about the chances of this renewal. As he put it, the progressive side of liberalism "has suffered an eclipse as striking and as complete as that which attended the doctrine of the divine right of kings after the Revolution of 1688" (ibid, p. 3).

61. See John Rawls, *A Theory of Justice* (Cambridge: Harvard University Press, 1971) and *Political Liberalism* (New York: Columbia University Press, 1993); Robert Nozick, *Anarchy, State and Utopia* (New York: Basic Books, 1974).

62. Kramnick and Sheerman, *Harold Laski,* pp. 440–49.

63. For a discussion of the broader implications of this conflict, see R. T. McKenzie, *British Political Parties* (New York: Praeger, 1963), p. 333 and n.

64. Kramnick and Sheerman, *Harold Laski,* p. 580.

**Transaction Books by Harold J. Laski**

*The American Presidency: An Interpretation,*
with a new introduction by James MacGregor Burns

*The Rise of European Liberalism,*
with a new introduction by John L. Stanley

# CONTENTS

# THE RISE OF EUROPEAN LIBERALISM

# PREFACE

THIS book is, in some degree, an historical background to its predecessor, *The State in Theory and Practice*, which I published last year. Since liberalism has been, in the last four centuries, the outstanding doctrine of Western Civilization, it seemed to me that an account of the factors through which it achieved its pre-eminence would help to explain some, at least, of the difficulties in which we find ourselves at the present time.

The reader will, I hope, take note of the fact that it is essentially an essay. Within a book of this size it is impossible to do more than sketch the main outline of the theme; and I am only too aware that, for adequacy, a much more detailed analysis would be required. The more I have worked at it, the more clearly I have come to understand how much more research is necessary, for example in the relation between law and economic development, or between the social composition of legislatures and their statutes, or again, between the idea of toleration and the economic effects of persecution, before any really full account of the liberal idea can be written. If, however, this preliminary study tempts any reader to examine some of these issues, to undertake, for example, that detailed study of Linguet that is so long overdue, I shall be well content.

My debts, for so small a book, are large. Above all, I am grateful to the members of my graduate seminar at the London School of Economics and Political Science who have helped me by criticism and a sceptical friendliness. What I owe to Professor Tawney's great

9

book on *Religion and the Rise of Capitalism* I can only record in a general way. My colleagues Mr. H. L. Beales and Dr. W. I. Jennings have, in endless discussion, helped me greatly to clarification.

Part of the book was delivered at Trinity College, Dublin as the Donellan Lectures in February of this year. I have to thank its Provost and Fellows for an hospitality as generous and kindly as even that great foundation could offer.

I have tried to avoid overloading these pages with notes. For the reader's convenience these have been collected at the back of the book. I have limited them, so far as I could, either to essential references which would save the student a considerable research, or to hints upon further reading which, from my own experience of his habits, I have thought it possible he might value.

H.J.L.

LITTLE BARDFIELD
*January* 1936

CHAPTER ONE

# The Background

I

IN the period between the Reformation and the French
Revolution a new social class established its title to
a full share in the control of the state. In its ascent to
power, it broke down the barriers which, in all spheres
of life save the ecclesiastical, had made privilege a
function of status, and associated the idea of rights with
the tenure of land. To achieve its end, it effected a
fundamental change in the legal relationships of men.

Status was replaced by contract as the juridical
foundation of society. Uniformity of religious belief gave
way to a variety of faiths in which even scepticism found
a right to expression. The vague medieval empire of
*jus divinum* and *jus naturale* gave way to the concrete and
irresistible power of national sovereignty. The control
of politics by an aristocracy whose authority was built
upon the tenure of land came to be shared with men
whose influence was derived solely from the ownership
of movable capital. The banker, the trader, the manufacturer, began to replace the landowner, the ecclesiastic, and the warrior, as the types of predominant
social influence. The city, with its restless passion for

change, replaced the countryside, with its hatred of innovation, as the primary source of legislation. Slowly, but, nevertheless, irresistibly, science replaced religion as the controlling factor in giving shape to the thoughts of men. The idea of a golden age in the past, with its concomitant idea of original sin, gave way to the doctrine of progress, with its own concomitant idea of perfectibility through reason. The idea of social initiative and social control surrendered to the idea of individual initiative and individual control. New material conditions, in short, gave birth to new social relationships; and, in terms of these, a new philosophy was evolved to afford a rational justification for the new world which had come into being.

This new philosophy was liberalism; and it is the purpose of these lectures to trace, in general outline, the history of the forces by which it was shaped into a coherent doctrine. The evolution, of course, was never direct and rarely conscious. The pedigree of ideas is never straightforward. Into the development of liberalism there have entered winds of doctrine so diverse in their origin as to make clarity difficult, and precision perhaps unattainable. To the evolution of liberalism have gone contributions of the first importance from men unacquainted with, often hostile to, its aims; from Machiavelli and Calvin, from Luther and Copernicus, from Henry VIII and Thomas More, in one century; from Richelieu and Louis XIV, from Hobbes and Jurieu, from Pascal and Bacon in another. The unconscious impact of events was at least as responsible as the deliberate effort of thinkers in shaping the mental climate which made it possible. The geographical discoveries, the new cosmology, technological invention, a renewed and secular metaphysic, above all, new forms of economic life, all made their contributions to the formation of its motivating ideas. It could not have become what it was without the theological revolution we call the Reformation; and this, in its turn, received much of its character from all that is implied in the revival of learning. Much of its character has been shaped by the fact that the breakdown of the medieval *respublica Christiana* divided Europe into a congeries of separate sovereign states each with its own special problems to solve and its unique experience to offer. Nor was its birth an easy one. Revolution and war presided over its emergence from the womb; and it is not beyond the mark to say that there was hardly a period until 1848 when its growth was not arrested by the challenge of violent reaction. Men fight passionately to retain those wonted habits in which their privileges are involved; and liberalism was nothing so much as a challenge to vested interests rendered sacred by the traditions of half a thousand years.

The change it effected was, on any showing, an immeasurable one. A society in which social position was usually definite, the market predominantly local, learning and science rather in society than of its essential texture, change usually unconscious and, as a general rule resented, habits dominated by religious precepts which few doubted at all and none successfully, in which there was little capital accumulation and production was dominated by the needs of a market for local use, slowly broke down. With the triumph of the new order in the nineteenth century, the church had given birth to the state as the institutional arbiter of human destiny. The claims of birth had been succeeded by the claims of property. The invention of invention had made change, instead of stability, the supreme characteristic of the social scene. A world-market had come into being, and capital had accumulated upon so immense a scale that its search for profit affected the lives and fortunes of societies to which European civilization had previously been without meaning. If learning and science were still the handmaids of property, their significance was appreciated by every class in society. If religious precepts still counted, their power to dominate the habits even of their votaries had disappeared.

Not, indeed, that liberalism, even in its triumph, was a clear-cut body of either doctrine or practice. It sought to establish a world-market; but the logic of that effort was frustrated by the political implications of the nationalism which surrounded its birth and flourished with its growth. It sought to vindicate the right of the individual to shape his own destiny, regardless of any authority which might seek to limit his possibilities; yet it found that, inherent in that claim, there was an inevitable challenge from the community to the sovereignty of the individual. It sought relief from all the trammels law might impose upon the right to accumulate property; and it found that the vindication of this right involved the emergence of a proletariat prepared to attack its implications. No sooner, in a word, had it achieved its end than it was compelled to meet a defiance of its postulates which seems certain to change the order it had brought into being.

What, then, is the liberalism we have here to discuss? It is not easy to describe, much less to define, for it is hardly less a habit of mind than a body of doctrine. As the latter, no doubt, it is directly related to freedom; for it came as the foe of privilege conferred upon any class in the community by virtue of birth or creed. But the freedom it sought had no title to universality, since its practice was limited to men who had property to defend. It has sought, almost from the outset of its history, to limit the ambit of political authority, to confine the business of government within the framework of constitutional principle; and it has tried, therefore, fairly consistently to discover a system of fundamental rights which the state is not entitled to invade. But, once more, in its operation of those rights, it has been more urgent and more ingenious in exerting them to defend the interests of property than to protect as claimant to their benefit the man who had nothing but his labour-power to sell. It has attempted, where it could, to respect the claims of conscience, and to urge upon governments the duty to proceed by rule rather than by discretion in their operations; but the scope of the conscience it has respected has been narrowed by its regard for property, and its zeal for the rule of law has been tempered by a discretion in the breadth of its application.

Liberalism has usually, by reason of its origins, been hostile to the claims of churches. It has tended, less perhaps to the Erastianism of Hobbes, than to view religious bodies as associations like any other within the community, entitled to tolerance so long as they do not threaten the existing social order. It has been favourable to representative self-government even when this has involved admitting the principle of universal suffrage. It has, in general, supported the idea of national self-determination. As a rule, though by no means universally, it has been tender to the claims of minority-groups, and to the right of free association. It has been suspicious of the control of thought and, indeed, of any effort, by government authority, to impede the free activity of the individual. I do not mean that its history is a conscious and persistent search for these ends. It is more accurate, I think, to say that these were the ends its more ultimate purposes caused it to serve; and I shall seek later to bring out the implications of this difference.

But liberalism, as I have urged, is hardly less a mood than a doctrine. Its tendency has been sceptical; it has always taken a negative attitude to social action. By reason of its origins, it has always regarded tradition as on the defensive; and, for the same reason, also, it has always preferred to bless individual innovation than to sanction the uniformities sought for by political power. It has always, that is, seen in both tradition and uniformity an attack upon the right of the individual to make of his own affirmations and insights a universal rule made binding not because authority accepts it, but because its inherent validity secures for it the free consent of others. There is, therefore, a flavour of romanticism about the liberal temper the importance of which is great. It tends to be subjective and anarchist, to be eager for the change which comes from individual initiative, to be insistent that this initiative contains within itself some necessary seed of social good. It has,

16

accordingly, always tended to make an antithesis (as a rule an unconscious one) between liberty and equality. It has seen in the first that emphasis upon individual action for which it is always zealous; it has seen in the second the outcome of authoritarian intervention of which the result, in its view, is a cramping of individual personality. The outcome of this is important. For it has meant that liberalism, though it has expressed itself always as a universal, has, in its institutional result, inevitably been more narrow in its benefit than the society it sought to guide. For though it has refused to recognize any limit in theory, whether of class or creed, or even race, to its application, the historic conditions within which it has operated effected a limitation despite itself. It is the meaning of this limitation which is the key to the understanding of the liberal idea. Without it, we cannot explain either the triumphs or the failures in its record.

For what produced liberalism was the emergence of a new economic society at the end of the middle ages. As a doctrine, it was shaped by the needs of that new society; and, like all social philosophies, it could not transcend the medium in which it was born. Like all social philosophies, therefore, it contained in its birth the conditions of its own destruction. In its living principle, it was the idea by which the new middle class rose to a position of political dominance. Its instrument was the discovery of what may be called the contractual state. To make that state, it sought to limit political intervention to the narrowest area compatible with the maintenance of public order. It never understood, or was never able fully to admit, that freedom of

17

contract is never genuinely free until the parties thereto have equal bargaining power. This, of necessity, is a function of equal material conditions. The individual liberalism has sought to protect is always, so to say, free to purchase his freedom in the society it made; but the number of those with the means of purchase at their disposal has always been a minority of mankind. The idea of liberalism, in short, is historically connected, in an inescapable way, with the ownership of property. The ends it serves are always the ends of men in this position. Outside that narrow circle, the individual for whose rights it has been zealous has always been an abstraction upon whom its benefits could not, in fact, be fully conferred. Because its purposes were shaped by owners of property, the margins between its claims and its performance have always been wide.

I do not mean that the triumph of liberalism did not represent a real and profound progress. The productive relations it made possible immensely improved the general standard of material conditions. The advance of science was only achieved through the mental climate it created. All in all, the advent of the middle class to power was one of the most beneficent revolutions in history. No doubt, also, its cost has been very great; through its coming, we lost the power to use certain medieval principles the recovery of which would, in my view, represent solid human gain. But no one can move from the fifteenth to the sixteenth, still more to the seventeenth, century, without the sense of wider and more creative horizons, the recognition that there is a greater regard for the inherent worth of human personality, a sensitiveness to the infliction of unnecessary pain, a zeal for truth for its own sake, a willingness to experiment in its service, which are all parts of a social heritage which would have been infinitely poorer without them. These were gains involved in the triumph of the liberal creed. They are not, of course, at any point gifts equally shared in the civilization to which they came; and their achievement was accompanied by its full meed of tragedy. But without the liberal revolution, the number of those whose demands upon life would have been satisfied, must have remained much smaller than it has been. That, after all, is the supreme test by which a social doctrine must be judged.

## II

Liberalism came, then, as a new ideology to fit the needs of a new world. What entitles us to speak of novelty? There are the geographical discoveries. There is the breakdown of feudal economic relations. There is the establishment of new churches which no longer recognize the supremacy of Rome. There is a scientific revolution which altogether alters the perspective of men's thought. There is a growing volume of technological invention which leads to new wealth and increased population. There is the discovery of printing with its inevitable implication of widespread literacy. There is the consolidation of vague and inchoate localisms into centralized and efficient national states. Born of all this, there is a new political theory which, as with Machiavelli and Bodin, makes the relation of man to man, instead of the relations of man with God, the foundation of social enquiry. There is the immense colonizing effort of Spain and Portugal, then of France and England. Out of all this were born new habits and new expectations. These came into conflict with a tradition of thought and practice which, in three centuries, they so reshaped that a society was born whose distinguishing characteristics would hardly have been recognizable to a medieval observer. It was a different society; and it knew that it was different. It had the sense of expansion, the feeling of spacious exhilaration, which come to men who know themselves to be engaged in the remaking of social foundations.

What was the essence of this new society? Above all, I think, its re-definition of the productive relations between men. For they then discovered that, to exploit those new relations in all their fullness, they could use neither the institutions nor the ideas they had inherited. The reason for the need of this transformation is a simple one. By the end of the fifteenth century the capitalist spirit began to attain a predominant hold over men's minds. What does this imply? That the pursuit of wealth for its own sake became the chief motive of human activity. Whereas in the middle ages the idea of acquiring wealth was limited by a body of moral rules imposed under the sanction of religious authority, after 1500 those rules, and the institutions, habits, and ideas to which they had given birth, were no longer deemed adequate. They were felt as constraint. They were evaded, criticized, abandoned, because it was felt that they interfered with the exploitation of the means of production. New conceptions were needed to legitimize the new potentialities of wealth that men had discovered little by little in preceding ages. The liberal doctrine is the philosophic justification of the new practices.

I do not mean to imply that the idea of wealth for its own sake was a new idea suddenly born at a particular time; no doubt it is as old as civilization itself. It is clear that what we term the capitalist spirit was present in men like St. Godric[1] or Jacques Coeur[2] or the Florentine bankers long before the end of the fifteenth century. But before that time it did not begin to colour the whole mentality of society. Before that time the criteria of legitimate activity were not, so to say, derived from the pursuit of gain merely, taken as an end in itself, but were determined by moral rules to which economic principles were subordinate. The medieval producer, whether in the realms of finance or commerce or manufacture, attained his individual end through an activity which, at every stage, bound him to rules of conduct which assumed the achievement of wealth to be justified only within a framework of ethical principle. He was entitled to sufficiency; but he must attain sufficiency by the use of means deemed morally adequate. He must not make value a mere function of demand. He must not pay only such wages as the labourer can exact. Hours of labour, quality of material, method of sale, the character of his profit, all of these, to take examples only, are subject to a body of rules worked out, at their base, in terms of certain moral principles the observance of which is deemed to be essential to his heavenly salvation. The middle ages are permeated by the idea of a supreme end beyond this life to which all earthly conduct must conform. The pursuit of wealth for its own sake is deemed incompatible with that idea. Wealth was regarded as a fund of social significance and not of individual possession. The wealthy man did not enjoy it for himself or for its own sake; he was a steward on behalf of the community. He was therefore limited both in what he might acquire and in the means whereby he might acquire it. The whole social morality of the middle ages is built upon this doctrine. It is enforced both by the rules of the church and by the civil law.

This spirit begins to disappear with the emergence of the capitalist spirit as predominant. A social conception of wealth gives place to an individualist conception. The idea of divine sanction for the rules of behaviour is gradually replaced by a utilitarian sanction. And the principle of utility is no longer determined by reference to social good. Its meaning is taken from the desire to satisfy individual want—it being assumed that the greater the wealth the individual possesses, the greater will be his power to secure this satisfaction. Once this attitude begins to obtain its hold over men's minds, it develops a revolutionary power. It replaces the predominant medieval idea of subsistence—which implies a static or traditional society—by the modern idea of production without limit; and this, in its turn, implies a society which is dynamic and anti-traditional because, since the desire for wealth is endless, it must continually seek experiment and novelty. More, it implies a society in which there will always be a tendency to anti-authoritarianism, for authority is by its nature conservative, and fears the disorder implied in unresting experiment. The logic of this new spirit, moreover, compels it to shape the whole world to its purposes. Where the ideas and institutions it encounters inhibit the progress of its search for wealth, it seeks to transform them to its own ends. For it offers to its votaries tangible and direct satisfactions, obtainable in this life, which the previous outlook was unable to offer. In the competition of ideas it is able, therefore, to change the basis of social relationships. Men are willing to bring a new world into existence because they agree that the balance of the old must be redressed.

If we ask why the capitalist spirit triumphed, the answer, surely, is the sufficient one that within the confines of the older system the potentialities of production could no longer be exploited. Little by little, the new men, and their new methods, pointed the way to a volume of wealth unattainable by the older society. The attraction of this wealth aroused expectations which that society, given its premises, could not fulfil. Men therefore begin to doubt the legitimacy of those premises. The attitude to usury, the acceptance of the guilds as a rational way of controlling production, the notion of the church as the fit source of ethical criteria, all begin to appear as inadequate because they stand in the way of the potentialities revealed by the new spirit. Within the confines of medieval culture the idea of capitalism could not be contained. The capitalist begins, therefore, his task of transforming that culture to suit his new purposes. To do so, no doubt, he has to proceed piece-meal; and, of course, he is not successful until he has defeated a resistance which, all in all, may be said to have lasted three centuries. He seeks to establish his right to wealth with the minimum interference from social authority of any kind. In that effort, broadly speaking, he has to pass through two great phases. On the one hand, he seeks to transform society; on the other, he seeks to capture the state. He seeks to transform society by adapting its habits and customs to a milieu suitable to his purpose. He seeks to capture the state because, thereby, he has, at long last, in his hands the supreme coercive power of society and may consciously use it for his ends. He justifies his effort by persuading his fellows—not without a considerable dose of coercion in the persuasion—that in the pursuit of wealth for its own sake social good is necessarily involved. The man who becomes rich becomes a social benefactor by the mere fact that he becomes rich. That is the essence of the new spirit. That is the central clue to the great adventure of modern times.

It is important here to emphasize one fact in this development which the very gradualness of the evolution tends to obscure. The inner idea of capitalism is inherently a philosophy of life. Those who accept it do not need extra-capitalist sources to validate their activities. Their search for wealth as individuals colours and shapes their attitude to every department of behaviour. Unless this had been the case, capitalism could not have achieved the revolution it effected. There was no sphere of life in which it did not encounter norms of conduct resistant to its spirit. Without exception, it transformed them, or sought to do so. It begins by modifying old practices and institutions; it ends by abandoning them. It begins by evasions and exceptional privileges; it ends by making evasions and exceptions into privileges. Jacques Coeur may need a licence to trade with the infidel; his successor does not require any permission of the kind. Relaxation of guild restrictions may seem adequate at one stage; but a time arrives when nothing less than their dissolution is regarded as satisfactory. Early capitalist theory, at least until the end of the mercantilist period, regards the subordination of economics to politics as natural; but an inefficiently administered state interferes with the full exploitation of the economic resources of society, and men begin to recommend the principles of *laissez-faire*. The state which, as late as the early eighteenth century, is still widely regarded as a beneficent agent of capitalist purposes, has, by its end, come to be regarded as almost their natural foe. The whole ethos of capitalism, in a word, is its effort to free the owner of the instruments of production from the need to obey rules which inhibit his full exploitation of them. The rise of liberalism is the rise of a doctrine which seeks to justify the operation of that ethos.

Let me put all this in a slightly different way. Before the advent of the capitalist spirit, men lived within an economic order in which the effective social institutions, whether the state or the church or the guild, judged that activity by criteria derived from outside itself. They did not regard the individual interest as conclusive. They refused to accept material utility as a valid justification of economic behaviour. They sought to impose, they partly enforced, a body of rules upon economic life of which the inner principle was consideration for social well-being taken in the context of individual salvation in the next life. To this consideration they were prepared to sacrifice the economic interest of the individual on the ground that, by so doing, they were assuring their heavenly destiny. With that purpose in view, competition was controlled, the number of customers a

25

trader might have was limited, commerce was forbidden on religious grounds, prices and the rate of interest were fixed, feast days were compulsory, wages and the hours of labour were regulated, speculation was, within wide limits, prohibited. These are, of course, a selection only of much wider regulations which go to prove the non-economic standards by which economic behaviour was judged. The rules broke down because the spirit which informed them cramped the power of men to satisfy the expectations they could fulfil, given the means of production, when the motive of wealth for its own sake was substituted for the medieval ideal. Almost every element in the new outlook was present in the middle ages. Its inventions, for example, show the same eager zest for gain that we recognize as capitalist in temper. Even the division of labour is in keeping with medieval practice in so fundamental an industry as mining. But though the capitalist spirit was present, it did not set the tempo of economic life. We note it as an exception rather than as a rule. Men appreciated wealth; but the search for it had not come to occupy the dominating position that is characteristic of the sixteenth century. Social organization was not yet rationalized upon the basis that this search was the true way to satisfy the nature of man.

Once it begins to be dominating, the whole atmosphere changes. Every aspect of social organization is seen in a new light. There is a new spirit of enterprise, a feverish activity, a zest for innovation, different in their quality from what the middle ages can show. It is as though a new challenge has confronted man, and he is determined to show his power to meet it. There is a new scale of things in capital accumulation, in risk taking, in the organization of factories. The business man welcomes the new nationalism with its greater guarantee of internal peace; for this means not only greater security in enterprise, but, also, the way to evade the regulations of the guilds by the location of industries outside their privileged areas. He welcomes the attack on the church, for this means a blow at the old, impeding rules, and it unquestionably made important resources more available for capitalist exploitation than they were under their ecclesiastical proprietors. The great increase, moreover, in the width of the market made for a new attitude to production. Capital was more urgently demanded, and the need to produce it led to new forms of banking and finance. The wider market, again, made the means of transportation, its cheapness, also, more important than it had been at any time since the break-up of the Roman Empire. This, in its turn, was a further encouragement to the centralized state which made possible such improvements by organizing protection for its citizens; and the protection, often enough, took the very practical form of building roads and developing navigation. The progress of accountancy, also, makes possible a new economic foresight, an ability to organize production on a wider scale and with a greater power to take risk confidently, of which the consequences were momentous.

We must beware of thinking of this capitalist spirit as new in the sense that men suddenly, at the end of the middle ages, began to be acquisitive for the first time. The pursuit of gain is as old as recorded history. What is new is the emergence of a philosophy which argues that

social well-being is best attained by giving the individual
the largest possible initiative in action. It is new because,
if room for that initiative was to be found, the medieval
idea of a society with clearly distinguished classes to each
of which, under ultimately Divine sanction, customary
duties attached was no longer adequate. For it denied
what was patently before men's minds. It denied their
power to exploit the resources at their disposal in the
fashion which changed economic conditions had made
possible. They found that, to exploit them, new class-
relations were necessary. But new class-relations, in their
turn, require a new philosophy to justify the habits they
impose. The movement from feudalism to capitalism is
a movement from a world in which individual well-
being is regarded as the outcome of action socially
controlled to one in which social well-being is regarded
as the outcome of action individually controlled.

The essence of the Revolution that occurred is thus,
in a real sense, the emancipation of the individual.
And because that emancipation justified itself by the
wider satisfactions it secured to society, it gradually
broke down the main barriers which stood in its way.
In so regarding the change, however, we must beware of
two mistakes. We must not think of the change as sudden
because we recognize it as real. It takes, as I have
insisted, something like three centuries to accomplish.
It has to triumph over cross-currents of opinion derived
from habits and ideas which were as stoutly armed as
any in the history of mankind. And it did not, everywhere, make its way at the same pace. In the fifteenth
century, it looked as though Italy was to embody its
fullest expression. But political disunity, on the one

hand, and the economic consequences of geographical discovery, on the other, were fatal to the brief dream of Italian leadership. So, also, in Germany the intensity of religious war, and the ruin caused by that intensity, held back German development for something like two centuries. France, also, had to struggle against well-organized and powerful centrifugal forces before the age of Colbert permitted a great forward movement. England was more fortunate. Her feudalism had always a national foundation after the Oath of Salisbury; and the outcome of this is a political receptivity to the new spirit wider and deeper than in any other country save Holland. And in Russia, until the time of Peter the Great, the new spirit makes hardly any impact at all. The new philosophy, in short, is like a tide which seeps in slowly over the land it is to overwhelm. Its progress is aided here, and arrested there, by natural conditions so different that it is difficult, until the land finally disappears, to recognize that it has, in fact, been a unified movement; the more difficult, indeed, because, as it reaches its highest goal, we discover that it is already on the turn.

III

The new spirit encountered, as it arose, that theological movement we call the Reformation, and it played an essential part in the shaping of its doctrines. Here we have to be careful in the definition of its influence. A thinker so eminent as Max Weber has argued that the coming of Protestantism makes possible the triumph of the capitalist temper; and he has found

29

in the Puritan doctrine of the "calling" an ethos almost invented in order to facilitate its advance.[3] His theories have found widespread support. The capitalist spirit, so cautious an historian as Professor Tawney has written, found in Puritanism "a potent force in preparing the way for the commercial civilization which finally triumphed at the (French) Revolution".[4] What is the connection between Liberalism and the Reformation?

That the rise of Protestantism aided the growth of the liberal philosophy there can be no doubt at all; that this was in any way a part of the purpose of the Reformers is not, I think, supported by any important evidence at our disposal. The Reformation broke the supremacy of Rome. In doing so, it gave birth to new theological doctrines, it effected widespread changes in the distribution of wealth, it immensely facilitated the growth of the secular state. Because it was a grave blow at authority, it loosened the hold of tradition on men's lives. Because it called into question ideas which had long held sway, it gave a deep impetus to the temper of rationalism. Both its doctrines and its social results were emancipating to the individual. But this is not to say that the makers of the Reformation intended this consequence. They did their work in a mental climate in which they had to adjust their ideas to innumerable influences wholly alien from the objects upon which they concentrated. Sometimes, they adjusted those ideas consciously in order to win support vital to their effort; sometimes they made the adjustment quite unconsciously, with no real insight into its implications. The emancipation of the individual is a by-product of the Reformation. At no point is it of its essence.

For let us remember that the Reformation is, above all, a revolt against papalism. It is an attempt to rediscover the conditions of the Christian life. Its protagonists believed that the Pope was anti-Christ, that obedience to him, therefore, imperilled their salvation. They did not free the individual from his control in order to make the pursuit of wealth for its own sake the cardinal principle of social action; they freed him in order that he might become, as they thought, a better Christian. There was not one of them who would not have regarded with abhorrence any plain statement of the principles of a liberal society. In every fundamental sense, Luther was a conservative in all matters of social constitution.[5] He hated usury, he was hostile to the new mechanisms of finance, he believed, as Troeltsch has pointed out, in a social organization dominated by a supernatural revelation all the terms of which were medieval. He postulated, no doubt, the priesthood of all believers; but he did not affirm their right to believe differently from himself. They must believe the plain word of Scripture; and that "plain word" lays down a code of conduct which, in his interpretation, is at every critical point identical with the medieval ideal.

He laid down the right of princes to control the religion of their subjects; and, thereby, even if indirectly, he gave a mighty impetus to the secularization of politics. But Luther's theory of the state is no more than the urgent pragmatism to which every revolutionary is impelled; it is simply a search, on almost any terms, for the conditions of victory. Every concession made by Luther—and he is rarely consistent in his concessions—is a safeguard of the support he needs. He never hedged about the state with rights which entitled it to deny his religious premises. It was always, for him, subservient to an idea of a Christian social order incompatible with the new spirit that was emerging.

Weber and his disciples have, indeed, admitted this; it is in the work of Calvin, and not of Luther, that they find the main evidence for their view. That the ideas of Calvin differ profoundly from those of Luther is clear enough; but there is nothing in that mighty authoritarian which entitles us to proclaim him a protagonist of individualism. The proof, surely, is in what he made of Geneva,[6] its massive and tyrannical discipline, its strict subordination of commercial behaviour to religious precept, its passionate repudiation of liberty of conscience. The very essence of Calvinism is theocracy. No individual therein has a private personality. He belongs, as Choisy has said, to the collectivity of which he is part, and this collectivity, in its turn, belongs to a body of Divinely inspired rules from which it cannot depart save at the expense of its salvation. Compared to this absolutism, the famous letter to Claude de Sachins, in which he permits the taking of interest, weighs but little in the balance.[7]

For what does Calvin say in that text upon which so much has been built? He argues that the Scriptural injunctions against usury are not conclusive. He rejects the patristic theory that money cannot breed money. He considers that the problem must be judged upon the basis that men now live under very different conditions from those of scriptural times. Money, he concludes, can be lent out at interest so long as the conditions of the loan are equitable. There are seven conditions which constitute exceptions to this general thesis. Read in their light, Calvin does not appear as an innovator in any marked degree.[8] He recognizes that there are some commercial transactions in which payment for the use of capital is justified. But nothing he says adds anything, in my judgment, to the argument of St. Antonino of Florence,[9] or to that of the *Sontentiae* of Gabriel Biel,[10] both of whom recognize that the full doctrine of the just price is no longer workable. His attitude was in full accord with the later view of the medieval canonists. What it was to become is a different matter; but for that Calvin, surely, can hardly be held responsible.

We are told, however, to see in the Puritan doctrine of the "calling" a contribution to the emergence of an individualist economy. Here, I suggest, the time-factor is all-important. The Puritan conception is not a static thing. It changes from the sixteenth to the seventeenth century, and, again, from the seventeenth to the eighteenth. There is nothing in Calvin's own economic ideas which suggests any great divergence from the previous period; and the practice of Geneva, both in his day, and in that of Beza, proves the toughness of medievalism. The English reformers of the sixteenth century can hardly be accused of any tenderness for the new wealth. Each alike saw what Aquinas saw, a divine plan in the universe which called the individual to his special place in the economy of things, and warned him of the danger of seeking to rise above it. That is the attitude of Robert Crowley,[11] as good a Puritan as ever there was; it is the attitude of Thomas Lever;[12] it is the attitude of Hugh Latimer.[13] Their view of wealth, of the obligations of the individual, poor or wealthy, is that of Luther with all

33

its inherent medievalism. All of them, indeed, were led by the view they took of the "calling" to be the defenders of the old order against the new, to protest against the practices of the "new rich" of their time as contrary to the principles of the Christian life. They inveighed, of course, against indolence; and they would not have been Puritans if they had not praised the virtues of asceticism. But there is not an atom of progressiveness or secularity in their outlook. To live the way of salvation; to accept the place in life to which he has been called; to do diligently the duties of that place; to regard either wealth or poverty as God's gift in which there is an opportunity of "grace"; this is, I think, the essence of their teaching. It is as far removed as possible from the outlook of the men who were shaping the new society. When in the second half of the seventeenth century, the idea of the "calling" became infected with the capitalist spirit the new society was already a hundred and fifty years old, and, by that time, it had at least as fundamentally influenced the Catholic attitude as the Puritan. Weber and his disciples have committed a grave anachronism in their eagerness to prove a theory. It is as though they judged the response to social problems of the churches in the twentieth century by their responses in the eighteenth. We do not estimate contemporary doctrine by either the precepts or the practice of Secker and Watson.

## IV

To understand the impact of the Reformation, therefore, we have to look in other directions. Doctrinally, it sought to renovate and not to evade, the principles of the Christian life; there was no nourishment for liberalism in that outlook. What gave the Reformation its importance for social doctrine was the fact that it synchronized with, and, in part, was caused by, the great economic dislocation of its time. Faced by that challenge, the church had no answer to it. The result was to unleash against its foundations all the accumulated grievances of the middle ages. They were of the most varied kind, religious, legal, political, dynastic. They were given new point and dramatic substance by the refusal of the Papacy to weigh them adequately. As always, refusing reform, it invited a revolution. Its failure to set its house in order at the time of the Conciliar Movement was fatal to its effort to maintain its pretensions before the new conditions it encountered.

We can see this most clearly, I think, if we look at the characteristics of the English Reformation, and draw our inferences from them. Broadly speaking, there was nothing new in the nature of the English grievances. Provisors' appeals, Peter's pence, there had been protests against these for centuries. The effort, again, to make the wealth of the clergy bear its due share of national taxation was no new thing. The sense of ecclesiastical corruption, the resentment against clerical wealth, is an omnipresent note in medieval English literature. The English Reformation was not born of Henry VIII's libidinous temper. It was not even the outcome of a dispute about the nature of supremacy over the church. The roots of the change had been growing for some hundreds of years. We can see signs of it in the struggle between Henry II and Thomas Becket. It is implied in the attitude of Edward I to the bull *Clericis Laicos*. It informs the treatises of Wyclif, in one mood, and the poems of Chaucer and Langland in another. Something of its temper is represented by the rebels who, in 1381, executed Simon of Sudbury, the Archbishop of Canterbury; and another aspect still is indicated by the attitude of the Council of Regency, under Henry VI, to the claims of Cardinal Beaufort to an effective share in power.

On the very eve of the Reformation, Dean Colet, whose loyalty to the church is above suspicion, attacked it in terms that no adherent of the change would have disavowed. "All the corruption, all the decay of the church, all the offences in the world," he told Convocation at Saint Paul's in 1512,[14] "come of the covetousness of the priests". The picture he paints of that corruption is a terrible one. Pluralism, simony, a worldly temper, greed, nepotism, the commercial spirit, the temper of the usurer, absenteeism, abasement to the great for preferment's sake, all these are in his indictment. He does not hesitate to tell his clerical brethren that their enormous wealth permitted them a lazy life, given up to gluttony and lust. It is significant that his plea was widely popular. And it is significant, also, that he should demand the enforcement of old laws against "those daily newly invented arts of getting money". Colet looks backward to the past for the principles of his reformation.

We can find a similar indictment in Erasmus, who was well acquainted with English conditions.[15] There is the same outlook in the famous pamphlet of Simon

36

Fish,[16] important enough, in its popularity, not only to attract the favour of the King,[17] and an answer from Sir Thomas More,[18] but also to be translated into German and Latin. Fish pleads roundly for royal action against the clergy, and he sees in the confiscation of their wealth the means to a new national prosperity. That, with all its defiant exaggeration, the "Supplicacyon of the Beggars" should have been so popular is an index to the degree in which the leadership of the church had been undermined. The people was not anti-Catholic; but it was anti-papal with an intensity which had been gathering momentum for generations.

To understand the English Reformation, above all the ease with which it was effected, its anti-papalism must be borne in mind. It is minimal in matters of doctrine; it is maximal in matters of exaction. Its essential legislation is directed against practices which tended to impoverish the realm for the benefit of the church. Behind it lay the kind of solid experience embodied in Guilford's account of the probate of Sir William Crompton's will. Appeals, annates, pluralities, non-residence, provisors, clerical absorption in secular occupations, the crying evil of mortuaries, all these were dealt with drastically by the Reformation Parliaments. The sweep of the measures, and their completion by the abolition of the monasteries, enables us to understand how Fox could write to Wolsey in 1523 that the people "were continually crying out against clerical abuses".[19] They got a full response to their cry.

The English Reformation, in brief, did three things. It abolished papal jurisdiction; it relieved the people from a grievous mass of clerical taxation, widely abused and resulting in vast corruption; and it transferred a great volume of property from clerical to lay hands. What explains its acceptance? Not, I think, moral indignation against abuses, and certainly not a desire for a purer theology. The causes of its success go deeper than either of these, even though there were men profoundly interested in both. A good deal was due to suspicion of the foreign interest of the clergy. This cut across that deep sense of nationalism which marks the Tudor period. Clerical devotion to Rome, outspoken in the case of Fisher of Rochester,[20] was as profound as it was held to be dangerous; for it was held by the government that the wealth of the church might be used in defence of the Roman jurisdiction. That this suspicion was justified was shown by the experience of the Bishop of London when he tried to collect the fine imposed on the clergy[21]; and by the large part played by them in organizing the disaffection which resulted in the Pilgrimage of Grace.[22] It is, moreover, clear that there was a moment in 1536 when effective leadership in the North might easily have meant the threat of a national disintegration like that suffered by France during her religious wars; to deprive the church of its wealth was obviously to mitigate this danger.[23]

Another element of importance is the outcome, also, of the centralizing nationalism of the time. It was felt that, as Wyclif had urged, the confiscation of church property would enable money to be devoted to the national defence without imposing further financial burdens upon the taxpayer.[24] The point is also made with great force by Simon Fish; one of the keynotes of his attack is that the nation cannot stand the drain on its resources, in case of war, represented by the flow of money abroad.[25] The cost of the military and naval policy of Henry VIII was undoubtedly a real factor in stimulating the suppression of the monasteries. These preparations, wrote Lord Herbert of Cherbury, "seemed to excuse the King's suppressing the abbeys; as the people willing to spare their own purses, began to suffer it easily; especially when they saw orders taken for building divers forts and bulwarks upon the sea coast".[26] Then, as now, a spirited foreign policy produced unexpected ramifications.

There is no doubt that the general economic condition of the realm created a wide feeling in favour of confiscation. Pamphleteers and memorialists were luxurious in suggestion of what might be done with clerical wealth for the common welfare. The expense of defence might be met. The sufferings from the enclosures might be mitigated. A policy of public works, including, significantly enough, the building of roads, might be undertaken to meet the burden of unemployment. All such plans, as we know, came to nothing[27]; it may be doubted whether they were ever seriously considered. But there can be little doubt that it was under cover of them that the Reformation policy went through. It was evidence of the degree to which men had become disillusioned with the church that so many should think of its property as of a national fund to which the state could legitimately turn for relief in a period of difficulty.

But what, quite unquestionably, made the policy of suppression popular was the opportunity it opened up to the King, the nobility, and the upper middle class of self-enrichment. The grasping cupidity with which men, from great nobles like the Duke of Norfolk, to country gentlemen like Humphrey Stafford, and even unknown members of the urban bourgeoisie, petitioned, bargained and bribed to get their share of the spoils is highly significant.[28] It created a solid party in favour of maintaining the new order of things. It facilitated the building up of great estates, and, hence, the progress of the enclosure movement. It stimulated the accumulation of capital, and thereby, the number of men prepared to risk their surplus wealth in the new commercial adventures. There can be little doubt that the policy represented by the Reformation is, psychologically, the expression of nothing so much as the breakdown of the medieval economic order. The expansion of trade and industry requires a strong monarchy able to govern in the interest of that expansion. The church is unfavourable to it. Its practices—witness the attack of Latimer on the evil effects of feast days[29]—stand in the way of production. Its property not only has a penumbra of foreign allegiance but is unavailable for full exploitation by the new methods. It hinders, by its incidence, that favourable balance of trade which has come to seem so vital to the nation. Even the charity of the church is held to encourage idleness. Its whole organization, as an agency of social control, is antithetic to the new spirit. Its destruction, as an organization, offered the prospect of new wealth at a time when men were dizzy with the sense of new opportunities. Its own corruption supplied a justification for this greed to men eager to seize on any pretext of the kind. Thereby, as they thought, they might enrich themselves negatively by shifting the burden of taxation on to other shoulders,

40

and, positively, by obtaining their share of the spoils. To the new social order, the church, as it was organized, seemed a definite incumbrance. The principles for which it stood meant the withdrawal of great elements of wealth, land, labour, and capital, from the new uses to which they might be devoted. The contrast between the eager merchant and the avaricious landlord of the Tudor age, on the one hand, and the priest and the monk, on the other, left no doubt of the result of the struggle for the wealth of the church. When, at the Council of Trent, the Papacy awakened to the need for reform, it was already too late. For, by that time, it had lost the half of its empire. The new men were in the saddle. The new terms of exploitation had been laid down. It was no longer for the new spirit to make its terms with the church. It was now the business of the church to make its terms with the new spirit.

## V

It is, therefore, in this indirect fashion that the Reformation came to the support of liberal doctrine. It opened the way to individualism by confiscating wealth used to support principles which stood in the way of individual opportunity. With the disappearance of that wealth, the influence of those principles diminished also. In antithesis to them, there slowly emerges a secular conception of life which defines ever more narrowly the empire they can maintain. More than this, that secular conception, in its turn, affects the content of Christian principle so as to shape it to its own needs. The way in which this was done is complex and tangled.

Partly, it came from events which compelled the
churches to shift their point of view; in searching for
allies, for example, the weakened commonwealth of
Rome was no longer able to make its own terms.
Partly, also, it came from the fact that, in the struggle
to advance the new outlook, ideas developed, and that
in the most diverse realms, the long impact of which
was in the direction the new spirit required. In the
sixteenth century this ideological revolution has three
main emphases. It is, in part, an evolution of political
doctrine; a theory of the state as a self-sufficient entity
is built. Partly, again, it is a new theology; and in the
building of this researches are undertaken which undermine the hold of the faith upon men's minds. Finally a
new cosmology is built, the results of which are a new
scientific outlook, on the one hand, and a new metaphysics on the other. We move from Copernicus and
Kepler, from Cardan and Vesalius, to Galileo and
Harvey, to Bacon and Descartes. By the time we have
reached the seventeenth century man the individual
has a sense of mastery over the universe that is new in
both depth and aspiration. He is prepared, as it were,
to dispute with God for the right to supremacy over its
destiny.

Each of these elements needs separate consideration,
though none, in truth, is separate from the others. The
history of political thought in the sixteenth century is
the history of the effort of men to justify, with only
partial success, the implications of a new environment.[30]
They are confronted with the fact of a political power
divorced from the theological foundations in which it was
previously embedded. The old sanctions of obedience

are in process of disappearance; new sanctions have to be found. They can no longer build their common-wealths upon a Divine law of which Rome is the ultimate interpreter, for the right of Rome to inter-pretation is challenged by the half of Europe. They can no longer teach the coevality of political duty and religi-ous obligation; for each of these has, by revolution, become diverse. The problem they have to meet is, no doubt, the eternal one of the reconciliation of liberty and order. But the idea of liberty is now set in a new frame-work. It meets an environment of which the material emphasis is different from any known since the use of the papal dominion. The evolution that occurs is the outcome of this novelty.

Sixteenth century political philosophy opens with an expression of modernity which, whether for realism or power of insight, it was never to surpass. The whole of the Renaissance is in Machiavelli. There is its lust for power, its admiration for success, its carelessness of means, its rejection of medieval bonds, its frank pagan-ism, its conviction that national unity makes for national strength. Neither his cynicism nor his praise of craftiness is sufficient to conceal the idealist in him. He espouses Dante's dream of a united and renovated Italy with all his heart. But he is also an administrator to his finger-tips, an administrator with the courage to avow that he who wills the end must will the means also. He believes in liberty, but he has been taught by grim experience that power is the price of liberty. So that all which stands in the way of realizing power, and maintaining it, he puts, ruthlessly, on one side. Moral limitations on con-duct, an independent church, these are the admissions of weakness; and weakness is the sin against the Holy Ghost. Machiavelli's Prince might well stand as the portrait of the new man of his age. He knows what he seeks to achieve; he is ruthless in serving his ideal. He is frankly materialistic—unencumbered by any of that other worldliness so rooted in medieval practice. Utility is the keystone of his practice, with power as the criterion of utility. His aims are wholly secular; his state has its eyes fixed wholly on this earth. If religion enters into his calculations, it is only as an instrument of value in bending men to the service of his aims.

Machiavelli is a man of genius, and the man of genius is never, perhaps, wholly typical of his age. But it is highly significant that, on the threshold of a new time, a book should have appeared which so frankly commended its inner essence. For, after all, the character of his prince is not a caricature of the century which followed, but an index to it. We find him in all its typical men, in Cromwell and Walsingham in England, in the Guises and Catherine de Medici in France, even, under their special protective colouration, in Luther and Calvin and popes like Paul III and Paul V. He is in religious zealots like Ignatius Loyola not less than in splendid pirates like Hawkins and Drake. A new enterprise, a new efficiency, serve a new ideal. If, with him, that ideal is nakedly terrestrial that is because, in a double sense, a new world has swum into his ken. He outlined, once for all, the ideal of amoral power which is worthy of pursuit for its own sake. He revealed the secrets of an impulse so profound in the human constitution that few sacrifices were deemed too great for its satisfaction.

44

But not less significant, in the sixteenth century, is the indignation Machiavelli aroused. Until some such time as that of Bacon, his unashamed secularity of temper was meat too strong for men's digestion. They are not less eager for power than he is, but they seek to clothe their purpose in terms that will make it compatible with the moral climate of their time. The idea of a strong and self-sufficient state frees itself but painfully from the trammels of competing ends. It is helped by Luther's view of the Prince as a chosen instrument of God; with Luther, there is no church behind to act as the judge of his conduct. It is helped, again, by Calvin's insistence—he falters only upon a single occasion—upon the Christian obligation to obey constituted authority. It was helped, once more, by the Presbyterian conception—largely the work of Andrew Melville—of the two Kingdoms; for that already involved the admission of a temporal world outside the boundaries of religious control. It drew nourishment from the Jesuit theory,—so magistrally developed by Bellarmine[31]—of the indirect power of the papacy, since this was built upon the thesis that a state which abstained from persecuting the faithful might assume its right to freedom from ecclesiastical intervention. Above all, perhaps, it was aided by the angry passion of religious war. For the cost of civil strife in social misery and political anarchy was so intense that men, of whom Bodin is deservedly the most famous, arose to argue that the state should not perish for the sake of religious conscience. They sought, like the *Politiques* in France, to discover a plane of political action, a sanction, therefore, for the authority it requires, which should be free from the intrusion

45

of religious argument. That meant, on the one hand, toleration; a conception from which, with rare exceptions like Marsiglio of Padua, the middle ages were inevitably free. And, on the other, it meant an approach, however circuitous and doubtful, to the atmosphere in which Machiavelli built his commonwealth. Religion may not have abdicated its claims by the end of the century; but it has been put in fetters so strong that, after its close, there is no longer any danger that those claims may prevail.

The most striking result of political change in the sixteenth century is, so far as theory is concerned, the *Commonwealth* of Bodin.[32] Both in motive and in argument, that is a book no medieval thinker could have attempted. It would not be of its age if it did not pay some tribute to the idea of natural law; but its significance lies wholly in a different emphasis. It is a treatise on the avoidance of anarchy. It urges the need, in any political society, of a supreme authority which shall give laws to all, and receive laws from none. Bodin was the first writer of the modern world to see that, once a state is to be sovereign, there can be, legally, no challenge to its authority. Its will is, by definition, an unlimited will. He thus discovers a plane for its activities upon which the rivalry of any competing authority, such as the church, is *a priori*, impossible. Yet, superb as is the clarity of Bodin's analysis, he hesitates before the implications of his own construction. Having built a state theoretically incapable of restraint, he then suggests that there are certain principles to which it should yield primacy. These are Divine law, the fundamental laws of the commonwealth, and that "natural" law which should prevent a prince from despoiling the property of his subjects.[33]

Those limitations are clearly of high significance. They mean, I take it, that Bodin saw, and desired, the inevitability of a purely secular state, but realized, from his own vivid experience of the Valois monarchy, the dangers of unlimited power. The limitations he therefore sought to impose are, all of them, conceived in the spirit of his own time. On the one hand, under the conventional name of Divine law, they are an acceptance of the moral conventions of his generation; on the other, they are an effort to find some place for the consent of subjects to the actions of authority, with special reference to the need for security in matters of economic constitution. The emphasis, for example, on the irrevocability of the Salic law is the realist's grim recognition that Renaissance man was apt to take advantage of a woman's weakness on the throne. The ascription of a special sanctity to private property, so that its control is ultimately to be born of consent through law, is the outcome of his knowledge that men are never so apt to fight as when they conceive their property to be in danger. Bodin's theory of sovereignty is a conscious search for a formula of peace in an age racked by civil strife. It is a measure of the changed atmosphere he confronts that he should find his remedy in the idea of civil supremacy. With him, the uneasy duality of the middle ages is finally laid to rest. The struggle between ecclesiastical and civil power is decided in favour of the latter. And this means—it is notable that it should mean—that the sanctions of conduct are, in increasing measure, to be secular and not divine.

47

Bodin's thesis, at bottom, rests upon a foundation of utility which makes order the highest good; a typical outlook, let us remember, for the lawyer to take in an age of anarchy. It is an attempt to find the groundwork of obedience within the confines of law itself. There were competing hypotheses slowly worked out within the period. The most notable of them are the idea, by no means new, and with good Scriptural warrant behind it, of the Divine Right of Kings, and the doctrine, again a renovation, of the social contract. The reason for their re-emergence is obvious enough. It is a disturbed age, in which men felt themselves in the presence of revolutionizing novelty. All the combatants sought to prove, first, that they did not seek to fight, and, second, that they were justified in fighting. All of them, therefore, from Luther onwards, were driven to examine the foundations of political authority. That there must be obedience they were all agreed, not least the Reformers who shrank from no accusation so angrily as that which declared them to be the proponents of social confusion. But they were not prepared for obedience without conditions; and they invented principles to explain that their own ends were, in fact, universal and eternal principles which all reasonable men ought to accept. Mostly, their view of the state was set in the framework of the religious debate which gave its immediate context to the conflict. But, as I shall seek to show, behind that context there can be descried a wider horizon.

Perhaps the easiest way to see the significance of the argument is to look at it in the age of its greatest richness—that of the Counter-Reformation. And, in that age, there can be little doubt that the most remarkable discussion is that which arose in France after the fateful massacre of Saint Bartholomew and continued with passionate intensity until Henry IV's triumphant entry into Paris, over twenty years later.[34] The problem is the terms upon which order can be made from confusion. There are religious differences, economic conflict, dynastic rivalries, constitutional disagreements. Before St. Bartholomew, the Huguenots had protested that they accepted the authority of the Crown; they took up arms only against its evil advisers. After the massacre, they became more radical. Power, they argue, is a trust which binds its holders to good government. It is born of a contract between prince and people, in which the latter have the right to withdraw the authority they have conferred upon a tyrant. It is the mark of tyranny to persecute a subject who is doing his duty to his God. For that subject has made a contract with his maker to place allegiance to him before any human obligation. When, therefore, he is persecuted, the right of resistance follows. But that right is to be exercised under significant limitations. The solid men of property, under whose auspices the Huguenot theory was constructed, never forgot things like the Peasants' War in Germany, the anarchist communism of the Anabaptists, the danger, when rebellion is proclaimed as a right, that all solid principles may be cast in doubt. They therefore deny the right of resistance to the common man. His duty is a passive one, until he is summoned to the field by his natural leaders, the princes of the blood, the nobility, the constituted magistracy of the commonwealth. They are the judges of when legal rebellion may be undertaken. They will take care, we may assume, that no resistance will seek to overthrow the principle of private property as such. A rebellion in the name of religious conscience is not to be made a cover for undue social radicalism.

The pamphlets which urge this attitude are innumerable; some of them, like those of Buchanan and Beza and the author of the *Vindiciae*, have left a permanent mark upon political thought. But, after 1589, Henry of Navarre, a Huguenot, is King. Thenceforward the note of Huguenot argument changes. Its protagonists are all for accepting the Divine Right of Kings. They have a monarch on the throne in whose conduct they have confidence. The idea of resistance seems to them wholly evil. The powers that be are ordained of God; it is blasphemy to resist their decrees. After 1589, the Huguenots are a minority still, but they are a minority with hope. They know that, once Henry's title is secure, there will be no difficulty in the way of their toleration. They therefore expend all their energies to prove that the civil state rests on Divine foundations, that those who resist its decrees are guilty of blasphemy, and the enemies of the well-being of the realm. There is little sense in them of inconsistency. New conditions have made peace their objective in one generation, as older conditions had made for war in another. Their real anxiety is to survive, to pursue their way through life unimpaired. They take the argument most likely to serve that end as the proper foundation for a political philosophy.

The Catholics go in a reverse direction. Until 1589, their protagonists are full of horrified indignation at men who threaten the foundations of social order. The

state, they feel, is their state, and they exalt with enthusiasm the right of the prince to order its activities
simply because, from St. Bartholomew onwards, it
operates to their advantage. But, after the accession of
Henry IV, their view changes completely. A heretic
is on the throne; and the Ligueurs do not doubt that
rebellion is better than the acceptance of a heretic king.
They therefore preach the sovereignty of the people as
indefeasible. They argue that the people may confer it
or withdraw it at their pleasure. It is conferred, they
say, for the purpose of good government. But good
government is impossible without religion; and religion,
of course, must be the true religion, which is that of
Rome. The preachers of the League, therefore, develop
a democratic theory of political authority in the knowledge that the majority is on their side. It is, indeed,
hardly too much to say that the *Vindiciae* is the source
of later Whig, the sermons of men like Boucher of later
radical, philosophy. The Catholic view, of course, is but
a temporary phase, nourished on the fanatical passion of
a Paris mob which had tasted blood, and saw in the
return of the Huguenots to Paris a threat to their virtual
monopoly of trade and employment in the capital city;
we can understand their reaction to these radical
ideas if we remember the contemporary popularity of
anti-Semitism in Germany with the small shopkeepers
and professional men. The analogy is important, because,
even after Henry's conversion ended the Catholic need
for a doctrine of popular sovereignty based on contract,
the church used the argument of economic advantage
to foster the acceptance of hostility to tolerance of
heresy.

51

Amidst this shock of pragmatic opposites a different doctrine was being slowly evolved. Huguenot and Catholic alike appealed beyond utility to a theory of right, however limited the idea of right that theory was to serve. The party of the Politiques, who may perhaps trace their origin to the noble effort of Michel de l'Hopital for peace, have a very different outlook. They do not doubt the desirability of religious unity; they do not even deny the desirability of persecution, if it has the hope of being successful. But they insist that civil society must not perish for conscience's sake. The interests of peace come first; the religious interest is a secondary consideration. For them, it is more important that Frenchmen should recognize their common interests as citizens of France, noblemen, landowners and traders alike, than that they should make of France two nations and a ruined society on the ground of religious difference. If this, they say, is the great barrier to peace and prosperity, let us level it. Let us grant toleration, since the long agony of civil conflict makes it clear that war is not a successful highroad to national unity. Let us find a plane of political activity upon which men may meet as citizens regardless of their religious differences.[35]

This is the view that prevailed, and I do not need to stress the significance of its victory. It meant the triumph of the secular state. It meant that the status of political right no longer needed definition in terms of an ecclesiastical sanction. From the medieval angle, it put the worldly interests of men above what was regarded as their heavenly interest. It meant that the preservation of order was so much the highest political good, that the state would disregard any claim to its interference which would jeopardize the cause of order. Once that view was accepted, the self-sufficiency of the state had no longer to be argued. Behaviour would then be justified, not by its coincidence with an idea of right justified by its conformity with Divine law, but by its acceptable congruity with ends which the state chose to serve. And those ends, broadly speaking, would, henceforth, be essentially secular ends. No state, henceforth, will embark upon religious persecution purely in the name of some sacred truth. Its concern will, beneath that claim, always be a state-concern; even the Revocation of the Edict of Nantes has political unity rather than religious truth as its objective, and it aroused no enthusiasm in Rome. Once order has become an end in itself, the differences between men are concerned with fundamentally economic problems of what that order makes, with the response, in short, of the state to the rights claimed by the owners of property. And the criterion of the response, at this stage, is no longer that of Divine law. It is the criterion of a conception of utility related to material well-being. The pursuit of wealth as the basic social aim has become the corner-stone of political activity.

One further aspect of political doctrine in this epoch deserves some little emphasis. The sixteenth century is an age in which new legal principles were forged to meet the needs of a new society. These principles may be looked at from two points of view. From one angle, they are the birthplace of international law in its modern sense, that is, of a law governing the relations between states regarded as its effective units. On another side, public law begins to be sharply differentiated from private law with which, under the feudal system, it had been closely confounded. We get not only law-making in a sense much closer to the modern idea of legislative innovation. We get, also, a judicial revision of legal doctrine intended to suit commercial necessities of a new kind in men's experience.[36] It may even be asserted that nowhere is the fact of a new society so obvious as in the legal realm.

The need for an international law was increasingly obvious after the Reformation.[37] It was made clear by the geographical discoveries. What was to constitute valid title to a colonial empire? Papal authority no longer sufficed, since it could not bind the Protestant powers. A body of doctrine had to be formulated which rested upon a different sanction. And the need was made greater by the new fact of national unity. The state this unity makes possible has relations with other states much more intense, especially in the realm of commerce, than was the case a century before. The rise of new nation-states, like that of Holland, gives point to the need. The finality of religious difference, implicitly recognized by Bellarmine, involved a new international status for the Papacy. The ambassador of the sixteenth century is, almost consciously, a very different and superior figure to his fifteenth century prototype; and the new monarchies he represented, the new and wider functions he performed, needed new rules to define his position and its privileges. The discoveries, moreover, raised large issues of international trading rights involving treaty arrangements of a complex kind. Publicists, in these conditions, had to find a body of rules, secular in their sanction, which were binding upon men of diverse faiths. The impetus is clear; the sources which go to make that central stream which culminated in the work of Grotius are more varied. Moral principle, as in the noble work of Francisus è Victoria, has its quota to contribute. There is a stream of moral rationalism, ecclesiastical in purpose, but only partially so in method, which comes from Suarez and the great Jesuits of the Counter-Reformation. There is the element born of the new *raison d'état* of which, though only in part consciously, Machiavelli is the fountain head. There is the influence of the Roman law, with all its revived authority in this epoch, as it is related to the new problems by men like Alberico Gentili. The result is a body of doctrine of which the consequences were great.

For its basis is the idea that nature gives birth to a body of rational principles as clear and as immutable as those of mathematics and physics. The analogy is a startling one. For the notion of binding force, Grotius has already gone to the new science rather than to the old theology. His state is fairly built on the social instinct of man, and its practices are guided by that rule of reason which he takes to be nature's law. The purpose of society is conservation; and, for him, writing as a Dutchman who has watched the struggle for independence and commercial supremacy, peace is the highroad to conservation. If the unending mass of citation makes us realize how near in time is Grotius to the schoolmen, from the jungle they make emerges principle after principle which indicate that a new lesson has been learned. The distinction between just and unjust war, the desirability of arbitration, the exposition of the rights and duties of neutrals, the restraints suggested on devastation and pillage as incidents of war, these indicate not merely a new humanitarianism, but also a sense of new terms in the relationships states imply. It is important that the whole scheme is outside the theological scheme of things. It is important, further, that the development of rules for the protection of private property should occupy so much of his attention. And read in the context of his famous controversy with Selden over maritime rights, it is not difficult to see in its conclusions the charter of that new commerce to the empire of which no boundaries could yet be assigned.

The evolution of the civil law has more complex implications. Yet its essence is unmistakably secularization. The decline of the canon law reflects definitively the defeat of the claims of Rome. The Reception of the Roman law, in Germany, Scandinavia and Scotland as well as in the Latin countries, came because its principles were far better suited than feudal rules to an age which required uniformity and strong government. The appeal of Roman law lay not merely in the prestige of its associations, but in the fact that it exalted the state, and the prince as the embodiment of the state, as the unchallengeable sanction of political power. It had the further advantage that it suited the class-divisions of the new society far more creatively than feudal principles based on distinctions already largely obsolete. For it was important that the Roman law was made for an empire built ōn world-trade. Its conceptions of property, therefore, were far more adequate to the new economic order than those of the system it supplanted. If they acted with depressive effect on the poorer class,

that was probably a commendation in the eyes of the
men who adopted them. What was supremely important
was, that once the change had been made, the power of
the state rested upon a different level from that of any
possible competitor. The courts were applying a
doctrine nursed by a philosophy which did not easily
permit a challenge to secular power.

In England, of course, the direction took a different
turn,[38] since the Common law proved too tough for
civilian transformation. What is important with ourselves is less immediately new doctrine—this comes, a
little tardily, in the seventeenth century, than the fact
that the strong and popular Tudor monarchs broke the
last vestiges of feudal pretensions. That meant the decay
of the feudal courts, a consequential advance, accordingly, in the authority and prestige of the national
judges. New legislation, a new and powerful class of
officials largely composed of *novi homines*, the renovation
of the office of justice of the peace and its attachment by
unbreakable links to the Crown, these are the main
experiments of the period, and they all make for that
centralizing nationalism which was the most urgent
need of the age. Nor must we fail to note the significance of Parliament, different in quality from that of any
continental legislature. The Tudors, no doubt, were
despots; Professor Pollard has said of Henry VIII that
he was Machiavelli's prince in action. But they were
despots by popular consent. Whatever the divisions of
the nobility, the middle classes rallied to them. The
landowner and the merchant enabled them to use
Parliament as the instrument of a state using political
means for economic welfare. The Tudors made their

law prevail by infusing it with the spirit that the new order required. They recreated self-confidence and enterprise in the middle class by providing them with security. That is the temper which always nourishes a new social philosophy.

In this respect we must notice that security has its price. What the state did in aid of liberalism in the sixteenth century is different from what it achieved, or was even asked, to achieve, in later ages; and there is a difference in attitude between one country and another because the time-factor is different in the emergence of similar problems. Broadly, we may say that the contribution of the sixteenth century is the destruction of ecclesiastical authority in the economic sphere. This enables property-relations to develop unhampered by theological considerations. There emerged from this a secular state which sought, and found, its mission upon the basis that it replaced the church as the guardian of social well-being. It builds its own morality, based upon utility, to suit its new prestige. But, in this first phase, its habits are necessarily marked by practices inherited from the previous age. We have a long period of widespread state activity in which it is assumed that the rules of economic conduct are to be laid down by the state instead of by the church. Individual economic good is still set in the context of a community-good of which the state is the appointed guardian. Men are still too accustomed to intervention of authority in economic life to doubt its general validity. There may be occasional protest, like that of the English Parliament against monopolies, or that of the merchants of Antwerp to Philip II against the proposal to make a privileged

58

insurance corporation under royal patronage; in these, as in occasional similar instances, a significant plea for freedom of trade will be made. But the new order, while the sixteenth century lasts, has still far too great a need for the security built by its actions, to resent its interference in any wholesale way. The achievement of a secular state was a sufficient revolution for one period to effect. Doubts of interventionism have to wait until the suspicion is widespread that the effect of intervention is less admirable than the theory which lies behind it.

Mercantilism, therefore, is the first step taken by the emerging secular state on the road to the full achievement of liberalism.[39] Its acceptance is natural enough. The action of a strong government has secured peace; why should such a government not secure prosperity also? Industrial decay, large scale emigration, especially in distressed countries like France, a debased currency, the need to protect international economic adventure, not least in the colonial field, the general confusion of industrial rules and standards, the struggles, due to the general decline of authority, between master and employee, on the one hand, and between rival crafts, on the other, all pointed to the need of state intervention. The belief that the export of the precious metals is dangerous, the threat of foreign competition, the desire, accordingly, for a protective tariff, made men look naturally to the state as a source of aid in their difficulties. The wars and the unemployment caused by changing economic methods like the enclosures meant that legal provision must be made for the new race of sturdy vagabonds of whom the literature of the sixteenth century has so much to say. The root of the mercantilist idea is its recognition of the need for a new discipline, a code of economic behaviour which will make for prosperity instead of misery, for work instead of indolence. It was natural to look to the state, in these circumstances, as the great regulator from whose beneficent action abundance might be won.

Mercantilism, in the first stage, therefore simply transfers the idea of social control from the church to the state in the economic realm. It is, of course, a momentous transference. For the motive of state-action is no longer the good life, but the attainment of wealth, the enactment, by legislation, of the conditions that will make for wealth. This attitude can be seen with abundant clearness in Englishmen like Hales and Cecil, in Frenchmen like Laffemas and Montchrétien, in Italians like Serra. Their outlook in these matters is wholly secular. The recommendation of their policy is simply that it will add to the wealth of the kingdom. What is new in their outlook is its frank utilitarianism, their acceptance of the idea of plenty as a self-sufficient social ideal. This emerges, above all, in their attitude to the poor. It is not, I think, too much to say that they look upon the unemployed as social criminals; they detract from the wealth that is attainable. This is the spirit of the Elizabethan poor law; it is evident in the repressive measures against them recommended by Laffemas.[40] The whole spirit of their effort is to get people working; even the new charity of the religious revival in France has no other purpose. The Statute of Apprentices, the French rules for dealing with abandoned children, are all permeated by this desire. The interest of a mercantile class which has made productivity a god is written all over the new temper. To it is sacrificed the interest alike of the consumer and the working man. The whole trend of policy is to make a state responsive to the needs of the business man. When Laffemas recommended the fixing of wages by compulsory arbitration through a chamber wholly dominated by the employers he gave merely a specially vivid expression to the outlook of the new business man. He was using the political machinery of the state to establish the conditions upon which he believed its prosperity to depend. He invoked its coercive power to effect the discipline of social life which gave him security for his effort.

It is this approach which explains the rise of the idea of toleration. No doubt there are men, Acontius, for example, and Castellion and Robert Brown, who urge the desirability of protecting conscience on purely religious grounds.[41] But the history of toleration shows that it is the economic destruction wrought by civil war which creates the mental climate favourable to toleration. It comes because, at bottom, persecution is a threat to property. It endangers the conditions of sound business enterprise. It suggests that the foundations of state-action are still primarily religious in character. It was anti-individualistic in implication because it postulated the assumption that the end of the state must be judged by non-political criteria. It is too much to say that the sixteenth century was fully prepared to reject that assumption. But it is significant that, in England, Elizabeth had already ceased to persecute on religious grounds alone; she tolerated her Catholic subjects so long as they did not threaten the unity of the kingdom. She was more concerned for order than for truth, because she saw in order the key to material well-being. That is the outlook which, as I have shown, emerged also from the religious wars in France; the triumph of Henry IV is a victory for *étatisme*. What suffers defeat is the doctrine that no price is too high for the kingdom of heaven. It takes two centuries for the defeat to become conclusive. But, almost from the beginning of religious difference, it is significant that the economic influence is ardently on the side of peace.

One final point upon the evolution of political doctrine it is necessary to make. The rejection of religion as the principle entitled to make political policy might easily have resulted in a new absolutism. The state might have taken the place of the church as itself the sufficient criterion of good and evil. There might easily have emerged what, indeed, is implied in mercantilist theory, a religion of the state in which the interest of the individual would have been sub-ordinated to *raison d'état*. That attitude, certainly, is the predominant one in the sixteenth century. The political theorists, like Machiavelli and Bodin, are concerned that the state shall be strong; the economic theorists, like Laffemas, are concerned that it shall be wealthy; and the new administrators, men like Cecil in England, share their objectives. We can see, in men like Bacon, at the end of the age, that a strong state rather than a free individual, that *étatisme* rather than liberalism, is still the dominating conception.[42] In France, indeed, that outlook lasted still longer. It is not until the last twenty years of Louis XIV's reign that we begin to see the liberal ideal challenging the power of the state. Why did not the idea of the state as itself a religion persist?

We may answer that question by pointing out that interventionism as a doctrine is challenged almost as soon as it becomes a principle of state-policy. The most remarkable expression of that doctrine is, no doubt, the protests of the House of Commons against monopolies under Elizabeth.[43] It is, perhaps, too much to say that the new economic spirit favoured freedom from the outset of its emergence. It is, however, true to insist that it supported the policy of interventionism only so long as internal order and peace were in doubt. Once the state had crushed all internal rivals its attitude to regulation was criticized immediately it was felt as a handicap to individual effort. That was partly because the administrative ability of the state was inadequate to the intervention it attempted. It was partly, also, because its favouritism tended to make of the privileges it organized a way of benefit to the courtier at the expense of the trader; "all free subjects", the House of Commons told James,[44] "are born inheritable to the free exercise of their industry". Partly, again, as Pirenne has pointed out,[45] most of the new capitalists were parvenus who can, given order, make their way better in a régime of liberty, than when a price has to be paid for state-assistance. National economy, in a word, was a stage on the way to individual economy. It persisted so long, but only so long, as it was successful. It produces internal order, and it is welcomed on that ground. But it is, in its nature, arbitrary, capricious, and inefficient. Its habits are dominated by statesmen whose outlook only partially fits the requirements of capitalism. They want a state

63

which they can directly shape to their own purposes; and, the more fully internal order is achieved, the more certain they are that the high-road to such a state is their own domination of it. In these circumstances, they can have rules to govern the acquisition of wealth that they themselves have the main share in making. They can control the will of the monarch, not least in financial matters. They can limit the privileges of a landed aristocracy which tends to secure a monopoly of political office. The absolute state hinders the full exploitation of unfettered capitalism. Constitutional theory, with its substitution of rule for discretion, of civil liberty for monarchical caprice, is the answer of the business men to the failure of national economy to serve his needs. Mercantilism breaks down because the principles of liberty offer wider prospects of exploitation to men whose interests are bound up with the implications of unfettered production.

## VI

The new theology follows a similar path. Its main result is the substitution of reason for authority as the main criterion of the right to believe. In a sense, of course, this attitude is implicit in the very fact of Protestantism. Luther's bibliolatry is inevitably anti-authoritarian simply because he had no criterion save individual insight to which to appeal for validation of his own views. Even the rigidity of Calvinist logic had no better hold. The accusation of Bossuet,[46] that the variations of the Protestant sects opened the door to atheism is an irrefutable one. But, for my purpose, the importance of the theological change is less in the attack it made upon Rome than in the unlooked-for result it had in promoting a secular and individualist attitude to the world. We must examine how this came to influence the development of the liberal doctrine.

It did so, in the first place, because it promoted free thought in the religious sphere. Once the authority of Rome was called into question, the basis of dogma was bound to become the worth of the testimony it could invoke in its support. That testimony was examined from angles wholly new in their temper. Biblical scholarship not only denies the pretensions of Rome; it also multiplies the variety of permissible religious faiths. The re-discovery of classical antiquity made possible new intellectual allegiances in which Christianity itself could be called into question. No doubt infidelity was much rarer in the sixteenth century than the fantastic exhortations of the clergy would tempt us to believe. But the fate of men like Bruno and Vanini, the attitude of Rabelais and Montaigne, Bodin's reputation for impiety, the fact that Viret can find it necessary to invent the term "Deist",[47] is evidence enough of a new temper. And, as the imaginary voyages of the seventeenth century were to show more fully, the discovery of immense variations of human belief by the explorers led to the notion that a morality could be defined independently of the Christian sanction. All revolutionary periods are unfavourable to the hold of traditional religions upon their votaries. The age of the Reformation is no exception to the general rule.

It presented a spectacle of confusion inevitably hostile to the idea of religious authority. The war of

65

sects, with its passionate recrimination, naturally under-mined respect for it. That was seen clearly by Nashe;[48] and its results were summarized with his usual succinct-ness by Bacon when he wrote that "if there is one main division it addeth zeal to both sides, but many divisions introduce atheism".[49] As early as 1565 Acontius pro-posed the unity of all religious sects as the only way to preserve faith in Christianity.[50] Arminius attacked the sectarian spirit; but the remedies he recommended, prayer, forbearance, and a general council, were nothing so much as a confession of helplessness. In such an atmosphere the scepticism of Montaigne became the natural attitude of a cultivated man. For him, truth has ceased to be absolute in religious matters. "We receive our religion," he wrote,[51] "but according to fashion. . . . Another country, other testimonies, equal promises, like menaces, would imprint a contrary religion in us." The result of religious warfare was undoubtedly to weaken the hold of dogma upon men's minds.

And as soon as the hold of dogma was weakened, the empire of reason extended its boundaries. The know-ledge of other peoples, with moral principles as fine as the best Europe could show, with wealth as resplendent, with power not less impressive, made men see the Christian argument in a new perspective. It becomes one opinion, one morality, among others; even the Jesuit missionaries are prepared to doubt whether some of the savage tribes they visit do not show a nobler habit in all their paganism. Christianity begins to be viewed in the perspective of history and geography. The effect is to make it a part of nature and not the mistress of it.

66

And this outlook, in its turn, suggests that principles of life may be discovered which are those of Nature itself. From this, as with Rabelais and Montaigne, it is an easy step to argue that the life according to nature is the path a wise man will follow. Inherent in that view is, among other things, an earthly view of pleasure, a rejection of the ascetic emphasis of the middle ages. The motto of the Abbey of Theleme becomes an increasingly powerful canon of conduct. But to act as one will, one must have the means of pleasure; and these are the outcome of the conquest of material power. The decay of dogmatic faith, in fact, made once again for the growth of that secular spirit which justified activity by its power to secure material satisfactions. The lights of heaven are not extinguished; but their illumination seems more distant as the secular spirit grows.

And its growth is not least shown in the theological sphere itself. Secularism demands reason as its weapon; and by the end of the century nothing shows so much that religion is on the defensive as the fact that it is using the weapons of reason to defend itself. It can no longer impose its postulates; it has to commend them by proving that they are justified by rational inference. Nothing shows this more clearly than the character of the ablest defence of the Elizabethan religious settlement that our literature produced. Anyone who compares the *Ecclesiastical Polity* of Hooker with the spirit of the Reformers a generation before will feel that he has moved into a different world. "The natural measure", he wrote,[52] "whereby to judge our doings is the sentence of Reason determining and setting down what is good to be done." He has the scholar's respect for tradition; but it is not

a blind respect. "For men to be tied and led by authority", he argued,[53] "as it were with a kind of captivity
of judgment and, though there be reason to the contrary, not to listen to it, but to follow, like beasts, the
first in the herd, they know not nor care not whither :
this were brutish. Again, that authority of men should
prevail with men, either against or above Reason, is no
part of our belief. Companies of learned men, be they
never so great and reverend, are to yield unto Reason."
To its claims, therefore, even the voice of the church is
subordinate; and he insists that "without the help of
natural discourse and Reason", no knowledge can be
obtained which will secure the acceptance of the
prescriptions of faith.

From this standpoint the theories of Hooker are
almost wholly built upon a rational and utilitarian
foundation. The power of the prince over the Church is
accepted, not on ground of history or of scriptural text,
but of social convenience. The idea is inequitable that
the clergy should have the sole right of ecclesiastical
legislation. "We are to hold it", he wrote,[54] "a thing
most consonant with equity and reason that no ecclesiastical laws be made in a Christian commonwealth
without consent as well of the laity as of the clergy, but
least of all without consent of the highest power." Even
the laws of God are not immutable. "And therefore
laws though both ordained of God himself, and the end
for which they were ordained continuing, may not-
withstanding cease if, by alteration of persons or times,
they be found unsufficient to attain to that end."[55] It is,
therefore, in his view, legitimate to accept a doctrine of
evolution for the church. "I therefore conclude that

68

neither God's being Author of laws for the government of His church, nor His committing them unto Scripture, is any reason sufficient wherefore all churches should for ever be bound to keep them without change."[56]

It is not too much to say of this attitude that Bacon would not have disowned it in Hooker's own generation, and hardly Hobbes in the next. Its temper is largely Erastian; it is built upon the assumption that the state can equitably alter religious habits to suit new social needs. It shows that Hooker is the contemporary of those men of science who were shaping a new world. It is not, indeed, the work of an individualist in religious matters; there is no hint of that almost defiant anarchism with which, a generation later, Chillingworth was to defend the right of private judgment in religious matters. Hooker was as convinced as any of his critics of the need for order, rule and form in the ecclesiastical field. But his church is in this world and not above it. He seeks to square it with the needs of men living in a new society, to lay its foundations in such a manner that it shall be capable of further adaptation, if this be required. The very depth of his own Christianity only makes his outlook the more significant. Such a church as he conceives does not define the life of the society in which it moves, but expresses only the general habits of that life. It is consciously receptive to new influences. It has ceased to be the prisoner of tradition. Not since Erasmus had there been concessions of this magnitude to the requirements of a new time.

Hooker's attitude, no doubt, was to the left of most of his contemporaries; it is an indication of direction, rather than a definition of it. But it still shows, with much fidelity, the contours of the revolution that had been effected within eighty years of Luther's first great adventure. There is by then no institutional expression of Christianity with more than a partial validity in Europe; and there is already none powerful enough to challenge successfully the political state upon which it has come to depend for what social discipline it may impose. Increasingly, it is exposed to critical winds of doctrine which impair the full power of that discipline. Rationalism has arrived on the scene;[57] the new world, half in shame and half in silence, is granting it its letters of credit. That rationalism is secular in purpose; it is seeking to give mankind a material empire over nature as its primary objective. That rationalism, also, is individualist in temper; for the breakdown of the church's universal discipline means that the individual is himself increasingly able to frame the conditions of the discipline he will accept. And as it is individualist, so also it is naturalistic in temper. It is less and less moved by the cardinal dogma of original sin, more and more influenced by the antithetic principle of self-fulfilment. Individual effort has made so many in this age the masters of their own destinies, that the moral ideal they seek as binding is one that leaves room for that expression. But the channels of individual effort are in the period defined, above all, by the new economic opportunities. The typical man is the new merchant, the new administrator, the new explorer, the adventurer in new thought. All of them are, so to say, experimenting with themselves; they resent whatever may interfere with such experiment. They therefore begin to question dogmas the inference from which is the right to limit such behaviour in men as experience suggests will conduce to their greater advantage. Once this attitude becomes widespread, theology loses its self-confidence. Having begun by resting on the authority of faith, it now seeks to insist that the findings of reason are equally on its side. But such submission means one of two things. Either it is an appeal to the individual judgment, or it is a claim, on secular grounds, for the support of the civil power. In the one case it abandons the right to impose itself; in the other it seeks for authority for purposes alien from its own ends. Either view is an abandonment, more or less explicit in this age, of its title to dominate civil society.

This, then, is the real meaning of the theological revolution. By denying that there was no salvation outside the church, it left no authority save the state capable of controlling the conduct of the individual. The state assumed that task, but from motives, and for ends, quite different from those of the church. The latter thought of the individual in terms of his heavenly destiny; the former thought of him in terms of his contribution to material power. For the state, therefore, the church was transformed into one of its own instruments, a weapon it might use in furtherance of its own limited ends. The church had its profound suspicions of wealth as such; the state had no such suspicions. Its sanctions, accordingly, erode one by one those elements of religious principle which stand in the way of the accumulation of wealth. This evolution, of course, is never uniform and only partially conscious. There is a time when the state almost approaches the church in fear and trembling; as self-sufficient, it is itself too new

71

to venture easily to lay impious hands upon it. It requires an undermining of ecclesiastical authority far more profound than a single century can effect for the process to be complete. The age of the Reformation effects little more than its commencement. It is the age of challenge rather than the age of victory. It brings emancipations which are never more than half-complete. But the foundations of emancipation are laid. Protestantism meant that man might question the title of his church to allegiance. To vindicate his right to question there was no realm of enquiry he did not ransack for argument, and, at its end, he had completed that first and essential step which consisted in proving that he had justified his presumption in thinking out anew the terms of the human adventure. From that justification all else followed that was to be accomplished.

VII

Medieval theology was a metaphysic and a cosmology; with its defeat a new interpretation of the world was essential. The change in the direction of men's thoughts from a universe in which their main attention was concentrated upon the problems of the after-life to one in which their chief emphasis was upon the issues of the life we know was revolutionary in its consequences. It gave an altogether new impetus to the study of natural phenomena. It meant the analysis of experience by reason and the validation of hypothesis by experiment. As the new knowledge accumulated, it replaced an interpretation of nature in which magic and miracle were fundamental elements by one in which observed and regular sequence permitted the formulation of law and this, in its turn, conferred the power to predict. As the results of science began to make possible a greater power over nature, so its practitioners developed an ever greater confidence in the power of reason, unaided by authority or faith, to resolve its mysteries. Where these, indeed, stood in the path of reason they were resented; and the men of science became, though in large part without deliberate purpose, soldiers in that battle for the right to think freely which is one of the cardinal principles of the liberal faith. The root of their attitude was a rejection of the two great medieval principles of homocentricity on the one hand, and teleology on the other. It was not, of course, a rejection which came suddenly and it had to be fought for inch by inch. The martyrdom of Giordano Bruno, the imprisonment of Galileo, the caution of Descartes, the passionate mysticism of Kepler, the fact that a great experimentalist like Harvey could still take part in an examination for witchcraft, the deep and abiding interest of Newton in the conventional problems of dogmatic theology, all show how tough and resistant was the climate of medievalism. But, after the publication of the Copernican hypothesis, the shift of the scientific spirit to secularism is rapid. Knowledge for the sake of power over a tangible and visible world becomes its self-sufficient justification. That attitude allies itself with the new spirit of commercial enterprise to alter the sanctions of behaviour.

Nor must we forget the significance of the relation of the scientific spirit to technological advance.[58] A large part of the discoveries were made possible by the making of new instruments which multiplied enormously the power to observe. Jansen's discovery of the compound microscope, the work of Leonard Digges in telescopy, the great improvements in marine instruments, the achievements of Tycho Brahe in more accurate astronomical invention, all meant an insight into a new world. The development of mathematics in the hands of men like Vieta and Cardan put new weapons in their hands. Stevin laid the foundations of modern hydro-mechanics; and, at the end of the century, Kepler had put the science of optics on a new foundation. Not less remarkable was the work of Gilbert in magnetism and electricity; and its importance consisted hardly less in its method of experiment than in its actual results. The voyages of discovery gave an immense stimulus both to geography and to the biological science. In botany L'Eclus and Mattioli, Bauhin and Cesalpini mark an epoch. Vesalius may be said to have effected alone a revolution in anatomy; and Servetus and Fabricius laid the foundations of Harvey's fundamental discovery. Medical progress, too, was rapid. There is not merely advance in diagnosis and treatment; there is the manufacture of artificial eyes and limbs, the use of new drugs, the more specialized study of disease. A name like that of Ambroise Paré alone is indicative of a revolutionary approach.

It would take me beyond my allotted province to discuss in detail the relation between the scientific achievement of the age and its economic character. It is enough for me to point out here their close interrelation. The stimulus provided by the geographical discoveries to the art of navigation, and, hence, to astronomy and physics; the importance of the new methods of warfare to engineering and thence, once again, to physical science; the way in which the agricultural revolution produced the light plough and thence, through the enclosures, new methods and machines in weaving; the relation of the classical revival in architecture to the solution of new problems in structural mechanics; the stimulus to engineering and metallurgy effected by the development of deep-mining for both coal and metals; the need, emphasized by Agricola in 1556, for labour-saving devices in all aspects of heavy industry; constructional works for municipal water supplies, like those completed at Augsburg in 1558 and at Toledo even earlier; all these show an intimate connection between the work of the scientist and the evolution of industry. It is not, I think, excessive to say that the new outlook codified in the *Principia* of Newton emerged from a nexus of problems presented to science by business men.[59] In their search for wealth, they required new power over nature, new instruments to develop that power. Their needs defined new horizons for the scientist out of which emerged a new picture of the universe and a new control of nature. This partnership in experiment, here deliberate, there only half-conscious, is one of the most momentous events in the modern world.

We can see that significance in every aspect of the century's striving. But nowhere are its implications more clear than in the lives of two very different men who summarize in their outlook the ultimate burden of its teaching. Giordano Bruno is less, perhaps, the child of the Reformation than of the Renaissance; or, rather, the attitude he symbolizes is born of that conflict between old authority and new insight which defined its basic canon.[60] He is impatient of medieval dogma and the provincial outlook it engendered. He sees in the universe the order and regularity of inviolable law. His gaze into the infinite transcends even the vision of Copernicus with its sense of an infinity of worlds which reduces to pettiness a merely Christian theology. The keynote of his writings is their almost reckless luxuriance in a feeling of emancipation from tyranny. He is a Pantheist drunk with the knowledge of universal godhead; but a Pantheist, also, with a new sense of the majesty of the human personality to whom this insight has been vouchsafed. From his marriage of the philosophy of Cusanus with the science of Copernicus he produced a metaphysic which made entire abstraction of the accepted doctrines of his day. And with that feeling of emancipation there goes a claim to enjoy its power so intensely felt that he seemed almost to welcome the conscious defiance of authority it implied. He is driven to proclaim new truth with ecstasy. He has no sense of the caution which, in other men of his time, led either to silence or compromise. His sense of a mission of which he could not evade the fulfilment almost invited martyrdom; but his enemies might well have suspected that the flames which consumed his body were burning an old world also as they consummated his tragic fate.

Bruno makes evident, if in an extreme way, the degree to which the new science had freed his generation from the fetters of the old cosmology. His attitude is nothing so much as the proclamation of the right of modern man to follow his thought wherever it may lead. Professor Whitehead may be right in saying that "the cause for which he suffered was not that of science but that of free imaginative speculation"; but the point of his martyrdom is the fact that the new science had supplied the full perspective of his thought. That is true, also, of Francis Bacon. In him there is expressed, more magistrally than in any other figure of his time, the realization, first, that a new world has been born, and, second, that science has given to man the means of becoming its master. The discoveries, he tells us, "have changed the whole face and state of things throughout the world". He has little save contempt for the "degenerate learning" of the schoolmen (who) "did out of no great quantity of matter and infinite agitation of wit, spin out unto us those laborious webs of learning which are extant in their books . . . but of no substance or profit." What he pleads for is experiment, co-operative investigation of nature, the abandonment of prejudice, the establishment of right methods of enquiry. We must be empirical and rational. We must observe relentlessly, and take pains to record our observations. We must endow scientific research as a principle of public policy. As we do this, "human knowledge and human power meet in one; for where the cause is not known, the effect cannot be produced. Nature, to be commanded, must be obeyed".

To command Nature, indeed, is the highest end of Bacon's ambition; and the way to command it is to discover the rhythm it follows. His view is, if in a high sense, an essentially utilitarian one. He has little of Bruno's zest in knowledge for its own sake; his objective is knowledge for the sake of the power it confers. He is the foe of tradition, and of that species of authority which, for the sake of tradition, would set boundaries to the acquisition of knowledge. "The relief of man's estate", "the service of human convenience", "the amplification of the rule and power of mankind over the world", "the restitution of man to the sovereignty of nature", these are the purposes of science as he conceives it. The reader of the *New Atlantis* can still feel in its pages the sense of a new power which is to regenerate the universe. Nor is his vision limited to natural science. He calls for a new history. He makes of philosophy a method almost alien, in any traditional sense, from metaphysical speculation; for philosophy, with him, is little save the knowledge of nature. His attack on the academic deficiencies of his time proposes an ideal hardly yet, in the fullness he gave it, realized in our own day. His admission of usury shows him the statesman who puts commercial requirement before theological principle. His attitude to the church is purely Erastian; for him it is simply an instrument that the state may use in its pursuit of power.[61]

The idea of power, indeed, is at the heart of his whole outlook. In a fundamental sense he is the disciple of Machiavelli in that he makes his code of ethics one of which the criterion is ability to satisfy material appetite. Indeed, save Machiavelli, he is the least theological writer in spirit of his time. Efficiency and utility are his gospel; and he has no condemnation too strong for whatever interferes with their attainment. Man, as he sees him, is above all a creature moved by desire to fulfil his capacity. He seeks the conditions by which, in a world of ambition, vanity, fear, selfishness, a world, moreover, in which he knows that the medieval discipline has broken down, that capacity may be fulfilled at its maximum. The criteria he applies to conduct are those of the business man, with power, instead of profit, as the end to be served. In his conception of science, there may have been deficiencies which bound him, despite himself, to the older, Aristotelian outlook; he may, as Harvey bluntly put it, have written of science like a Lord Chancellor. But he wrote of it as a Lord Chancellor concerned to administer a vast terrestrial estate the boundless possibilities of which intoxicated him; and he would admit the validity of no principle of government which hindered the realization of those possibilities.

### VIII

By 1600 we may say definitively that men are living and working in a new moral world. The sources that have gone to its making are various indeed. But what permeates them all is the sense of a new wealth at hand for the seeking. What has been born of that new wealth is an attitude of criticism to tradition which is, in the long run, fatal to its power to impose a discipline upon men. There is hardly any element in life which is not seen in a new and creative way. The passion for novelty is intense; the avidity with which men read the record of geographical adventure is alone proof of that. The emergence, from that record, of ideas like that of the virtuous savage, the good life independent of Christian principle, the possibility of progress, relativism in morals and government, the far-off land where men may find peace and toleration, all these are of an importance beyond denial. They affected even the missionaries themselves, as the Jesuit narratives made evident. How greatly they shaped the minds of thinkers like Montaigne and Bodin is evident from every page of their writings. It is hardly an exaggeration to say that, already in the sixteenth century, there are laid down those general principles which, in the eighteenth century, formed the outlook of Voltaire and Adam Smith, of Hume and Diderot and Kant. Mankind is consciously engaged in a new human adventure in which it resents as fetters the characteristics of the old.

This it is which explains the emergence of secularism. The attack on Rome is above all an attack upon a way of life which stood as a barrier across the new path. Its sanctions were too absolute; they were devised, it was felt, for a static world which had departed for ever. The emphasis of Rome was so much upon this life as a mere preparation for the life to come that it interfered in a hundred ways with all the possibilities in which men felt themselves involved. Whether that interference was for good or evil, we have not to determine; it is enough for us that it was felt so widely as unjustifiable restraint. Secularism had the immense advantage over the Roman outlook that it implied advantages which were immediately measurable and tangible. It could be made the parent of a new outlook with wholly new postulates, and wholly new inferences for conduct to be drawn from those postulates. How largely they were drawn in the economic realm we have seen in the new attitude to usury and to the poor. Each changes because it interferes with the accumulation of wealth. Each is abandoned because it limits the exploitation of new opportunity. By the close of the sixteenth century it is the state and not the church which is the sanction of peace and order. The state develops its own principles of conduct; it is not too much to say that it develops its own theology. It is not too much to say that, after the Reformation, it looks upon religion as an instrument to use rather than as an end to serve. It has suffused the churches with its own ideology. It has made them agents in the emphasis upon utilitarianism as the criterion of moral ideals.

But the state, after all, is no more than a body of men who, at some given time, exercise the supreme coercive power of society in a particular way. The significant fact in the sixteenth century is the way in which that power is exercised. Predominantly, it is exercised for peace and material power. It is increasingly, incarnate in the Prince who directs it; there is little literature in the epoch which does not, in greater or less degree, assume that incarnation, for the influence of classical example, is weak before the need of the strong man who, in an age of anarchy, shall impose his will on his subjects. The sixteenth century prince is allowed wide powers because, the greater his authority, the better the chance of the economic revival which conflict hinders. And none are so eager for peace as the new merchants. It is their alliance with the monarchies that is most helpful in extinguishing the effort of the great feudatories to retain some vestige of independent authority. The rising bourgeoisie sees in a strong central authority the best guarantee of its own survival, the best hope of its own prosperity. The princes recognized the value of that alliance; and their legislation is, in large part, a deliberate effort to establish the conditions the bourgeoisie requires. The greater the wealth the bourgeoisie can attain, the more powerful will be the state. The prince should encourage and protect manufacturers, give them peace and a cheap and rapid justice, a disciplined working class schooled to work. We can still catch the note of this temper in the stately English of the preambles to Tudor statutes. We can still measure something of the price it involved in the tragic pleas of clergy and pamphleteers for a more generous attitude to the defeated in those who exploit the new methods.[62]

The bourgeoisie is rising; let us note that it has not yet risen. Its attitude to the state is still one of profound genuflexion. It is an ally conscious of the need to be humble, not yet daring to claim mastery. What it seeks, it asks for as privilege and not as right; the groundwork of its requests, so to say, is always an advantage to itself that the state may realize by yielding to them. We have not yet, at this period, reached the stage of individualism. Monarch and aristocracy still have an exceptional status; and the alliance between the lawyer and his business client is still far from complete. But each step in this period that the state has to take makes it more and more dependent upon the business men. The increased need for military defence gives industry, whether for the financing of policy or the manufacture of arms, a new significance. The effect is cumulative simply because the more intense the military effort of the state, the greater the fortunes the business men will make thereby; "artillery", as Bouillon noted in the seventeenth century,[63] "devours finance". And the nature of the new armament leads to a growth of the heavy industries upon a far wider scale than previously known. Not merely so. This, in its turn, poses problems, in ballistics, for example, which cements the partnership between science and industry, and makes the men of one group the supporters of the needs and outlook of the other. And the new militarist state, once more, is naturally bound to a policy of public works, especially in the field of communications. This means the development of loans, with the new significance it gives to the banker, and of the engineer. It emphasizes, in fact, the need of the state, if it is to maximize its strength, to act upon the principles which the bourgeoisie is applying in its own private sphere. It makes the state a capitalist state, almost despite itself. For the state, by 1600, is beginning to pursue ends it can only pursue successfully if it adopts as its own the fundamentals of the new economic spirit. The new ways of power have to be, increasingly, bourgeois ways.

And all this involves a rationalization of administrative principle to which is have large consequences. It is important that the chief officials of the state become laymen instead of priests; this was in itself something of a revolution. But it is not less important that, in large degree, the chief officials are also *novi homines*, adventurers whose attitude to their problems makes them very apt to sympathize with both the purposes and the methods of the new enterprise. We must not, indeed, push this fact too far. As soon as the Stuarts come to the English throne the disparity between the outlook of the state they envisage and that of the business men becomes immediately apparent. Yet the fact that by 1642 the business men are prepared to fight the monarchy for the right to control the state is evidence of how far the new conception of administration has made its way. Their temper is already foreshadowed in the sixteenth century in such things as the debate upon monopolies; and the way in which Peter Wentworth is prepared to use Parliament as a platform for the expression of grievance makes him in some sort the real predecessor of Pym and Hampden. We can at least say that, by 1600, the state has built the institutional instrumentalities it requires for new purposes. The English Parliament, no doubt, occupies a place apart. But the King's Council, the King's courts, the administrative departments, are all operating upon a new scale. The King's ministers, whether it is William Cecil in England, or, a little later, Sully in France, have a wholly new outlook. To them both the soldier and the aristocrat are subordinate. The lawyer is arising to independent political status, partly because the enhanced significance of national law has given him a new importance, partly because the very nature of the new regimé requires legal principles and standards of administration he is the type most fitted to define. The contrast is great between a chancellor like More, at the beginning of the century, and one like Bacon a century later; their criteria of good have no relevance to each other. The one has, with all his modernity, the typical aspects of a medieval saint; the other is the efficient courtier in whom personal advancement determines all standards of conduct. The author of the *Utopia* was not unaware of the passions and discoveries of the Renaissance, but he sought their subordination to the glories of the Catholic ideal. The author of the *New Atlantis* is wholly secular in temper. He stands for the world of the future, its frank materialism, its lust for power, its contempt for asceticism, its healthy acceptance of the natural man. Between the death of More and the death of Bacon a whole world passes. The difference between them symbolizes what was implicit in the transition.

In the sixteenth century, this is to say, the foundations of a liberal doctrine have been laid. There is a social discipline which finds its sanctions independently of the religious ideal. There is a self-sufficient state. There is an intellectual temper aware, perhaps a little uneasily aware, that a limitation to the right of speculation is also a limitation to the right to material power. There is a new physical world, both in the geographical sense and the ideological. The content of experience being new also, new postulates are needed for its interpretation. Their character is already being defined in the realm of social theory, not less than in those of science and philosophy. This content is material, and of this world, instead of being spiritual and of the next. It is expansive, utilitarian, self-confident. It sets before itself the ideal of power over nature for the sake of the ease and comfort this power will confer. In its essence, it is the outlook of a new class which, given authority, is convinced that it can remould more adequately than in the past the destinies of man. It has hinted at the philosophy upon which it proposes to proceed. In the next age it proceeds without hesitation to its fuller definition.

## CHAPTER II

# The Seventeenth Century

I

THE seventeenth century has been rightly termed the age of genius, for, even after three hundred years, the implications of its discoveries are not yet exhausted. Yet it is well not to emphasize too sharply its separation from its predecessor. The evolution from the one to the other is gradual rather than distinct. Its canon is merely the flowering of seeds planted in the earlier time. Newton and Descartes, Hobbes and Locke, Pascal, Sydenham and Bayle, only developed with genius the major insights of their forerunners. What, perhaps, differentiates it from the sixteenth century is less the character of its attitude than the scale and the intensity with which this is pressed forward. In the sixteenth century, the battle is yet to be won, even if the assurance of victory is present. In the seventeenth the triumph is so complete that the foe is hardly discernible upon the field.

What is the triumph that was won? It is in England that this is most clearly to be seen and there is no mistaking the meaning of the result. The victory is for utilitarianism in morals, for toleration in religion, for constitutional government in the sphere of politics. In the economic realm, the state becomes the handmaid of commerce; its habits are modified to the new medium this has come to require. Even its wars are for markets, for the power, that is, that accrues indirectly to economic domination. The prize of its conquests are colonies, by which is meant the opportunity to trade more widely. The men of the city began to play a conscious role in politics; at the end of the period they have founded, in the Bank of England, an institution which they know to be the cornerstone of the new house. Political parties have been born; the cabinet system has taken shape; the King is beneath, and not above, the law. The incidence of wealth has definitely shifted from the countryside to the town. The successful merchant is no longer a suppliant for the monarch's favour; he is aware that his interests shape the whisper of the throne. England in the seventeenth century is the triumph of bourgeois virtue.[1] It traces the outline of an empire. It puts the volume of its commerce beyond the reach of contemporary rivalry. It teaches King and aristocracy alike that their privileges may not be incompatible with its interests. Having achieved the internal administrative unity it requires, it determines, beyond peradventure, what that unity is for. Great as was the genius of Newton and Hobbes, that collective genius of the English middle-class which, in this age, wholly reshaped the framework of a Kingdom to its purposes, does not suffer by the comparison. For, in its achievement, it set the temper, and guided the spirit of its contemporaries not merely in the next age, but for two hundred years longer. From the revolution it effected nothing escapes. In establishing its supremacy, it changed both the substance and the manner of men's thinking.

We can see this in innumerable ways. It is evident, for example, in the change of the preacher's emphasis from the scholastic embroidery of Donne and Andrewes to the simple moral exhortation of Tillotson and Wake. It is evident in the change from Bacon's essays at the beginning of the period, to the light ease of Swift and Addison at its end. The superb mysticism of Vaughan and Crashaw passes, through the organ-like religious note of Milton, to the rationalist self-confidence of Pope. Society may still accept a rigid distinction of class. But the great man of science, like Newton, the great man of letters like Milton or Dryden, the great thinker, like Locke, begin to exercise an authority independent of court and patron. The refinement of manners penetrates to the middle class. Their houses, their furniture, their plate, begin to assume newly luxurious forms; sumptuary laws prove powerless before their wealth and self-confidence. They assume an interest in art; though, here, it is in Holland rather than in England that the bourgeoisie sets the standard of production. It is significant, too, that after Shakespeare the substance of its drama is almost wholly concerned with the passions of this world. Religious conflict hardly enters into its interests. There is, even in the Elizabethan age, a new sympathy, illustrated by Dekker's *Shoemaker's Holiday* (1600) with bourgeois aspirations; there, already, the zealous apprentice wins the rich man's daughter despite the rivalry of earl and gentleman. If, in the seventeenth century, English drama still centres about a life above the middle-class world, it is important that, with the Restoration, it has lost all need to subordinate itself to standards religiously defined. Its theme is the play of wit, the struggle between secular vice and secular virtue, the quest for pleasure, the conflict between youth and age. Its very licence is the measure of the degree to which the stage had freed itself from the need to defer to the church. When protest against its indecencies came, as with Jeremy Collier, the new drama begins to eulogize the typical bourgeois virtues and to make of success the supreme end. That Wycherley and Dryden and Congreve should give place to Lillo is a measure of the prestige the merchant has already won. In the seventeenth century, indeed, the Republic of Letters begins to assume its modern democratic form. The rise of the periodical press, greatly stimulated by the Civil Wars, has the twofold effect of making the average man a commentator on the world about him and, at least vicariously, a critical intimate of that great world in which statesman and courtier dwelt. It is significant of the new power of public opinion in the age that no authority is successful enough to introduce an effective censorship of the news; and that in the first years of the eighteenth century Swift and Defoe are already providing the political parties with their authoritative organs of propaganda. The periodical press may, as Pope bitterly complained, live by "new born nonsense" and "dead born scandal". But its general influence realized the ambition of Addison[2] of bringing "philosophy out of the closets and libraries, schools and colleges, to dwell in clubs, at teatables and in coffee-houses". The man of letters begins to constitute himself the interpreter of new knowledge to the multitude; and he is aware of the magnitude of his task. He should, wrote Dryden,[3] "be learned in several sciences, should have a reasonable, philosophical, and in some measure a mathematical head . . . he should have experiences in all sorts and humours and manners of men, should be thoroughly skilled in conversation, and should have a great knowledge of mankind in general." In the seventeenth century, in a word, while there is all the amplitude of learning which characterizes the sixteenth, it begins, both consciously and on a great scale, to adapt itself to a new audience. Latin rapidly ceases to be the universal tongue of the learned; and the bourgeoisie begins to enter its kingdom.

Not less important is the evolution of a new educational outlook. In this respect, as in so many others, Locke summarizes the results of a century's progress.[4] What is significant, in the first place, is the immense influence he attributes to environment; the child "is wax to be fashioned and moulded as one pleases". Here, clearly, is fully present the new sense of that power over nature which science was held to confer upon mankind. There is no sense, either, of original sin or predestinationist doctrine; the "blank page, void of all characters" will be what training makes it. Important, in the second place, is Locke's assumption that the child will be trained by suitable tutors in a good environment; education, for him, is a luxury that men of property alone can afford for their children. For the most part, the type of training he recommends is that of the gentleman. But the new spirit is pervasive in his ideas. The child is to be taught religion, but he is to be safeguarded against superstition from his earliest days. The curriculum, with its emphasis upon secular knowledge in general, and the sciences in particular, emphasizes "the ability to manage his affairs in this world with foresight" as essential; even the gentleman's son should learn a manual trade. And if this theory is contrasted with Locke's specific for the education of the poor, his view of their place in the community is obvious. "Knowledge and science in general", he wrote, "are the business only of those who are at ease and leisure"; it befits, that is, people who already possess property to give them a place in the world. The children may be taught religion, and some handicraft like weaving or knitting; by these their useful employment in this world, and their destiny in the next, may be assured. For Locke, that is, the world is already divided, so far as education goes, into the two fundamental classes of rich and poor. For the one, the purpose of training is an ability to govern, whether in affairs of state, or in the management of their private affairs; for the other, a pious and useful obedience is the end of existence. There could hardly be a clearer expression of what the rise of the bourgeoisie had come to imply. It had for Locke, so to speak, fought its fight and established its title to share with the gentleman in the direction of governance; henceforward its problem was to discover the educational means to maintain the equilibrium it had achieved.

Seventeenth century England, moreover, sees the emergence of a new attitude to religion. It becomes rational, even worldly, in character. There is much less interest in mysticism or enthusiasm; a shift in the emphasis of discussion from problems of dogma to problems of conduct. Partly, of course, the rise of deism, in itself a proof of decline in the religious spirit, is responsible for this; partly, also, men are fatigued with the unending warfare of the sects and seek to concentrate discussion

on identities rather than differences. What Bossuet
said of Christianity generally, in the post-Reformation
period, is true of England after the Restoration in a
special degree. "There are Christians", he wrote,[5] "who
rob Christianity of all its mysteries. They transform it
into a philosophic sect adapted simply to the senses.
. . . They open the way to deism, to, that is to say,
a disguised atheism." This temper is abundantly evident
in Locke with his insistence upon the danger of the
inner light, and its enthusiasm, as the ground-work of
belief; and it is, of course, from Locke that the English
freethinkers of the eighteenth century take their rise.
The fact is that, by the end of the sixteenth century, the
difference between religious principle and economic
practice had become so wide that a restatement of
religious sanctions was imperative. The importance of
that restatement lies in its being made in the seventeenth
and not the sixteenth century. For, by then, the great
outlines of the commercial revolution are complete.
The rise of the middle class is no longer a claim to be
challenged, but a fact to be accepted. Religion has to
accommodate itself to this new order.

How this accommodation was effected Professor
Tawney has shown in a classic analysis.[6] "To the Puritan", he has written, "a contemner of the vain shows
of sacramentalism, mundane toil becomes itself a kind
of sacrament." We do not need, in Max Weber's
fashion, to search out scattered texts to prove how the
Puritan prepared the path for capitalism's triumph.
For, in the first place, he did nothing of the kind; and,
in the second, in adapting the framework of his creed
to a new environment, he was wholly unconscious of any

92

desire to serve new gods. Nor is there, in any case, a single Puritan doctrine which presents a united front to economic requirement. The supreme Puritans of the century, John Bunyan, George Fox, even Richard Baxter, were not the men to compromise with Mammon. The two first wrestle as passionately with the Devil for the right to salvation as any medieval saint. They are not less unworldly in temper. They are not less possessed of the deep conviction of sin. To rescue themselves by grace, to make each item of their lives permeated by its spirit, to will themselves into salvation, this becomes the temper of their effort. They abhor indolence, which offers temptations to frail mortality to desert the way. They shrink from amusement and pleasure which offer worldly satisfaction where there should be spiritual delight. The mood of their religion made them men of steel, Ironsides in very faith, who could not but succeed in the thing to which they put their hands.

It was a mood tempered into unbreakable determination by the persecution they encountered. We can see something of its lofty indignation still in Milton's passionate sonnet against the massacre of the Vaudois. That is but an item in a long and terrible record. We cannot too often remember that wherever the Puritan encountered the state it was, for him, not merely an engine of repression, but, more, an engine of repression concerned to destroy the saints of God. They knew the state, until the Toleration Act, as an instrument used to harass and attack them; it was no wonder that they came to suspect the purposes of its action. They saw it used always either to enforce truth they knew to be contrary to God's teaching, or to penalize those of their brethren who stood by the faith. For them, the state meant imprisonment, confiscation of goods, poverty for themselves and their dependents. They heard from the exiles of Flanders and France what it meant abroad. How should they not argue from their experience that the less power it possessed, the smaller the sphere of its operations, the greater the freedom they might enjoy? For them, to urge the desirability of toleration was a simple lesson from the teaching of their daily lives. The tolerant state was the state which set truth free to be believed. More, to achieve that state was to win a victory for God. To fight, therefore, against its omnicompetence, to build a philosophy which limited its power, was the means of something more than economic benefit. It became also a sacred obligation. This is the fundamental reason why, both in England and France, the theory of a liberal state found such widespread acceptance among dissenters.[7]

And this attitude joined hands with the religious spirit of Puritanism at a point where its influence became decisive. It was an inference from their faith that they should pour, as I have pointed out, all the energy of their spirit into all their daily lives. So they could win the favour of God. But how not conclude that the proof of the favour of God was success? How not infer, if wealth follows effort, that the man who attains it is the chosen vessel of the Lord? How avoid, in the desperate struggle to survive, the tendency to accept the methods which succeed as blessed of God because they succeed? We must not assume that these Puritans are any less rigorous than Anglican or Catholic in their insistence on the religious sanction of economic practice.

Ames, Baro and Baxter, are all concerned with salvation
and not with the construction of a secular ethic for the
business man. But the Puritan moralist, and especially
Baxter, is aware that his teaching is to apply to a life
which, from the very nature of man, is a vale of tears.
He is conservative not less than any of his religious
rivals in his emphasis upon the supremacy of religious
rules. But, in large part unconsciously, the very virtues
that his experience made him foster weakened the
effect of his precepts upon them. "The sly and forbid
practice" of usury, for example, begins to find root by
subtle exception and refined distinction. The difference
between the private world of the inner light and the
public world of commercial practice begins to be emphasized. A new attitude to poverty develops which
begins to equate failure with the absence of grace. A
sense that private advantage makes for public good
permeates, especially after 1660, the whole outlook of
Puritanism. It is not too much to say that, by the end
of the seventeenth century, it has come to possess one
standard for the owners of property and another for
those who live by wages. When the predominating position of the Puritan in industry is remembered, the significance of his dualism becomes momentous indeed.

The habits of the seventeenth century state, that is
to say, brought out in Puritanism those elements which
made it, quite contrary to its inherent principle, an
agent in the promotion of a secular outlook. More,
because it was always the religion of a minority, it made
it individualist in temper. From its hatred of the state as
persecutor, it moved easily to the doctrine that man must
rely upon himself, that his prosperity is the outcome

of his own energy. Persecution made him tender for
the rights of property; he can even come to accept
the idea of state-action against enclosures as undesirable. He can come to see virtue even in the idea that
the cash-nexus is the only bond between man and man.
For while he may emphasize the duty of charity to one's
neighbour, this does not interest him in the question of
higher wages. While he may protest against the evil of
extortion, he will come, as with Defoe, to see in the
"luxury, pride and sloth" of the wage-earner their
efficient cause. And, after the Restoration, he is the
essential part of the commercial class which is staking
its existence on the conquest of an economic empire
from Holland and France. There is little he is not prepared to do for the achievement of that victory.

We must not think of Puritan dualism as solitary in
its age. It represents, with different ways of expression,
an outlook which gained momentum over the whole of
Europe as the century proceeded. It is more emphatic
in England than, save Holland, elsewhere, only because,
in England, the Revolution of 1640-88 gave the commercial class the status of full political recognition
earlier. But we can see the sweep of the outlook, if we
turn, for a moment, to seventeenth century France.
For there is the golden age of the French monarchy
which, after its triumph over the Fronde, shapes all
institutions and thoughts to the service of its supremacy.
It is an age of widespread religious renovation—the age
of the Jesuit College, of Port Royal, of the Oratorians,
of ecclesiastical charity upon a wider scale than France
has ever known. It is, moreover, the great age of the
preachers, Catholic and Protestant alike; the richness of

a period in which Bossuet, Bourdaloue, Massillon, Fléchier, Fénélon, on the one side, Claude, Saurin, Jurieu, on the other, exercise their magistral sway. It is the age which produced, in the *Pensées* of Pascal, perhaps the most influential apologetic Christianity has known since the Reformation. It is an age, also, in which the battle for religious supremacy was waged more fiercely than in any other part of Europe with all the authority of the Crown behind the fight for orthodoxy.

And yet behind the apparent emphasis upon Christian principle the growth of the bourgeois spirit is unmistakable. We can see that growth in countless ways. It is implicit in the very existence of Jansenism which, whatever its errors and exaggerations, is a noble protest against the worldliness which had invaded religion. We can see it in Molière's plea for a natural ethic[8]—the direct descendant of the gospel of Rabelais and Montaigne. La Rochefoucauld preaches a naked gospel of success; the misery of the Fronde, on the one hand, and his own restless ambition on the other, combine to produce in him a doctrine that Machiavelli would not have disowned. And the truth of La Rochefoucauld's picture is implicitly affirmed by La Bruyère[9]; for the whole essence of the *Caractères* is their admission that the worldling of the Court has triumphed and their resentment at pretensions which exclude the bourgeois from privilege. We can see it, once more, in the genial Epicureanism of La Fontaine and Saint Evremond. For them, the wise man is he who follows the life of impulse and makes the attainment of pleasure the end of existence. We can see it, also, alike in the Cartesian

philosophy and the scepticism of Bayle. The emphatic
"je pense, donc, je suis" of Descartes makes, as Bossuet
saw,[10] man and not God the Master of the universe;
while the immense influence of Bayle is wholly directed
to the erosion of traditional belief. The battle for religious principle in seventeenth century France was lost
before the armies took the field.

This is, of course, a record of a challenge between
fundamentals. Let us note, however, that the sermons
of the French preachers of the age are full of emphasis
upon the bourgeois virtues. They are untiring in their
emphasis upon the obligation to work, upon the need
for regularity of discipline, upon the duty of obedience
to superiors. Bourdaloue hardly tires of insisting upon
man's duty to accept his allotted station and to perform
its obligations faithfully. The social order is divine;
and diversity of condition, even the existence of the
poor, are the will of God. They decry the evil of rebellion; religion itself is threatened by the existence of civil
disharmony. And their very protests are a measure of
their failure to impede the coming of the new order.
The unending desire for wealth, the restless ambition
of the time, the love of display, the hope of finding
security and ease, the yearning to found a family, confidence in one's own foresight instead of trust in the
Providence of God, the separation of the life of this
world from the life of the Christian, the acceptance of
the morality of the *honnête homme* rather than the morality of the gospels, these are the vices they attack. They
lament unceasingly the growth of unbelief. They admit
the rise of an ethic which knows how to secure
honourable conduct without invoking the sanctions of

Christianity; the church no longer presides over their destinies. One has only to compare the change of temper from the sermons of Bossuet to those of Massillon to see the degree to which the new spirit has triumphed. For there is as little relation between Bossuet with his sense of a Providence whose awful decrees one may not dare to examine, of an agonizing mystery at the heart of the universe which it is not given to human beings to solve, and Massillon, with his sweet reasonableness, his desire to move the debate from the plane of dogma to that of ethics, as between the passionate mysticism of Donne, with his sense of a god who is found in contrite agony, and the quiet, almost benevolent, precepts of Tillotson. The seventeenth century in France may be an age of belief; but the faith is powerless to affect the progress of the relentless tide.

For the forces which assisted the capitalist spirit in England were at work in France also, though with some retardation; for historical reasons, feudalism resisted the rise of the bourgeoisie to political status longer in France than in England. The political element apart, though its importance was enormous, there is a similar progress to record in each country. In France, as in England, the barriers which religion oppose to its development break down. In France, as in England, the price of religious controversy is the growth of unbelief. In France, as in England, science and philosophy cease progressively to pay homage to theological censorship. In both countries, also, the search for profit, the extension of the scale of economic enterprise, puts the problem of the poor in a new perspective and results in the emergence of a new state-discipline for their control. In both countries, though in less degree in France than in England, the rise of the bourgeois leaves its mark upon art and literature. In both countries there emerges the new force of public opinion—a force which seeks to grasp the contours of policy and to control them. Each of them develops a wider administrative technique, and there are new men, with new ideals, to staff the departments of state. If England had Pym, Cromwell, Somers, France had Richelieu, Mazarin, Colbert, whose ends are wholly secular ends. It is, indeed, significant that, at the close of the century, a diarist like St. Simon can regret the absorption of political office by the *novi homines*, and make a plan of government which is to restore the nobility to something of its ancient authority.[11] He has the wit to see that a centralized monarchical despotism leaves it no future.

But nothing, I think, shows so plainly the degree to which capitalism had made its way in France, despite all superficial differences, on lines parallel to these of England and Holland, as the character of the criticism encountered by Louis XIV in the last twenty years of his reign. It comes from the most varied sources. A great military engineer like Vauban, a great ecclesiastic like Fénélon, combine with administrators like Boisguillebert and Boulainvilliers to emphasize their view that despotic government and imperialist adventure are ruining the resources of the kingdom. The same picture is implicit in the terrible account given by La Bruyère of the condition of the peasantry. And the critics have, in their different ways, the same remedies to recommend. They want some form of constitutional government and an end of religious persecution. They recognize that material well-being is incompatible with arbitrary authority. They realize that the results of the Revocation have merely added to the wealth of France's rivals. A rational fiscal system, security of property, a means of expressing grievance for those who have substance to contribute to the national wealth, a hint, at least, of freedom of trade, these are their demands. They were, it is notable, all of them demands that the English people had finally translated into achievement in the same period. They differ remarkably from the simple plea for good government on any terms which, Claude Joly,[12] apart, is about the sum and substance of the myriad political pamphlets of the Fronde. They differ remarkably, also, from the tones of passionate eulogy which, from Lebret to Bossuet, greet the creation of Louis XIV's system. The critics are done with Richelieu's *raison d'état*, they are done, also, with Bossuet's defence of divine right. By 1700, the foundations of the omnicompetent state have been decisively undermined. It remained for the eighteenth century to discover how to give a new social order its letters of credit

I must not, of course, be taken to accept the view that French liberal doctrine in the seventeenth century is fundamentally akin to that of England. I am arguing only that similar causes are at work there, though with retarded effect. The great distinction between the two lies in the individualist note which begins to pervade the whole English habit of thought. English constitutionalism in the seventeenth century makes its specific contribution to the liberal idea in two ways. On the one hand it seeks to lay down rules by which the character of authority must be guided; on the other, it seeks to infuse these rules with the idea that their end is the protection of the citizen from interference outside the course of law. To secure this constitutionalism, further, it seeks to deprive the sovereign power of the two main instruments by which despotism becomes possible—control of the armed forces of the state and of finance. The Revolution of 1688 was only the completion of the objects aimed at in the middle-class rebellion which Cromwell headed against the attempted Stuart despotism. Habeas Corpus, triennial Parliaments to be dominated by political parties one of which will be the constant ally of the commercial interest, religious freedom within wide limits, the abolition of government control of the press, a judiciary independent of the executive power in the performance of its legal function, finance and the army in the control of an elected legislature, with these achievements the English merchant may sleep comfortably in his bed. His property is safe alike from the assault of state and church for the simple reason that, equally with the country gentleman, he now has at last his hands on the levers of political power. In the full sense, he is a person, able to make and unmake governments. He has not only willed order; he has decided what purposes that order is to shape. It is because he achieved these things in the seventeenth century that he could so largely define the effective liberal doctrine which emerged in its full maturity in the eighteenth century.

Two things must be added. Liberalism as a way of life, as, most notably, a theory of the state, was largely outlined by the experience of England (in a lesser degree of Holland) in this age. It is important to note how largely it is a compromise. It was made possible by revolution, and there was a period under Cromwell when that revolution seemed likely to travel much farther than its authors desired. They sought a limited monarchy; they achieved it, but only after a brief experiment with republicanism. By achieving it, they built the solution they effected upon the basis of an alliance between the aristocracy and the middle class. The landowner and the man of commerce went into partnership at the Revolution to exploit possibilities in which the interest of both urban worker and landless peasant were only indirectly involved. After 1688 there is no threat in England from the middle class to the fundamental lines of the compromise then effected. The civil war, in the second place, was won for the middle class by an army of apprentices, workmen and peasants who developed, during its course, radical ideas whose daring seems more suited to the nineteenth than to the sixteenth century.[13] We must not miss the significance of the social revolution which failed in the Puritan Rebellion. The Levellers and the agrarian communists of that day, in a lesser degree, also, the Baptists and Fifth Monarchy men intimate the emergence of a proletarian ideology. They make it clear that the victory which was achieved was not their victory. They emphasize the fact that the constitutional liberties which were conquered may have suited a class of property-owners but failed to fulfil the dreams of those who had nothing but their labour-power by which to live.

103

II

English political thought in the seventeenth century passes through certain distinct phases. From the accession of James I until the outbreak of the Civil War, its main theme is the limits of monarchical power.[14] A peaceful compromise between opposing views proved impossible. From 1642 until 1660 we therefore watch a revolutionary struggle in which the royalist cause is beaten in the field. But, as always in a revolution, issues were raised in its continuance far different from those intended by its makers; for whereas the Parliamentarians fought the Crown in order to establish the legislature as the effective centre of law-making power, the sufferings of the army, its sense of the high mission it had accomplished, led many of its members to seek the transformation of a political into a social, revolution.[15] The dissidents failed. They had neither the numbers nor the organization necessary to achieve their purpose; and the whole mental climate of the generation was unfavourable to it. But the importance of their effort was great, if only for the light it throws on the very limited character of the Revolution they assisted in making. The Restoration which followed on the death of Cromwell only supplied a traditional penumbra to the new foundations his victories had built. Henceforth, it is recognized that political power is a trust the purposes of which shall be defined by Parliament. James II sought to evade that conclusion. The result was the "glorious revolution" of 1688 which defined the Cromwellian compromise in precise terms. The philosopher of the revolution was Locke; and his theories defined the essential outlines of Liberal doctrine for nearly two centuries.

This is, of course, to summarize with deceptive simplicity a debate that was, in fact, infinitely more complex in character. Neither the Royalist party nor the Parliamentarian had a single point of view. On the King's side were advocates of the Divine Right of Kings, of a utilitarian theory of monarchy, of tradition and order against novelty and rebellion. Some of his protagonists, like Laud, stood for a thoroughly medieval view of social relationships, in which a partnership between the King and the Anglican Church simply replaced the claim of Rome to settle the canons of social behaviour. Others, like Clarendon, are aware that wider foundations for the state are required than Divine Right merely can supply; but they shrink from the rigorous logic of Hobbes which, as Filmer saw, can as well justify a Cromwell as a Charles. And their motives are devoid of any unity. Charles' clerical supporters, for the most part, simply saw in their exaltation of the monarchy the one means of beating a Parliament whose victory meant the triumph of Nonconformity. The legal supporters, like Sir Matthew Hale, saw in the joint sovereignty of King and Parliament not only the one effective guarantee of order, but also the realization of a fundamental law of the kingdom which it meant social confusion to abrogate. The different theories hinge upon the social ideal of the particular doctrinaire. Moderate royalists, like Hunton, are for compromise between the conflicting claims. They see the force of the Parliamentary plea for a share in government; the evils of absolute rule force them to that conclusion. But to abolish kingship is for them to violate certain essential rules which both law and history have shown to be invaluable. The royalists were in the difficulty that they dare not, with Hobbes, simply insist that order is in itself the highest good; they are not less interested in what that order makes. They are aware of what Filmer called the "anarchy of a mixed monarchy". But experience of Charles in action compels them to preach a theory of sovereignty in which its attributes are controlled by a fundamental law intended to inhibit its uncontrolled exercise. They stand by the monarchy on grounds, in part historical and in part psychological, in character. Historically, because they are not prepared for the break in tradition which republicanism implies; psychologically because the implications of monarchy seem to them a guarantee of social peace such as no alternative régime can justify. It is the linch-pin of the class-structure of society. Remove that, even, as Filmer said, put the ground of obedience upon a merely secular foundation, and there is no reason why men should not question these whenever they think fit; and the outcome of that questioning is fatal to property and security. Heylyn, Fearne, Filmer, Hunton, all show this sense of dismay.[16]

"They have cast all the mysteries and secrets of government before the vulgar", wrote Clement Walker of the sects in 1661,[17] "and taught the soldiery and the people to look into them and ravel back all governments to the first principles of nature." To understand the meaning of that complaint is the essence of the problem by which England in the seventeenth century was confronted. The antagonism to the Stuarts before 1641 is a dislike of controls which are at least as much social as religious. Government interfered in these years not merely to persecute religion, but to control wages, prices, foreign exchange, the general conditions of agriculture and industry. The poor law, the enclosures, the monopolies were all administered with a rigour which interfered with the business man's desire to conduct his affairs in his own way. When, for example, in 1621 the employers in the clothing industry desired to lockout their workers, they were ordered by the Council to keep the men at work.[18] Whatever the inefficiency of the régime, its energizing principle was that expressed by Laud when he wrote[19] that "if any be so addicted to his private, that he neglect the common state, he is void of the sense of piety, and wisheth peace and happiness to himself in vain". Strafford had no different view; and he was unmoved by the social importance of the men he over-rode.[20] The Stuart despotism was an effort to control the whole of life in the interest of a corporate well-being which regarded the individual interests of particular citizens as completely subordinate to it. It is this corporate well-being which explains the unending interference of the High Commission as Laud engineered its activities. The spirit of the adventure is symbolized not merely by Prynne and Bastwick in the pillory, not merely, either, by the countless Puritans who emigrated to the new world, but by a stern attack on the claims of private property which descended even to criticism of the printing trade for bad work.

And the control attempted had grave demerits. It may have been efficient and impartial with Strafford; for the most part, it was prejudiced, vexatious, costly and arbitrary. It enforced holidays and saints' days which interfered with trade. It made, as in the bullion crisis of 1640,[21] for grave economic loss. In agriculture, as Pierpoint told the House of Commons,[22] it threatened the security of property; on this count the hatred aroused by Laud's high-handedness is testified by Clarendon. The monopolies were loathed. They were held responsible for the rise in prices, and they are held to infect the whole kingdom with corruption. They, too, are attacked on the ground of interference with the rights of property. There is, too, a dislike of the big commercial companies; they deny the opportunity of "all free subjects" to be "inheritable to the free exercise of their industry".[23] Commercial liberty is felt to be the basis of trade efficiency; it is better, wrote a merchant,[24] to leave regulation "to the judicious merchant whose labour is to profit himself, yet in all his actions doth therewith benefit his King, country and fellow-subjects". It is too much, perhaps, to say that there was any widespread dislike of government control of industry as such. But there is hatred of the particular means of control adopted by Charles and his agents, a conviction that it interferes in realms better left alone, a dislike of the corruption and arbitrary rule that it involves, a sense that it leads to impoverishment and insecurity. It is out of all these motives that the Civil War emerges. It is the outcome of an accumulation of particular grievances, all of them aggravated by misgovernment, which, in their total effect, lead to a demand that the content of freedom be given a new institutional basis. To guarantee that content the Parliament asked for control of the army and finance, and the dependence of prerogative upon its own will. When Charles refused these terms, there was no alternative to conflict.

Misgovernment did not become tyranny in 1641 because the Puritans had a passion for democratic government. The constitutional system which emerged was not, either, an expression of their desire to let the ends of government be defined by popular consent. There are democratic elements in Puritanism; and the idea of popular consent as the basis of the state has an important place in Puritan political theory. More than this we cannot say, because more than this the evidence does not permit us to say. The men who made the Revolution of the seventeenth century were seeking to find ways of limiting the operations of authority which would give them security of person and property. The roads thereto, in their conceptions, were extraordinarily diverse, and they changed frequently during the course of the conflict. What would have satisfied them in 1641 would not have satisfied them in 1644, nor again in 1646, or 1653. Once they are engaged in war, there is no interest not concerned to formulate a programme. The incompatibilities [formulated were so profound that, as in all revolutions, their evolution was marked by imprisonment and execution. The revolution that Cromwell made was far from the Revolution that Lilburne conceived as desirable; and what would have satisfied the latter would still have seemed to Gerard Winstanley inadequate and incomplete. To grasp the real character of the debate, therefore, it is upon the differences that emerged, rather than upon their identities that we must lay emphasis.

What are those differences? Above all, I think, they

lie in the social composition of the Puritan party. If they could agree that they disliked unlimited royal prerogative, a persecuting church, the practice of monopolies, there was not much else upon which they could agree. Cromwell and Ireton were as eager as any royalist to see the safety of the state entrusted to the men of solid property. Lilburne represented the small men of the city who felt that the big men of commerce were not less their enemies than king or bishop. Winstanley speaks for the new landless proletariat who have come suddenly to the consciousness that property itself is the enemy. Conditions in war time sharpened these social differences. The high cost of living, new levels of taxation, profiteering, an army and navy with their pay in arrears, throughout the whole period there is the sense of bitter disillusion which finds its grim expression in the tragic prescriptions of Milton's last political pamphlet. Where men hear what the gentry of Norfolk call "the loud outcries of multitudes of undone and almost famished people, occasioned by a general decay of trade, which hath spread itself throughout the whole nation",[25] men begin to take thought for their particular interests. The rich man begins to sigh for the order which means prosperity and self-confidence. He begins to resent the Utopia-making of poor and ill-taught fanatics who, owning nothing, think of the state-power as a fund by which they can live. In these circumstances, the spirit of accommodation advances quickly; and it was this advance which makes possible the compromise of 1660.

Once, in short, the Civil War had made it certain that no new dispensation would involve either unlimited

kingship or an absolute church the divisions between
the Puritans were fatal to their retention of power. The
men of substance feared that the radicals would subvert
the very idea of property itself. They were not going to
exchange a state dominated by Charles and Laud for
one dominated by Lilburne or Wildman or the Diggers
of St. George's Hill. We can see in innumerable utter-
ances the growth of this spirit. "The well-monied man
that is prudent, by God's blessings gets up and above
his neighbours," says one characteristic writer. "Grace
in a poor man is grace, and is beautiful," another tells
us,[26] "but grace in a rich man is more conspicuous,
more useful." "If", says another writer still,[27] "the man
be gracious and religious, that is great and rich, he will
make sweeter harmony and melody in God's eares,
than if he were poore and in low estate." The complaint
against the Quakers, who sympathized with the sufferings of the poor, is not least that their membership "was
made up of the dregs of the common people";[28] for
even to an ardent social reformer like Hartlib the able-
bodied vagrant is not a victim of society but a self-
created burden upon it, who deserves punishment.[29]

It is not too much to say that the Restoration was a
combination of men of property in all classes against
a social revolution which they vaguely felt to be threat-
ening. The very Cavalier Parliament which their
enthusiasm elected soon made Charles II realize that,
whatever was restored, it was not the old order of things.
The new England was emphatically the England of
Hobbes and Harrington, of Petty and the Royal Society,
an England, as an acute French observer remarked, in
which religion was "preaching and sitting still on

Sundays".[30] It was an England which did not doubt
Harrington's natural law that political power follows
upon economic power, that, also, in a generation, was
to accept his dictum that there is no civil liberty which
does not include religious liberty as well.[31] Even the
revival, under the later Stuarts, of the Divine Right of
Kings is merely a passing phase;[32] as soon as James II
threatens the security of the Church of England, Dean
Sherlock shows that a good Anglican can argue as well
upon one as upon the other side of the question.[33] What
disappears in the first half of the seventeenth century
is enthusiasm for any regulations of social and economic
life which does not emanate from Parliament. It had
been tried and found unsafe. It threatened prosperity
by injuring security and impairing initiative.[34] It stood
in the way of what men could achieve if they were left
to themselves. Parliament was a different matter. When
it acted, it stood for the solid and substantial part of the
nation. Its control was hardly resented because, at
least by responsible delegation, it was a self-imposed
control.

In the seventeenth century, this is to say, there were,
effectively, two revolutions. The first, of which the great
protagonist is Cromwell, is the revolution that succeeded. Built on a multiplicity of grievances, its real
result was to make an English state apt to the purposes
of men of property. For that end, after all its hesitations,
it wins for them the civil and religious freedom they
require if they are to make their way in the world. It
ends the tutelage of the church over matters of economic constitution. It rejects the notion that there is any
inherent connection between poverty and salvation.

It establishes the counter thesis that the rich man is, as such, a public benefactor. It frees him from the danger of arbitrary taxation and arbitrary imprisonment; it assures him of the control of the army. Its measure of good becomes the utility of Hobbes, even if it is a little ashamed frankly to avow it. Given this environment, it feels energetic and strong for the new wealth there for its exploitation. It has ended the disciplines, religious or regal, which stands in the way of its attainment.

The other revolution, which failed, was a social revolution, more clear in the evils it attacked than the remedies it knew how to prescribe.[35] It was the effort of men who suffered profoundly from the emergent social order, who fought on the side of Cromwell against tyranny in state or church. When they had enthroned Cromwell in power they found, to their indignation, that the new dispensation brought them no more benefit than the old. There was still one law for the rich and one for the poor.[36] There was still private property in land instead of "the ancient community of enjoying the fruits of the earth" to which they had looked forward. The "young men and apprentices of London" were still, as Lilburne knew so well,[37] conscious that their masters looked no better than before to the interests of humble folk. The working tailors who, in 1649, complained of "divers rich men of our trade who . . . weaken the poorer sort of us"[38] are representative of a widespread feeling in many trades and cities. The levellers' plea for work or maintenance, for annual parliaments and universal suffrage, the abolition of taxes on food and imprisonment for debt, met with wide response in the army. The radicals felt that liberty is inherent in the fact of human existence as such, not, merely, in the man who can purchase it with property. They sought, therefore, to build a state in which, because the common man was sovereign, its power would be utilized to realize certain moral principles inherent in the nature of the universe. They were not fully agreed upon them. Lilburne's ideal was, probably, a community of small property owners, with religion free and generous provision for the poor, Winstanley's an agrarian communism in which the means of production were owned and exploited by the society as a whole. Whatever their differences, the radicals shared the beliefs that the state must have a positive character, and that it could not be unified while it was divided into rich and poor. In such a division, they saw, the only effort the state makes is for the protection of wealth. They who had fought against one despotism were not willing to endure another. They realized, as Peter Chamberlin put it, that the men who in 1641 departed from their King "to ease their purses and their consciences", would be equally willing to "forsake their fellow subjects from the same Cause."[39]

This social revolution failed because it was premature. Its protagonists lacked both the numbers and the organization necessary to give it coherence and strength. The whole impact of economic conditions was on the other side. The circumstances made for the rule of that body of property-owners who constituted, as Harrington saw, an aristocracy by the very fact of their possession of economic power. For their ends, they did not require a positive state; they needed liberation from authority, and not subordination to it. What would aid them most was a social discipline in which wealth as such was highly regarded, in which indolence was penalized, in which taxation was high enough to pay the costs of maintaining order, and low enough to permit thrift and accumulation. We see this attitude making its way throughout this period. It is triumphant because all the facts were, as yet, on its side. It multiplied wealth, it increased population, it conferred security and freedom upon the owners of property. From 1660 until the Industrial Revolution its implications were unchallenged. If it put a heavy penalty upon failure, it put its limit to the opportunities it offered to successful men. They were the state; and it is intelligible enough that, in the intoxication of their freedom, they should be convinced that they have discovered universal truth.

That, certainly, is the mood of their most representative prophet. The triumphant note of the *Two Treatises*, the exuberant commonsense of the *Letter concerning Toleration* proclaim in Locke nothing so much as the successful missionary of a new faith. The very currents of thought that go to his making are significant. The friend of Sydenham, Boyle and Newton, the administrator of commercial empire, the man who had experienced exile and confiscation of property for the sake of his beliefs, he summarizes in himself the outcome of an age. Rationalism, toleration, constitutional government, without excess in any, these are his watchwords. He stated his case in such a way as to make that bridge from the particular to the universal that is always the sign of a doctrine conscious of victory. His emphasis upon the "natural right of life, liberty, and property" is his century's insistence that a man's effort shall not be without its reward. His atomic view of society as a body of individuals living together for mutual convenience leads easily to a state the functions of which are limited by the powers they confer upon it. He has no difficulty in regarding that state as made to protect the interests a man will have who by effort accumulates property. For God, as he tells us, has given the world to "the use of the industrious and rational", and the state, by their own consent, is there to protect their exploitation of it. He has the full sense of indolence as sin, the corresponding insistence on the obligation to labour and the recognition of the successful man's good fortune as an enrichment of the commonwealth. If property is the outcome of labour, clearly it is entitled to security, for it is "the great and chief end, therefore, of men's uniting into commonwealths".

They are to be secure in what they have, and, therefore, they are to be free. By freedom Locke means that men shall not be bound without their own consent. His state is nothing so much as a contract between a group of business men who form a limited liability company whose memorandum of association forbids to the directors all those practices of which the Stuarts had, until his time, been guilty. It is not accident that makes him list as political evils, forbidden to the state, exactly the things which led to the Revolution. It is not accident, either, which makes him construct a non-sovereign state; he is too aware of the implications of Filmer and Hobbes to permit of omnicompetence. It is, again, of design that religion should appear to him a purely private affair with which the state has no concern save as it promotes disorder; the exceptions being the denial of tolerance to exactly those outlooks acceptance of which still shocked the moral conventions of his generation. He is, in short, constructing the foundations of a society in which the landowner and the farmer, the merchant and the shopkeeper, have the right to confidence. His security is a security for them, his liberty the kind of liberty they could, with their property, expect to achieve; and the kind of governmental machine he constructed for their control is one that, from the very habits he imposes upon it, they may expect to operate in their own way.

There are, no doubt, loose ends in Locke's social philosophy, just as there are loose ends in his metaphysics. As the latter made Berkeley an idealist, Hume a sceptic, and Kant the protagonist of *a priori* categories, so his social philosophy led, through Ricardo to Marx in economics, to anarchism, with Godwin, in politics, and, in the religious field, to a state indifference to all forms of ecclesiasticism which, as Rousseau saw, made some form of civil religion essential. Yet the very illogic of Locke is his strength. His generation wanted to be told that Nature justified their social requirements. He provided them with their justification. He gave them a specific for order, the limits of which admitted exactly the freedoms they desired. He gave them a theory of toleration which enabled them to exclude from its benefits exactly those whom they desired to exclude. He gave them a theory of property which made its owners worthy of protection by reason of the effort involved in its accumulation and the social good this represented. He reconciled the contradiction between authority and freedom in such a way as to offer the rising middle-class exactly the ideas that they were seeking. It is no wonder that, within a generation, Addison could salute in him the "glory of the English nation".

There is a fertility and breadth in English political speculation in the seventeenth century unrivalled upon the Continent of Europe. What is notable there is less, Spinoza apart, the quality of the thinking than the emphasis of its content. Frenchmen like Bossuet, Pufendorf, even Leibniz hardly do more than repeat certain obvious commonplaces with ample learning and an ornate style. Partly, that is due to the fact that neither France nor Germany has yet fully achieved national unity against the disintegrating influences of feudalism. When France has done that, under Louis XIV, the emergence of constitutionalism is immediate.[40] In Holland, Spinoza is remarkable for his ability to turn the grim realism of Hobbes to the service of the liberal idea. His plea that the state is unsafe which denies civic rights and freedom of conscience, even when it has the power to do so, is not merely a protest against the reactionary principles of the Gomarist party; it is also a summary of that Dutch experience of the relation of political freedom to commercial prosperity which so greatly impressed Petty and Sir William Temple. In his sense of freedom as proved by reason to be the condition of the good life, and in his refusal to accept any principle of which reason cannot offer a demonstration, Spinoza was unique among his contemporaries. He had all the insight of Hobbes, together with a passion for justice from which the latter was wholly free. But Spinoza was without great influence in his day partly because, as Leibniz said, he was "unbearably free-thinking", and partly because the suppression of his book by William III made it the possession of a limited circle. The ideas it promulgated were either advanced in other ways or by other thinkers more in harmony with what his generation could digest.

Mostly, the continental theory of the state in the seventeenth century arrives at its objective not frontally, but by a side-door. It seeks to place the right to govern on a wholly secular foundation. It emphasizes categories like contract and property. It insists upon an absolute sovereign power vested, as a rule, in the prince; but it seeks to construct, also, a system of natural rights which shall infuse the idea of law with rational ends. Its weakness is the simple one that it is pursuing two disparate objectives at the same time. On the one hand, the need for unity in internal government compels the exaltation of princely power; on the other, the abrogation of ecclesiastical sovereignty makes it search for moral principles to limit his authority. This means the evolution of a political code in which the emphasis separates life and practice in a way that was ruinous to creative thinking until Rousseau renewed the continental theory of the state in the eighteenth century. This is true even of such radical thinkers as Althusius.[41] At bottom his elaborate system is little more than a specialized adaptation of Monarchomachic theory to the case of Holland. It was artificial and insipid because so specialized. Such influence as it had was limited to professional lawyers largely engaged in technical exercises which did not touch the mainstream of political thought; for despite the four editions through which his work passed, none of the major figures of the century felt it necessary to discuss his ideas. Bayle dismissed him in a few, brief lines; and the fact that Rousseau quoted him on a single occasion does not appear to mean more than that that magnificent sciolist had read his Bayle.[42]

What, indeed, is more interesting than the formal treatises on politics of the seventeenth century is the indirect way in which a new thought is emerging. In part, this can be seen in the new humanism of the theological treatises, most notably in the great Jesuit compilations. Few people now would argue that Pascal was justified in his attack on probabilism; even one of his most learned admirers can speak of the Jansenist doctrine of grace as one of which the results are "appalling".[43] No serious student, either, would condemn Jesuit morality on the basis of such libels as the *Théologie Morale des Jesuites*.[44] The truth is that, from Lainez onwards, the Society had the insight to realize that the excessive rigour of medieval standards was a hopeless canon of behaviour for the new world to which they belonged. As men of experience, they strove to save all that they could of what was best in the old by making concessions at any point which did not, in their judgment, imperil the essential. The work of Bellarmine and Suarez, of Lessius and de Lugo, is notable, above all, for its endeavour to find the basis of a secular society in which a practical compromise can be reached between the claims of church and state. None of them doubted the primacy of the ecclesiastical claim, or the need, indeed the obligation, to fight for the primacy. But all of them realized that, in the new climate of opinion, to ask for too much was to risk the loss of all. That worldly men abused their concessions is no more proof of laxity in their ideals than in the analogous cases of Calvin and Baxter. It is proof only of how complete was the empire the secular attitude had won. Fairly to judge them, we must compare the total impact of their teaching with that of those who were preaching a wholly secular ethic, with men such as Hobbes in England or La Rochefoucauld in France. When we do that, the wonder is, not that the Jesuits conceded so much, but, rather, that they conceded so little. They were fighting a rear-guard action in a battle in which the power of religious faith was no longer adequate to withhold the demands of the ambitions and hopes it sought to control.

But the essential outlook of the age is in a still different realm again. The Jesuits show that the ablest of practical enthusiasts had to admit the claims of a secular politics with a secular code of conduct. The Utopians of the seventeenth century show that behind the formal façade of absolutism on the Continent, new ideals of politics were being rapidly defined. They are important because, under the guise of romance, they are clearly criticizing the society in which they live, and suggesting more adequate principles of its regulation. Their works show the profound impact that the voyages of discovery had made upon men's minds. That would, in any case, be obvious from the popularity of such collections as those of Hakluyt and de Bry. In his remarkable book,[45] Professor Atkinson has shown how impressively their result has been written into the pages of Leroy and Bodin and Montaigne. The *New Atlantis* of Bacon and Campanella's *City of the Sun* make it evident that the liberation effected from the old ways of thought has a universal significance. But the "extraordinary voyages" of the French writers of the seventeenth century have the additional importance that they are a vehicle of social criticism. Foigny, Vairasse and their predecessors foreshadow not merely the work of Fénélon, but also that of men like Rousseau two generations after them. The translations of their romances alone is testimony to their popularity. They show how profound is the acceptance of a new world.[46]

The characteristics of these writers may be summarized briefly. They are, first of all, definitely rationalist in temper. They criticize the wars waged between Christians. They are sceptical about the truth of the miraculous and the validity of revealed religion itself. They deny that war and the life of reason are compatible. Foigny praises liberty as of the essence of human personality, and argues with conviction that men, to be free, must be equal in status. He is a deist; and it is significant that he makes religious belief a matter on which men do not speak in public; that is the only way, in his view, to avoid the endless dissension that would otherwise arise from differences of opinion. He is even capable of criticizing, under a thin veil of disguise, the authenticity of the Old Testament—a dangerous adventure, as Bossuet taught Richard Simon, in the France of Louis XIV. He paints an ideal commonwealth, in which there is equality of the sexes, and all that limits a man's liberty is frowned upon. It is difficult not to see in the *Terre Australe* a conscious manifesto of rationalizing liberalism.

This spirit is even more obvious in the *Histoire des Sévérambes* of Denis Vairasse. Here are lauded deliberately "la santé du corps, la tranquillité de l'esprit, la liberté, la bonne éducation, la pratique de la vertu, la société des honnêtes gens . . . les maisons commodes" which the imaginary commonwealth offers its citizens in contrast to the France of Louis XIV. The sexual ethics of the Sévérambes read like an attack on the asceticism of Christianity. There is the same note of insistent feminism as in Foigny. Town-planning, elective monarchy, the encouragement by the state of the arts and sciences, a hierarchy of state officials concerned to see that all work and that all have the necessaries of life, the absence of differences of wealth and social status, are all carefully described. There is no death penalty; and though the public practice of a single religion is alone permitted, all are allowed liberty of conscience. The idea of natural law, mild, beneficent and rational, is consciously opposed to the stern substance of the civil regulations of contemporary Europe. God is regarded as unknowable; and the simple religion of the Sévérambes is commended for its supreme "conformity to natural reason". There is a warm eulogy of education, and an account of some of the inventions by which the inhabitants have improved their material conditions.

How the literature of the extraordinary voyage reached its apogee with works like *Télémaque* and *Robinson Crusoe* is a subject into which I cannot here enter. Nor can I attempt to show how widespread was the interest aroused by the technique it employed. Men so different as the youthful Fontenelle and the Spaniard Gracian bear their part in its evolution. The voyages of travellers both to the East and the West are all laid under contribution by the makers of these fantasies. What I can alone emphasize is their implications. They are the work of men eager to contrast the splendour of nature with the evil of civil society, the "natural" man, with the contemporary European. They are critical of property, rank and dignity, religion in its orthodox forms, intolerance, the sexual customs of the old world. They are enthusiastic about science and education, the beneficent influence of liberty, the value of an egalitarian element in social relations. No doubt their influence was a limited one; no doubt, also, they were read more for the interest of the wonders they had to relate than for the social philosophy they sought to expound. But their importance is quite beyond question. They make it evident that the voyages of discovery had broken down that provinciality of medievalism which equated its own outlook with universal and eternal principles. They show, also, a growing, even an ardent rationalism, an appreciation of the possibility of experiment in matters of social constitution. Their emphasis on the blessings of liberty, especially when the narrator is, like Vairasse, a Protestant who had visited England, is also notable. They show the growth of a new attitude to the principles of government which, obscure and diffident though it may yet be in expression, is significant of coming change. The extraordinary voyages are linked to the work of free-thinking advocates of toleration like Bayle, on the one hand, and to social reformers like Fénélon, on the other. Their significance is even enhanced by the fact that they lie outside the mainstream of social doctrine. They show that a liberal philosophy has its appeal beyond the conscious exponents of a new political faith.

### III

The philosophic thought of the seventeenth century makes it plain that the human mind had largely freed itself from dependence upon theological authority. Its predominant notes are secular and rational. It is confronted by the new mechanical explanation of Nature, and it evolves a doctrine to fit the postulates of that explanation. If the idea of God is still omnipresent in its speculations, it is not unfair to say that he has little connection with the dogmatic requirements of orthodox ecclesiasticism.[47] It breaks the essential traditions upon which the churches depended for their power. Even where, as with the Cambridge Platonists, or those Quietists for whom Fénélon fought in vain, it develops a mystic outlook, the inner emphasis of that tendency is an individualist one; and its necessary result is, accordingly, away from the dependence upon corporate authority. The real burden of the century in philosophic speculation is to make the universe a pattern the laws of whose design have to be thought out afresh and on new terms.

The whole impact of the new philosophy is one of liberation. That was why men so different as Bossuet and Bishop Parker of Oxford could see in Cartesianism the battle-ground of a great conflict with the church;

125

that was why, also, the university of Utrecht could forbid any philosophic teaching which proceeded in independence of Aristotle. The inference from Descartes is of a universe the laws of which man discovers by the research of reason; and to set bounds to the free play of his speculation is thus, also, to set limits to his knowledge of those laws and the power they may confer. It leads also to that scepticism the agonizing results of which are written eternally in the passionate sentences of Pascal. It produced a spirit of criticism, a realization of the incertitudes of human knowledge, which made the idea of toleration seem the only rational position for a philosopher to adopt who knows the degree to which man may be deceived.

The influence of psychology is in the same direction. Its essence is the way in which, as with both Hobbes and Locke, it comes to regard the appetites of men as natural, and thus to argue that, in a society like ours, reason should be the judge of the measure in which they are to be satisfied. It thus ends the case for medieval asceticism because it is built upon a rejection of the dogma of original sin. It is hedonistic in its emphasis; and it therefore prepares the climate which liberalism needs by acclaiming the individual's right to make his terms with a universe in which his own view of fulfilment is limited only by his knowledge of what a rational man will seek to attain. Its implication is strongly individualist. The process of life is, for man, a continuous search for satisfactions which confer the sense of power. We can see that attitude in a saint like Spinoza, on the one hand, and a worldly aristocrat like La Rochefoucauld, on the other. Man is conceived as plunged into a struggle for existence in which his triumph is attained by his power to dominate his environment; and that power, in its turn, is a product of appetite fulfilled. With Hobbes this individual passion for power is so relentless that only the strong hand of despotic government can control its operations. We are, so to say, saved from our passions by reason which shows us the way to limit their claims. It teaches us to create Leviathan whereby we may wrest security from what would otherwise be a brutal condition. In the whole atmosphere of this speculation enlightened self-interest is made the key to social construction.

The gulf between the sanctions of this outlook and that of the medieval world is a startling one. It is reinforced at every point by the nature of the environment it encountered. It is rational; it is materialist; it seeks naturally to curb the power outside the authority of a man's self. It tends to measure the validity of that power by the effect it has upon individual desires. Thence it is not a large step, as with Locke, to make the authority of government a function of consent. Thence, also, it is easy to make the catalogue of the things to which a man will naturally consent a list of the needs he feels most deeply in Locke's own time. It is notable that even the philosophers most alien from him in method either, like Hobbes, make contract the foundation upon which the state is built, or, as with Spinoza, by making self-preservation the fundamental assumption of his ethics, arrived at a plea for freedom in politics as the only way of life a rational man would desire. We can see, in short, in the burden of the century's philosophic message, a continuous effort towards the emancipation of the

individual from bonds by which he had been restrained.
The philosopher confers upon him his right to interpret
the universe for himself. The moralist and the psycho-
logist unite to tell him to follow the promptings of his
nature so far as his reason warns him they may wisely
go. The influence of both is towards the erosion of the
theological authority which warned him against free
interpretation and rational self-interest. Even his Christianity is to be reasonable; and, increasingly through
the century, his need to avow acceptance of its dogmas
grows weaker. For, as the age unfolds, the degree to
which its historical aims are on the defensive grows ever
more evident.

The rationalism of the age, in fact, attacks the central
position of the churches—their reliance upon the historic
evidence which provides their dogmas with their
ultimate validity. That evidence is assailed in diverse
ways. Partly it is direct assault. Cappel's discovery[48]
that the Old Testament was an Aramaic rescension of
ancient Hebrew texts was, as Buxtorf saw, a fatal blow
to its claim of inspiration; and the very fury of such
Puritan assaults upon him as those of Lightfoot and
Owen only testify to the importance of the discovery.
In the last quarter of the sixteenth century van Maes
had already shown the composite character of the
Pentateuch. Now Hobbes and Spinoza went much
farther. The former showed without difficulty that
Moses could not have written the Pentateuch, that
Joshua, the books of Judges, Samuel and Kings, are
all far later than the events they record. He cast new
light upon the Psalms and Job. If his rationalizing hand
stayed itself before the New Testament, it was with a

sting in the tail of his caution. Spinoza may be said, without exaggeration, to have laid down the lines of the modern approach to scientific exegesis; and with the tools he largely invented, the idea of inspiration vanished before a ruthless application of critical radicalism. To the impact of these works must be added the results of Richard Simon's enquiry; after his history of the canon, that "matchless author", as Dryden called him, made it more easy for piety than for reason to accept traditional claims. Spencer showed how much Jewish ritual had been influenced by the rites of neighbouring pagan religions. Even the discussion of chronology, with the realization of the light thrown upon its problems by the geological evidence, show the degree to which accepted notions were called into question.

It is no doubt true that, especially in England, the seventeenth century is, *par excellence*, the age of biblical enthusiasm; we may well believe that the masses were content with the new magic of the Authorized Version, even unaware of the debate upon these themes that was being conducted. But the significance of this scholarship is only properly seized when it is read in the light of the growing tolerance of the time. Many winds of doctrine contributed a cleansing influence. The example of America was impressive. The growth of religious freedom in the new world set an example to the old of which the influence is immediately apparent in the literature. The spirit of Montaigne that "it is overvaluing one's own conjectures to cause a man to be put to death because of them" finds a hundred advocates in the seventeenth century where it found one in the sixteenth. No single cause can be assigned to this development. With Chillingworth, Jeremy Taylor, and the Cambridge Platonists, it comes from the vivid sense that persecution is incompatible with a religion of love. With Petty and Sir William Temple, it is the outcome of a realization, emphasized by the experience of Holland, that toleration and economic well-being are inextricably inter-related. With Pufendorf, writing in the light of the wise experiment of the Elector of Brandenburg, it is a gospel of expediency.[49] Much came, no doubt, from sheer weariness at the endless war of the sects. Much more came from the growth of an indifference to all revelation of cultured men; Selden's "'tis a vain thing to talk of a heretic, for a man can think no otherwise than he does" represented an attitude which grew in vigour throughout the age. The claims of science and philosophy lent it their aid; and it was assisted by the ever-wider recognition that church and state occupy quite different spheres. When a devout Christian like Roger Williams could write that "all civil states with their offices of justice in their respective constitutions and administrations, are essentially proved civil, and therefore not judges, governors or defenders of the spiritual state of worship," he was laying the foundation for the settlement which Europe was to adopt. The reception accorded the refugees from the persecution of Louis XIV shows that intolerance had, by 1685, lost its main hold. Men had by then come to think of religion as a matter rather for their private lives than for their public relations. Expression might continue to be cautious, right down to the French Revolution; but by the close of the seventeenth century men found it too costly to be any longer a natural adventure.

It was, indeed, above all its cost that was the ruin of religious persecution. Tolerance came because intolerance interfered with the access to wealth. The emigration for conscience's sake, whether to America from England, or to England, Prussia, Scandinavia and Holland from the half of Europe, rapidly impressed itself on men's minds as a source of gain to the tolerant, of loss to the persecuting, nations. The root of the rationalism which, after the Restoration, began to make its way on an ever-increasing scale was the perception that persecution, being incompatible with peace and order, was a final hindrance to prosperity. It is out of that motive that there grows the wide examination, from so many sides, of the religious claim, whether papal or protestant, to control. It is because of its cost that men examine its implications. It is because of its cost that the basis of power is transferred from right to utility. The crisis of authority in the seventeenth century is rarely an attack against authority as such; antinomianism was an exceptional outlook. The crisis arose out of a search for such a basis for the action of authority as would make its behaviour compatible with the new order of things. Conformity by compulsion was obnoxious to every trader to whom a persecuting state meant loss of business. It was then easy for him to infer that it was contrary to the law of Christ. After a century and a half of warring sects he was grateful for Locke's demonstration that the state need only concern itself with those patterns of religious faith which inherently troubled the commonwealth.

Writers like L'Estrange might exhaust themselves in proof of the evil influence of Nonconformist opinion;

they might collect pages of proof that Dissent and rebellion were interchangeable terms. What impressed their neighbours was, as one commentator put it, "the gaols . . . crowded with the most substantial tradesmen and inhabitants, the clothiers . . . forced from their houses, and thousands of workmen and women, whom they employed, set to starving".[50] The climate of opinion was rationalist because the price of belief favoured all doctrine which, by attacking persecution, made for security. That attitude was favoured by the increasing alliance between the trading class and the aristocracy. It was fostered by the extravagance and inefficiency of the government. It drew nourishment from the patent experience of Holland and from the realization that the more things were left alone, the more they seemed to prosper. The courtier and the priest might be startled at the pretensions of the rising bourgeoisie; they might feel, with L'Estrange, that there was no traditional principle they were not prepared to call into question. But what was far more impressive than his argument was the way in which the solid tradesman was a bulwark of law and order immediately he was left alone. Parker might think of the trading corporations as "so many nests of faction and sedition".[51] But that was not their attitude when the policy of James II threatened to undermine parliamentary government and the Established Church. Dissent showed then a loyalty at least as great as that of the average Anglican. The political inference was clear that it deserved its reward. It was found that the "godly discipline" might reject episcopacy, but it meant effort, thrift, soberness. It was a nurse of civic virtues not less apt than those of the Anglican to promote the prosperity of the realm. It was discovered that the solid Puritan man of business was no more anxious than the Anglican landowner to embrace doctrines of social and political radicalism. What he objected to was simply a social order which threatened the fruits of his enterprise. He did not see why he should suffer loss in the interest of a court favourite. He hated taxation which supported what seemed to him the extravagant revelries of a dissolute court. He was prepared, fully as much as the country squire, to pay for good government. But he was insistent that good government must include his interests, and he was prepared to fight for the shaping of its principles to that end. As soon as he had achieved it, he became as devout a conformist to its implications as the men who had criticized the purity of his allegiance.

This, then, is the environment in which the philosophy of the seventeenth century made its way. Its basis is an economic individualism hostile to state interference because the latter inhibits the full realization of material possibilities. It struggles, if slowly, yet with success, to separate economics from ethics because their juncture meant the imposition of rules fatal to individual success. It conceived of social relations increasingly in atomic terms. Its radicalism was the negative radicalism of men who are conscious of an energy that can conquer the universe if only they are left alone. They are fighting a theocratic ideal, whether the god of that ideal be church or state, because seventeenth century theocracy hampers, instead of forwarding their mission. Out of their situation they evolve the weapons of conflict. They fight Rome, the Church of England, the King, the courtier, in the name of the new opportunities they are exploiting. Their need to be free in one realm makes a philosophy of freedom for all. Its inner urgency produces a logic which, if stated, as by Hobbes or Spinoza, with naked consistency, startles them by its implications not less than it shocks their opponents. But they cannot escape, any more than other men, the obligation to erect their particular necessity into a universal creed. They did not consciously seek for secularism. What they wanted promoted its acceptance because that could be won on no other terms. And its acceptance becomes rapidly surrounded with a halo of religious approval. To choose gain rather than loss becomes the path of Christian duty. But when the choice of gain cannot be made if state or church bar the way, then both, because they stand in the path, must be removed from it. The liberal need, in a word, is a doctrine woven from the texture of bourgeois need. It is the logic of the conditions they require for their ascent. The pattern of the creed is set by their necessities.

So, as they went forward, they took with them in their rise ideas and principles they did not seek consciously to promote. They required a secular and tolerant state. But to achieve this kind of state they had to undermine the theological framework of unity upon which it had been erected, out of whose slow erosion it had emerged. To effect this erosion they had to accept a new philosophy fatal, in the end, to the religious principles they themselves held. The contrast between Baxter and Hobbes, between Descartes and Bossuet, is decisive in this field. The Puritan and the Catholic alike are as eager as any medievalist to set boundaries to the research of reason and the empire of secular things; they are both half-conscious that they are engaged in an impossible task. The Catholic philosopher and the English Deist may pay a formal tribute to the traditional duty of their time; they may be cautious, even timid, in their mode of expression. But behind a half-traditional façade, each is in fact intoxicated with the sense of a boundless empire for reason which makes individual man not by revelation but by enquiry, not by faith, but by self research, the master of the universe. The philosopher of the age is as aware of the power he may attain as the business man; he knows, also, that the condition of its attainment is that he be left alone. The economic individualism of the one is matched by the intellectual individualism of the other. Each is concerned to require of authority that it holds its hand from his particular vineyard. Each is prepared to prove the social advantage of leaving him unhindered in his quest. To the one the end is wealth, to the other knowledge; but the man who seeks for knowledge is moved, not by a pointless curiosity, so much as the passionate conviction that knowledge is the key to power. To restrain him in his search is, therefore, to impede that acquisition of power out of which there come both wealth and glory.

That, above all, is the impact of the advance of science in the seventeenth century. I am not concerned here to trace the outline of its incredible achievement in this period. What is important for us is less the achievement itself than its implications. It is vital, first, that it gave an interpretation of the universe which rendered obsolete the competing theological view. It established, thereby, the self-sufficiency of a reason free of the need to take account of metaphysical assumptions sanctioned by the churches. It was frankly materialist in outlook. It conquered its contemporaries by showing them that, in accepting its views, they were acquiring a power over Nature not to be attained in any other way. The status it attained is shown by the establishment of bodies like the Royal Society, the French Academy of Sciences, the Accademia dei Lincei.[52] It wins government recognition of its importance. It obtains endowments, it is asked to solve the practical problems that business men confront. The magic of its discoveries enthrals the age. Its vogue is so universal that, as early as 1665, Glanvill can write of the Royal Society that "it had done more than philosophy of a notional way since Aristotle opened shoppe".[53] The scientific journal and the museum add to its prestige. The observatories of Paris and Greenwich make it plain that it is regarded as an investment in the control of nature. The great man of science becomes at once a part of the national glory. He is felt to have conferred new splendour upon his time. Leibniz, Huyghens, Boyle, are filled with the ecstasy of discovery. Its extent was so great that Sprat could say, in 1667, that the interest in science was so strong "that there seemed to be nothing more in vogue throughout Europe". We can see that interest in Pepys and Evelyn, in Molière's satire on the blue stockings of the day, in the growing number of popular works on science, like Fontenelle's *Plurality of Worlds*.

It creates a new mood of self-confidence. "In these last hundred years", wrote Dryden, "almost a new

Nature has been revealed to us—more errors of the schools have been detected, more useful experiments in philosophy have been made, more noble secrets in optics, medicine, anatomy and astronomy have been discovered than in all these doting and credulous ages from Aristotle to us."[54] This sense of superiority is evident in men as diverse as Joseph Glanvill in his belief that "no age hath been more happy in liberty of enquiry than this",[55] in Campanella, and Sir Thomas Browne. Even a pietist like Milton, when, as in *Paradise Regained*, he warns men against the intoxication of the new knowledge, shows a wide acquaintance with its import. The difference here between the emphasis of science in the literatures of the Elizabethan and the Caroline periods is in itself the proof of the new horizons that had been descried.

The effective inference drawn is the idea of progress.[56] The new knowledge is so immense and so vital that men have a conviction of superiority. The older ages cease to be golden and become dark. Men become certain that there is greater wisdom and greater achievement, that the possibilities which open before them entitle them to look forward rather than backward. They tell themselves that they are the masters of nature. They infer from that mastery the rights of reason, the ability to shape their own environment, the absence of a need any longer to believe in the doctrine of original sin. This is the real significance of the struggle between the Ancients and the Moderns.[57] What gave the latter their victory was essentially the sense of scientific achievement. After Fontenelle, it is almost tacitly assumed that each age adds to the accumulated store of its

137

predecessors, and even a stout defender of the past, like Boileau, has to make fatal concessions to his opponents. For the most part, indeed, the critics of the idea of progress are either, like Temple, engaging in a genial literary exercise, or, like Swift, venting the spleen of thwarted ambition upon mankind; and it is perhaps a sufficient commentary upon the battle to note that Swift's most savage attack became, within a few years of its publication, a nursery tale for children.

The sense of progress made for the growth of optimism. This, in its turn, is evidence that the new synthesis is succeeding. The men who want liberty and reason have now the sense that victory is on their side. They have reduced the world to a mechanism the laws of whose operation are revealed by knowledge. They can apply the methods of science to every aspect of life. Already, in the second half of this period, the statistical view of nature is, as with Graunt and Petty, being made to reveal results in the social sphere. The obvious consequence of the evolution is the triumph of the rationalist spirit. And rationalism, once more, is bound to be secular in temper simply because in that alone can it find the atmosphere which sanctions its results. After 1660, when the fundamental compromise with religion has been effected, there is a new optimism because there is a new security. And that security begets the faith in the ability of men to wrest happiness from Nature through their knowledge of its processes. The happiness stifles the spirit of doubt; the agony of a Pascal is not repeated. Utility pervades the mental climate and adjusts all values to its mood. It is alien from superstition. It is enamoured of experiment. It has a growing conviction of the innate dignity of human personality, a difficulty in believing that such dignity is compatible with the right to persecute; just as the geographical discoveries, so the scientific, reshaped the habits of thought.

We must not, of course, read more into this evolution than it imports. There is still incredible superstition; there is still, as notably in Spain and Italy, a wide theatre for religious persecution; and, apart from Holland and England, the number of those anxious to plead for any form of limitation upon despotic government is small. Those who are are, most frequently, men like Jurieu who, having a minority cause to expound, find naturally in a quasi-democratic theory the sanction of its claims.[58] What is most typical is the effort to give effect to the compromise that has begun to define itself so successfully. We can see its temper, in perhaps its most characteristic form, in the work of Bayle; at its most characteristic because he so widely foreshadows the whole atmosphere of the century that was to follow him.[59] In matters of political constitution, he is a monarchist, partly because he is a loyal Frenchman, but partly, also, because he sees in all theories of popular sovereignty a threat to the preservation of order. But his monarchism is built on a passionate defence of toleration, a defence which accepts the findings of science and philosophy with pride, and insists that they are fatal to all claims of dogmatic religion. The vast *Dictionary*, itself the most popular work in the generation that followed its appearance, is nothing so much as an immense encyclopædia of tolerance. It pursues the claims of reason through the whole realm of recorded knowledge, and establishes them by the Voltairean method of reducing opposition to them to absurdity. The *Thoughts on the Comet* of 1680, paralleled almost at once by the work of Bekker and Góngora, marks, as no other book, the degree to which the hypothesis of nature as uniform was fatal to the old superstition.[60] Gibbon's remark that "he balanced the false religions in his skeptical scales till the opposite quantities annihilated each other" is an effective summary of his influence; but it is inadequate in its failure to point out that the impact of the equilibrium which emerged is one in which morality has no need of religion. Bayle left Christians with the difficulty that, if their chief doctrinal positions were to be maintained, they were really driven implicitly to accept Manichaeism. Few more powerful dissolvents of faith have ever been constructed than his work. And it has in it a note of contempt and defiance of traditional belief which makes it evident that men no longer sought the ancient harbour with the confidence of old.

The scientific revolution, this is to say, is one expression of a social revolution in process of finding its categories of action. It is not merely popular in and of itself, though the marvels it revealed gave it a hold on the imagination similar to that aroused by the conquest of the air in our own day. It is popular because the conditions it demanded for its success were those also that the economic climate demanded for its success; it lent powerful psychological aid to the rationalizing force of capitalism. It bred also in its votaries the qualities and the temper that the new business life demanded—precision, experiment, daring, the search for authority in the facts themselves. Its triumphs invited patronage, and that involved, at least implicitly, a policy of intellectual enlightenment in the patron. Its triumphs, again, conferred the sense of power over the stubborn facts of nature, the same sense that the business man had when his enterprise justified itself by its returns. If its work in the scientific societies showed the value of organization in achieving results, its most resounding discoveries were, for the multitude, associated with the names of individuals. It was the most significant of the conscious agents in breaking down the power of the old by the emphasis it threw on the significance of the new. Thereby, its ethos penetrated with remarkable rapidity into the most disparate spheres of life; its influence is nowhere so marked as in its contribution to the formation of the idea of progress. It seemed to justify the faith in reason as the key that, ultimately, would unlock all doors. It therefore encouraged optimism, and with that encouragement, the belief that men, when free, may hope perpetually to improve their condition.

Nor must we forget an inference from all this that was bound, sooner or later, to be drawn. If reason can reduce chaos to law in the realm of nature, it is bound to be argued that it is capable of the same achievement in the realm of social fact. The full consciousness of that possibility, indeed, belongs to the eighteenth century; and it was then attempted, as Hume was to see, with a confidence unwarranted by the results. But, already in the seventeenth, Hobbes was seeking to formulate a universal system in which sociology has its due and allotted place. Already, also, though, no doubt, in very different ways, Harrington, Spinoza and the political arithmeticians are trying to wrest a body of laws from the chaos of social fact, and to imply an obligation to obey those laws as the inference which makes good government possible. The science of the seventeenth century denied the place of arbitrariness in the cosmos; and the politics of the age move, if at a laggard pace, in the same direction. The authority denied by the one is the authority of faith; that of the other will be, as with Locke, the discretion of a monarch who seeks obedience to an unlimited will. From Grotius onwards, the idea of natural law in the social world is born of the desire to arrest the right to arbitrary power. It will produce a body of natural "rights" which it will be wary of announcing as coincident with positive law, but which it will seek to proclaim as a code of behaviour the rational man will follow. It is notable that most of these will seek to protect the individual as he goes about his daily business; they are nothing so much as a specific for prosperity. They are what the business man needs if the hazards of his enterprise are to be minimal in character. At first, indeed, natural law in the social world is, outside of England and an occasional thinker of the continent, Althusius, Claude Joly, Jurieu, little more than a tactful admonition to the Prince; it is Bossuet's distinction between the "absolute" and the "arbitrary" monarch. But as the century ends, it is becoming more than this. It is shaping itself, as in the France of Louis XIV's later years, into the demand for a constitution. And, in eighteenth century France, as in seventeenth century England, when the framework of social institutions resists the demands of natural law, revolution takes by force what is not yielded to persuasion.


IV


It is customary to call the period between the Reformation and the French Revolution the age of mercantilism; and it is certainly true that until the latter part of the eighteenth century, there was no wide appreciation of liberalism in the economic field. But we must beware of thinking of mercantilist theory as a coherent body of doctrine in the sense of the classical economy of the nineteenth century. It was, as Adam Smith was careful to note, "political economy considered as a branch of the science of a statesman or legislator", not as a study of "the nature and causes of the wealth of nations".[61] It assumed, that is, the inevitability, perhaps even the desirability, of a government which regulated the economic affairs of the commonwealth; and, for the most part, its discussion turned upon the principles that regulation should adopt. Its debates centre around problems which mostly assume interventionism, and, for that reason, its analysis of elementary postulates is naturally rare. It is not difficult to understand why despotic governments in this period should accept these views; they inherited the notion that economic life was subordinate to regulation from the medieval society out of which they emerged. And there is hardly a doctrine that we call mercantilist that is not capable of intelligible defence in the light of this fact. To multiply the precious metals, for instance, was an obvious objective to any ruler who desired an ample treasury for

143

almost unceasing war. Military grounds, too, explain the enthusiasm of many mercantilists for a large population as a source of strength. The intensity of national rivalries explains why self-sufficiency should be regarded as an ideal, especially when there was ground for the belief that the trader as such is only too eager to subordinate his patriotism to the spirit of gain. The ideals of List and Fichte, the revival, in our own time, of economic nationalism, make it easy for us to understand their theory of the balance of trade. The view that in commercial matters my neighbour's loss is not necessarily my advantage is one of the truths most difficult to persuade men to accept.

To grasp the essence of mercantilism certain aspects of it need special emphasis. Its doctrines are the confused and contradictory efforts of men to persuade their governments to support one interest rather than another. The exporter of cloth has a different policy to urge from that of its manufacturer; and the sheep-farmer has a different view again. The governments wavered from time to time between the encouragement of monopolies and their prohibition. There are periods when alien immigrants are encouraged, and periods when they are frowned upon. Sometimes the export of bullion is eagerly advocated; sometimes its export is attacked as meaning the loss of the nation's wealth. We cannot understand mercantilism until we think of it as expressing an environment in which diverse interests are in constant competition to assure that the regulation is favourable to them. We cannot understand it, either, unless we think of the state as inheriting the church's function of defining the habits of permissible economic behaviour; with the important corollary that the stronger the government, the more natural was the expectation that it would impose its definitions. The seventeenth century state is winning order from the chaos of the sixteenth century; that chaos is largely rooted in an economic revolution. It would have been remarkable, therefore, if it had not sought to preserve order by the obvious means of controlling the factors which made for disorder—the currency, the conditions of employment, the flow of trade and immigration, the relief of the poor, the supply of the precious metals, the relations of the trader to foreign markets and colonies, the navigation laws with their obvious bearing on supremacy at sea, the heavy industries with their direct relation to the implements of war. Regulation was rooted in the insecurity of the age. In such a period men always fly for safety to the state. They seek from the authority of its supreme coercive power regulations in which their property is safeguarded. That has been the experience of our own time not less than of the earlier period.

What, therefore, is notable is not the absence of any economic liberalism in the seventeenth century; what is notable is the fact that it should be able to issue a challenge at all. What, also, is significant is the coincidence of the challenge with the growth of constitutional government. The rising bourgeoisie adapts, first, religion, then culture, to its purposes; the state is the last of its conquests. It is seeking freedom not as a universal end, but as a means to the enjoyment of the wealth that is open to it. It attacks its antagonists where they are weakest. It makes of the state first ally, then enemy, in the pursuit of its objective. It is inhibited by the medieval economic order; it uses secular power to destroy its discipline by attacking the church. That means a century and a half of warfare during which the Crown and middle class in partnership make a new discipline to replace the old. At this stage, the bourgeoisie is not ready for a total re-definition of legal relationships. The Crown is strong; the landowning aristocracy is strong; the traditional belief in regulation is still implicit in all the major social experience. It is only when the new order of things has firmly established its foundations, when freedom in the economic sphere seems an obvious inference from its attainment elsewhere that the bourgeois moves to the final assault. He has then supreme coercive power in his hands. The chief use of the state to him is merely as a police agency. He bids it keep outside that realm of economic action he now proposes to exploit on his own terms.

We can see the first beginnings of this attitude in the seventeenth century, mainly in England, and predominantly in England after the Restoration; for the period of the Commonwealth, though it is one of passionate constitutional debate, is also one of profound revolutionary disturbance and that consequential distress which promotes, rather than diminishes, state interference; so, also, during the French Revolution, the advent of the Jacobins to power intensified economic interventionism. So, also, in 1917, the victory of Lenin was a victory of a policy which utilized state-power for a maximum economic control. The history of the seventeenth century is a protest against interventionism until the outbreak of the civil war. There then comes a period of regulation wider and deeper than that which evoked disapproval under the first two Stuarts; this is the response to the distress evoked by conflict. After the Restoration, the movement towards *laissez-faire* gains new momentum. By the end of the century, the attitude is prepared out of which Hume can urge, and Adam Smith demonstrate, the full philosophy of economic liberalism.

The mercantilist, we must note, is deeply conscious of a possible antithesis between the national interest and the trader's well-being. "Private advantages", wrote Fortrey,[62] "are often impediments of public profit." This disharmony is often emphasized, by Roger Coke, by Child, even, we must remember, by Adam Smith himself.[63] It is the consciousness of this disharmony that is behind the effort at regulation. The state controls exports and imports, the quality of production, the conditions of labour, lest the avidity for profit of the trader injure society as a whole. "What does the merchant care," it was said under the Commonwealth, "so that he be rich, how poor the public is? Let the commonwealth sink, so that he gets his profit." We must put the current of economic liberalism as, in this epoch, but a weak eddy in a general tide flowing against it. Nonintervention means that the gentry lose to the trading class, the workman to his employer, the domestic producer to his foreign rival, the manufacturer to the import merchant, the monopolist to the proponent of a free trade, the native employee to the alien immigrant. Each of these groups is for regulation on its own behalf. It is only gradually that some of them will come to

147

argue that the common good lies in freedom from any
intervention.

A variety of circumstances combined to make regulation disliked. The administration was ineffective. The
impotence of the government before smuggling,[64] its
inability, with any uniformity, to control wages or the
regulating apprenticeship were the source of continuous
complaint. Such things as the failure of the fish days
and the breakdown of the aulnage[65] point in the same
direction. The settlement laws were deeply disliked, and
they were felt to impede that mobility of labour which
industrial organization required. It was important, too,
that, after 1660, the authority of the Privy Council
declined greatly;[66] for it was not only the main instrument of regulation, but its place as the source of policy
was taken by a parliament in which the interest of
business men had an increasing place. The abolition of
feudal tenures, the eagerness of the squirearchy for
enclosures, the ineptitude of the monopolists in the
utilization of their privileges, particularly evident in the
breakdown of Cockayne's ill-starred project,[67] the
inability to operate effectively the attempts at the
standardization of industry, all worked in the same
direction. The decay of the guilds, the rise of industries
which flourished in places where they had little or no
authority, the growth of new processes beyond their control, all worked in the same direction. There is hardly a
species of regulation in the century which does not give
rise to wide and angry protest of some kind. It is rarely
universal; it never fails to evoke some counter-protest
in its turn. It is, indeed, rarely a protest against the idea
of regulation in itself. But its cumulative force moves

irresistibly to that conclusion. The condition of state control was an administrative machine which could invent the necessary expedients of successful control. That was lacking, and lacking increasingly, in the seventeenth century. It came, therefore, to be felt as a handicap on successful enterprise. It impeded access to wealth which lay there ready to be attained. By 1700 the protests have become an attitude of mind. In the eighteenth century they develop into a philosophy.

We can see that attitude developing as the political arithmeticians begin their work of analysis. The change in the attitude to usury arises out of the growth of trade on borrowed capital. "It is certain", wrote Bacon,[68] "that the greatest part of trade is driven by young merchants upon borrowing at interest." That realization led Selden to remark that "'tis a vain thing to say that money begets not money, for that no doubt it does".[69] Malynes, Barbon, North, have all a clear insight into the view put pithily by Locke when he said that "to receive profit from the loan of money is as equitable and lawful as receiving rent for land, and more tolerable to the borrower".[70] There is, that is to say, a new sense that risk is entitled to its return, a doubt arising from this view whether state intervention to control the rate of interest is wise. Petty, indeed, went so far in this connection as to condemn "the vanity and fruitlessness of making civil positive laws against the laws of nature"; he has the clear sense, put with irresistible force by Bentham a century later, that general economic conditions make the price of money a simple result of supply and demand. The relation of this temper to the growth of banking is obvious. There is too much

149

profit in the possibilities it opens for the state to maintain easily the thesis of regulation. The number of legislative changes in the rate of interest during the century shows that the older view of control is losing its hold.

"Trade is in its nature free," wrote Davenant,[71] "finds its own channel, and best directeth its own course; and all laws to give it rules and directions, and to limit and circumscribe it, may serve the particular ends of private men, but are seldom advantageous to the public." That argument sums up an evolution that had been long proceeding. As early as 1641 Robinson had seen the folly of limiting imports.[72] Within fifteen years of the Restoration Roger Coke[73] was stating the outlines of the free trade position in terms that Barbon and Dudley North merely repeated after the Revolution. "They that give the best price for a commodity", wrote Child,[74] "shall never fail to have it"; and from this he drew the inference that a policy of embargoes was fatal to its own objective. The merchants of leather took a similar position; let there be freedom and many thousands will be employed to the national advantage. As early as the reign of James I, Mun had pleaded for the right to export bullion, and described the state of employment as "a remedy far worse than the disease".[75] Roger North insisted on the futility of wage regulation by judicial assessment.[76] The Privy Council itself noted that the Statute of Apprentices "has been by most of the judges looked upon as inconvenient to trade, and to the increase of inventions";[77] and it was out of a mass of petitions seeking the enforcement of the traditional rules that the House of Commons resolved in 1702 that "trade ought to be free and not restrained".[78] That was the acceptance of Sir Josiah Child's plea for new ideas. "To improve and advance trade," he argued,[79] ". . . begin the right way, casting off some of our old mistaken principles in trade, which we inherit from our ancestors." His protest against attempts to standardize methods of manufacture is still more emphatic. "All our laws," he wrote,[80] ". . . if they were duly put into execution, would in my opinion, do more hurt than good." The guilds and their restrictive practices are stoutly condemned in similar fashion. Roger Coke traced the decline of towns to their influence.[81] The author of *Britannia Languens* called them "oppressive oligarchies".[82] Child thought it a vulgar error to urge that the practice of industry should be limited to their members.[83] Neither Parliament nor the law courts paid much attention, after the Restoration, to pleas in favour of customs in restraint of trade;[84] Chief Justice Holt, indeed, may be said to have won his eminent place in our legal tradition by the zeal with which he gave legal force to the theories of *laissez-faire*. The poor law is attacked as a burden on industry, "a discouragement", in Roger Coke's words,[85] "to all industrious and labouring people, when lazy and idle people shall be maintained in their idleness from the fruits of their labour and industry." North particularly attacked restraints on the movement of labourers as detrimental to "the sort of men we call undertakers, who are very instrumental in the public by advancing manufactures".[86]

Two remarks of Charles Davenant summarize the implications of the new doctrine. "No imagination", he wrote,[87] "can be vainer than to think that trade is to be ruled and circumscribed by art; it must be suffered

151

to take its own natural course." "Nowadays," he wrote again,[88] "laws are not much observed which do not in a manner execute themselves." Even Dean Tucker, half a century later, would not have repudiated those sentiments. They are the case for individualism on its most fundamental grounds. They assume that economic liberty is in the nature of things, and that regulations are foolish if they require supervision to give them authority. With this philosophy, what Professor Tawney calls "the triumph of the economic virtues"[89] reaches maturity. The tradesmen have the sense that, as Steele put it,[90] "the world is all before them." Like Pistol, they will take out their sword to open it. But the sword is now an economic sword whose bearer has an independent body of secular doctrine as the justification of its use. If he is to be, as Bunyan said, a "doer" and not a "talker", he must have freedom as the condition of doing. No doubt he is to have freedom for God's work. But by a magic sleight of hand God's work has come to seem a matter of private faith and not of economic works. The rules of the latter are those of reason, which means thrift, effort, prudence, those book-keeping virtues which show a balance on the credit side of the ledger. It is the outcome of the recognition, emphasized by North, that knowledge has become "in great measure mechanical". Men have attained a science of the economic nature of things independent of mutable human nature. It was what may be seen in its "visible foundations", as Petty and Graunt are displaying these in their statistical tables that is to outline the new code of behaviour. And the law they give is the law of freedom. If it operates to bless only the successful, that is the reward of their energy and industry. We are to have a nation of freeholders and merchants defining the conditions of their prosperity. It is in this prosperity that national salvation is to be found.

"The advancement of private persons", wrote Joseph Lee under the Commonwealth,[91] "will be the advantage of the public." But to advance, he must have property, the condition of the social adventure, and, after a century of continuous crisis, its security must be safe from state invasion. Locke, whose goods had been confiscated, and who had spent ten years in dreary exile, had no doubt of that need in the gospel he bequeathed to the eighteenth century. In that state of nature which reason already rules private property exists by the law of nature; the state comes into existence to make certain men's title to it. "The supreme power", he wrote, "cannot take from any man any part of his property without his own consent." We can understand well enough how grateful a doctrine this must have seemed to men already convinced that the able-bodied poor were idle vagabonds whose poverty was fault and not misfortune. Locke builds for them a state in which there is, effectively, to be no regulation without their own consent. The philosophy has been founded that enables them to limit regulation in accordance with their own conception of its wisdom. A state has been made in which property is the effective title to citizenship. In such a world, it becomes natural to assume that self-love and social can be equated with each other.

This non-interventionism is not a merely English phenomenon even in the seventeenth century, even though conditions there were more favourable than

elsewhere to its evolution. It is emphasized also by the
Swiss merchants. It has, as Pirenne has pointed out, a
continuous pedigree in the Low Countries from the
sixteenth century. In France, in the later years of
Louis XIV, there are the beginnings of a reaction
against Colbertism which soon begins to assume significant proportions. Fénélon is for free trade; Vauban and
Boisguillebert begin to make the case against excessive
regulation.[92] The devastating effects of the Revocation
open men's eyes to the evils of a positive state. The
revival there of the debate on usury, though its main
emphasis is in a later period, is evidence of the European
character of the notions we have been discussing. We
have only to read the pages of Savary[93] to note the rise
in France of the "honnete homme" of commerce with
all the typical features of the English bourgeois. He has
the same hopes; he has the same ambitions; and it is
symptomatic of the new atmosphere that Louis XIV
opens to him the avenue, if indirectly, to the ranks of the
nobility. In France, as in England, the stage was set
for demands for freedom. Self-made men, there also,
are not willing to be bound by rules which threaten
their ascent. They are too near the new security the
unified monarchy has given them as yet to challenge
its foundations. Yet within a generation of the death
of Louis XIV they are making ready for a new
world.

One final word on the seventeenth century is necessary. With its close, the foundations of a liberal philosophy have fully emerged. The secular state has established itself; rationalism in science and philosophy are no
longer seriously challenged. Even the case for religious

freedom now arouses only a sporadic doubt. But, as that philosophy has emerged, its links with a property-owning class are unmistakable. Its basic ideal is security; and those whose security it above all considers are the men who have made their way. It is not too much to say that, steadily as the years proceeded, it hardened its heart against the poor. That is seen not merely in the breakdown of the system of public assistance. It is implied in the new attitude to charity of Steele in one generation and Defoe in the next. It would, I think, have shocked a medieval Christian to read in the *Religious Tradesman* that the poor are not victims of misfortune, but of their own "idle, irregular, and wicked courses".[94] If we have an occasional eulogy of high wages, far more frequent is the sense of horror at the excessive demands of the workers. There is a growing suspicion at their effort to combine for self-protection, a growing sense, both in parliament and in the courts of law, that the nexus between master and man is purely economic, a relation, not a partnership implying reciprocal social duties.

There is a veneration for the status of birth and its privileges; but that is being matched by a kindred veneration for wealth and its claims. The state is becoming a fellowship of the successful man; its rules are to be made to protect the implications of success. This is what is really involved in the defeat of the "hot gospellers" of the commonwealth. When we speak of its democratic doctrines, we must remember that the idea which prevailed was not that of Lilburne or Winstanley or that put forward with passion by Colonel Rainsborough in the Army debates. It is the ideal of Ireton to whom the state is a society of property owners; and that, at bottom, is Locke's ideal also.[95] The dislike of regulation is a dislike of limitations upon the right of property to do what it will with its own. The good citizen is the man who has achieved, or is achieving, prosperity; the law is to be the law he conceives himself to need. The freedoms sought for are the freedoms he requires. The dangers against which precautions are to be taken are those which threaten his security. Out of the moral crisis of the seventeenth century there emerged a liberalism, indeed, but one attuned to the implications of the religion of success.

That is not a religion which differs very profoundly from age to age. It is the creed of the Pharisee who makes outward possessions the test of character, and associates social merit with conformity to a law which he has shaped to his own purposes. We need not deny his sincerity; we are justified, I think, in deprecating the narrowness of his vision. It is unable to transcend its own environment. It is so confident in its own energy and power that it cannot see that the lame, the halt, and the blind, are not so of their own vision. In effect, it tells them that if they, too, will become men of substance, they may share in the benefits of the state it has made; it lacks the imaginative insight to realize that the class-relationships it has built make this an impossible adventure. Its enclosures separate the peasant from the land; its rules of commercial ownership leave the industrial worker with nothing but his labour to sell. Having made inequality an implicit article of its faith, it then invites to freedom those who are denied the means of reaching it.

156

Its universal, in a word, is a particular woven from a special logic unaware of its inherent limitations. Admission to the common good it organizes is always an essay in the conditional mood. Men may achieve that privilege if they have already proved their worth. But the proof is the attainment of that very status in society which is by the nature of the system denied to most men who seek it. It is not, of course, difficult to understand their outlook. They came in an age which was entitled to pride in its immense achievements. They took, as most men will take, the short view of their meaning. They were hypnotized by the spell the new wealth cast upon them. They saw great fortunes made by parvenus who the day before, as it were, seemed to be nothing; not unnaturally, they inferred that the career was open to the talented and that to make the rules in their interest was to make them in the interest also of the common good. They refurbished the content of Christian principle to give new sanction to their enthusiasm. Philosophy, even science, were harnessed to its service. They were unaware that they were imprisoning human nature in categories too narrow to contain it. They did not even know that the criterion by which they judged human objectives was conceived essentially in economic terms. The men who doubted or opposed their purposes were either failures, like Lilburne and his followers, or, like Bourdalone, men who stood by the ancient ways. They had found, as they thought, a method of reconciling individual ambition with social good. It was only in the next age that the old truth would be re-affirmed that a man must lose the whole world to gain his own soul.

Yet, even in this unconsciousness, there is, nevertheless, a sense of the direction in which they were moving. The perception that political power, by an inescapable natural law, follows economic power, was the pivot of Harrington's writings; and though there is a liberal flavour in his proposals, their keynote is the assumption that those who have a stake in the country ought to rule the country. While he was in prison in Newgate, Richard Overton, radical though he was, ardently declared his faith in an inviolable individualism. "To every individuall in nature", he wrote,[96] "is given an individuall property by nature, not to be invaded or usurped by any." Richard Harley, writing in 1710, had no doubt that the change in the distribution of property was the cause of the civil wars. "The single authority of his prerogative", he wrote,[97] "proved but an artificial and precarious power, unable long to hold out against the real and natural power of property, which was now so largely vested in the people that when they had found the way to put their affairs into a method, and came to feel their own strength, they were able to bear down all before them." So deep is this sense, indeed, that men did not hestitate to make the claim one which should determine the structure of the state. In the debate on the proposal to re-establish the House of Lords (February 3, 1657) we are told[98] that "the commonwealth's men fell in, and showed, that where the cause is taken away, the effect must cease; that as the House of Lords had anciently a natural right to a superior jurisdiction, in that their property was five parts of six of the whole nation, so it is now more natural for the commons to have that superiority, their proportion of propriety being ninety-nine parts, or more, of a hundred; and therefore moved, that if they would have another house, it might be so bounded as might suit with the people's interest".

The "people's interest", clearly, is the business man's; he will not be sacrificed to the King and the aristocracy. The men of property are to have an "absolute power" to "dispose of all they have as they please".[99] To secure that end, they must capture the machinery of the state. When they have done this, they may "who are English subjects . . . blesse God for His goodnesse who hath made us absolute proprietors of what we enjoy, so that our lives, liberties and estates doe not depend upon, nor are subject to, the sole breath or arbitrary will of our Soveraigne".[100] It is clear enough how emphatic a wind of doctrine went to the making of Locke's hypotheses. He summarized, he did not innovate, when he said that "the supreme power cannot take from any man any part of his property without his own consent".[101] He shared the view of his contemporaries that the men of property are the natural rulers of society. He understood the attitude that made John Houghton say that "the majority of the poor are very expensive and lazy, especially the manufacturers".[102] The inference from this view was clear enough to Addison within a generation of the Revolution. "It is here in England", he wrote in the *Spectator*,[103] "come into our very language, as a propriety of distinction, to say when we would speak of persons to their advantage, "they are people of condition. . . ." The consideration of fortune has taken up all our minds, and, as I have often complained, poverty and riches stand in our imaginations in the place of guilt and innocence".

The Revolution of the seventeenth century was not an attack on the institution of Kingship as such; it was directed, as Dryden said,[104] against Kings who were felt to be "a clog on trade". It was because business men revolted against interference with their economic opportunities that

"the springs of property were bent

And wound so high they cracked the government."[105]

A conception of nature had been evolved of which the major premiss was the convenient one that the operations of the state must correspond to the will of those who owned economic power. The idea of natural rights therefore meant, as it meant in Locke, the idea that property could be controlled only as it consented to be controlled. Liberty, accordingly, became the obligation in government to refrain from such interference with the rights of property as its owners might resent. The laws may "regulate the right of property", the possession of land may be "determined by positive constitutions"[106] but those laws, in their turn, men of property will shape. Religious precept is no longer valid against their prescriptions, for, as Locke showed, churches were properly to be regarded as merely voluntary associations with which the state should only concern itself as they affected public order. The church had lost, as Richard Harley realized,[107] authority and prestige when it sided with the Crown against business men. A "natural" social order had begun to find the institutions it required to give effect to its inherent purposes. It had shaped all the contours of civilization to an appetite for acquisition which recognized no boundaries to its claims.

## CHAPTER III

# The Age of Enlightenment

## I

THE creative centre of liberal thought in the eighteenth century is in France. There, the problems to be solved demanded a greater effort, the need for change was more profound. In England, no small part of the mental climate necessary to a liberal evolution had already been achieved. A framework of constitutional government had been erected which, if its basis was more narrow than its admirers were willing to admit, yet offered opportunities far greater than those of any continental people. English political thought, in the seventy years before the French Revolution, did little more than work out the implications of Locke's philosophy. Even Adam Smith may not unfairly be said to have developed with magistral emphasis a doctrine of which the postulates were already in existence before his time. There is novelty in Burke; but the true emphasis of his doctrine was in a conservative direction. His concern was to persuade his epoch to accept the finality of the Revolution settlement; and it was rather to the protection than to the enlargement of its implications that he devoted his superb powers. Price and Priestley[1] did little more than demand formal recognition for a status for the Nonconformists which was already largely implicit in the practice of the English state. They made their obeisances both to the American and the French Revolutions; but their effort was a rhetorical gesture rather than an index to novelty. It won no wide response from those to whom it was addressed. The average Englishman of the eighteenth century was, if I may use a paradox, at peace even when he was at war. He felt that he had made his bargain with fate. It was with the details rather than with the principles of the system under which he lived that he concerned himself. The whig compromise had made room for the bourgeoisie within its confines. It was not necessary to disturb it until after the Napoleonic wars.

But eighteenth century France is a society in ferment, and the pressure of new ideas is inexhaustible. The *ancien régime* was challenged in the name of new ideas. All the genius of the period was on the side of the novelties; its outlook permeated even those who had most to lose by its victory. The system could not meet the challenge. To the new ideas it opposed an outworn discipline the sanctions of which were destroyed by its association with bankruptcy at home and defeat abroad. The monarchy was, at long last, compelled to take counsel with the middle class; and when it refused to accept the terms which the latter proffered, the result was its overthrow. As in the England of the Puritan rebellion, it was discovered that traditional institutions cannot be uprooted without a conflagration. Just as Hampden and Pym begat Lilburne and Winstanley, so Mirabeau and Mounier, in their turn, begat Babeuf and the *Enragés*. As Cromwell made possible the new equilibrium of the Restoration, so Napoleon made effective the compromise of the Charter. As 1688 made an England in which the middle class established their title to a predominant share in statehood, so, after a generation of passionate conflict, 1815 gave the French bourgeoisie their letters of credit. Meanwhile, in America, a middle-class state had, if in exceptional circumstances, been founded.[2] The history of the nineteenth century is the record of the use made by that class of a power which it elevated to a universal plane.

It is not, of course, that the French Revolution was a sudden event. Its coming was predicted a generation before its advent. Men felt that they were living in dangerous times. The preparation for the final explosion was gradual and cumulative. It was effected by a concerted attack on every element of privilege in the community. There was not, indeed, any effort before 1789 to attack directly the monarchical principle; even Robespierre was a monarchist when he entered the National Assembly. But the church was ruthlessly dissected. Its theology and its social ethic were subjected to a criticism more merciless than any it has undergone before or since. The claims of the nobility, the legal system, the habits of government, the economic basis of society, all these were examined afresh and, in large part, upon the dangerous assumption that most of the traditions they represented were evil. It is the age of reason; and the philosophers used the weapon of rational criticism to declare that freedom is good and restraint in its nature bad. They sought quite consciously to evade whatever limited the right of individual personality to make its own terms with life. There was no form of effort they neglected in this task; there was no institution, however venerable, they did not seek to influence or invade. They penetrated, as with Turgot, the councils of the administration. They transformed the Academy into an organ of propaganda. The novel and the theatre became weapons in their attack. That salon which, in the seventeenth century, had been taught to speak the language of polite culture, was, in the eighteenth, instructed with ardour in the habits of social reform. The government might imprison; a term in gaol became a passport to social distinction. The church and the Sorbonne might thunder their denunciations; they aroused ironic amusement in their hearers. The diarists, the chroniclers, even the reports of the police, depict for us, the more truly because they are unconscious of their implications, the picture of a new society struggling to be born. It is a society which rejects the tenets of the past because it has new needs of which those tenets take no account. It is a society, also, which we can watch, as it emerges, breaking into pieces the old self-confidence of its opponents. Where, in the seventeenth century, they were assured and insistent, in the eighteenth they were dubious and hesitating. There is no architect like Richelieu, even like Mazarin, in this age to give the old régime a sense of mastery over its subjects; it cannot even find a Colbert to bring efficiency to its service. It perished because even the men who ruled it knew in themselves that their critics were right. When Malesherbes gave, as Director of Publications, shelter to that encyclopædia which symbolized the erosion of the old order, it was admitting its impotence before the demand for a new social scheme.

We must not, indeed, think of the *philosophes* as an organized fellowship which shared a common body of integrated ideas, nor must we imagine that their influence was other than sporadic in character. What Voltaire desired was very different from the ideals of Rousseau; and if there is an alliance between Turgot and the Physiocrats, there are also distinctions of importance to be made in their ideas. Holbach and Helvetius, again, share much of the Voltairean outlook; but neither their programme nor their methods coincided with his. Much of what he wanted Mably would have approved; but the latter has an outlook which, at important points, denies all that is vital in the philosophy of Voltaire. In a sense, moreover, the most remarkable attitude of the century is that of the Abbe Meslier; and while he would have joined the philosophers in their attempt to overthrow, it is certain that he would have fought them as passionately as Bolsheviks fought social democrats in their endeavour to fulfil.[3] There are important differences in their attitude to England; to Voltaire, it was a constant inspiration, to Rousseau and Holbach a warning rather than an example. And there are vital streams of thought in the period, of Diderot in metaphysics, for example, and Linguet in social theory, that we cannot fit into any neatly patterned scheme. The age is one of momentous confusion. Men rather feel themselves dissatisfied than know with any coherence what they will do about their dissatisfactions. They know that they want freedom; but what freedom is for, and upon what principles its limits are to be traced, upon these matters they can hardly be said to have made up their minds.

And there is the resistance to the new ideas. Religion may have been on the defensive but, at least, it is active in self-defence. We tend to forget that for every attack

165

launched by the philosophers, there are a dozen defences some of which were widely popular. And some of the defenders are men whose ability and solidity are beyond dispute; Fréron,[4] Bergier, the Abbe Guénée, the lawyer Moreau, these are not mean names. That savage attack on the new ideas which Palissot called the *Philosophes* was one of the most successful plays of its epoch. Men like Rousseau and Necker were proud to defend the necessity of religion; and President Hénault represented a very widespread attitude when he protested that Voltaire's impieties were socially dangerous. If there were great ladies like Madame du Deffand, to whom religious feeling was unknown, there were many others like Madame de Montbarey whose devout life would not have shamed a disciple of Port-Royal. The memoirs of the duc de Croy point in the same direction. Booksellers like Hardy, historians like J. N. Moreau, make us realize how little a simple piety could be touched by new doctrine; and the portrait painted of his father by Rétif de la Bretonne makes us realize that the faith which inspired counter-revolutionary feeling was widespread among the comfortable peasantry.[5] If the theatre was popular, there was still a wide audience eager to applaud the traditional attacks upon its morality. If there was a decline in superstition, there was still, within a few years of the Revolution, an eager faith in miracles.[6]

This is not all. The political literature that has survived is mostly that of the party which was victorious; the names we know are of the Left. But Lefevre de Beauvray could publish in 1770 his widely read *Dictionaire Social et Patriotique* which rejects all the new ideas, and can write that liberty "leads to the subversion of all social order". Writers like Gin and Dubuat-Nancay found a ready public for their defences of the traditional monarchical system. Madame du Deffand, who called Turgot "un sot animal" finished in entire disillusion with the philosophers whose outlook she had done so much to promote on the significant ground— the permanent tactic of conservatism—that they mistook licence for liberty and insolence for equality. We have novels which mock the philosophers as well as those which praise them, and we are warned against the type who, the more eagerly he reads the new books, the more ardently he neglects his wife. The moral hold of the old institutions and the old ideas was weakened; there is no doubt of the urge for novelty in thought and habit. But there is no doubt, also, of the tenacity with which the old defended themselves; nor that they were supported both by the rigorous arm of authority, on the one hand, and by a large population which approved of the ancient ways, on the other. The makers of liberalism had to fight for their victory.

But the struggle is always proceeding in an atmosphere which leaves no doubt of the result. His generation, after all, canonizes Voltaire; that final visit to Paris in 1778 sets the seal of triumph on a half-century of labour. Even the counter-influence of Rousseau is, until after the Revolution, an indirect support to his cause; for Rousseau, as the protagonist of a religion of sentiment rather than a religion of dogma, is in the central stream of the Protestant tradition. But we do not need to assess the standing of the great names to recognize the victory of the new spirit. Testimony to the fact that it is entering upon its empire is omnipresent in its opponents themselves. That duc du Croy, whom I have quoted as the embodiment of an older ideal, has moments when ambition compels him to subordinate its habits to a worldly temper.[7] The sermons of the age are full of lament over its secularism. Charity is no longer respected; the rich no longer see the danger of their wealth to salvation. The holiness of poverty has disappeared; in its place has come an appetite without limit for worldly goods. There is everywhere a restless ambition among men which will not allow them to rest content with their allotted station in life; their attitude to work is wholly different from what the church can approve. They are unmoved by denunciations of money-getting so long as they are successful. Men are so eager to be rich, groaned Father Croiset, they spend so much of their days and nights in seeking wealth, "that they have hardly the leisure to remember that they are Christians".[8] The love of wealth, the passion for comfort, these, the preachers insist, have made men wholly forget the claims of religion to regulate behaviour.[9]

The same admission is apparent in the revival, which dates from the late seventeenth century, of the debate upon usury. The volumes are endless in which churchmen of ability and knowledge like Liger[10] and Hyacinthe de Gasquet,[11] will seek to argue that commercial advantage is useless if it is purchased by obedience to rules which imperil men's souls. But they know that they are arguing in vain. No one can now read their angry denunciations without realizing the awareness of these clerical moralists that they are dealing with a lost generation. They will even tell the people, though a people who have no access to their books, that they labour in suffering for the sombre manufacture of profits in which they have no share. They will attack the usurers who, so they say, immolate upon the altar of their avarice the flesh and blood of the poor. Yet they are half-hearted in their denunciations. These business men may neglect the law of the gospel; nevertheless they are honest and worthy men who labour for the state's increase. "There is not a business man nor a banker," writes one of their critics,[12] "nor a single merchant who does not believe he knows more about usury than all the Holy Fathers and theologians in the universe. For business men, these understand nothing of affairs; they know only what they can find in their books, and these books are all of them useless in business matters." The business men think so for a very simple reason. "Theologians argue", wrote one of the advocates of the new order, "that merchants should suspend all business dependent upon loans . . . since it is impossible to maintain a social order by means of contracts without interest . . . (to do so) would be to overturn at once all classes in society, and to banish from its proceedings liberty and the uninterrupted movement of the exchanges in which every one finds his special advantage."[13]

The clerical moralists, in fact, were defeated because they could not effectively answer a straightforward question. Is interest on money necessary, asks their critic, to make possible that commerce which supports at least one-third of the inhabitants of the globe? To the bourgeois the answer is obvious. "The special character of my religious faith", wrote the author of a *Letter to the Archbishop of Lyons,*[14] "is not to reap eternal happiness until I have secured my good fortune in this world." There is, in short, a final conflict between the prescriptions of business and the prescriptions of the Catholic faith. The business men needed a moral code the prescriptions of which arose, not from the deductive insight of medieval scholasticism, but from the felt requirements of commercial enterprise. The church refused its accommodation to these. And what, in this context, is of significance is the fact that what the church refused to supply, the philosophers had already provided. From this aspect, the value of Voltaire to the business man was effectively beyond measure. Himself engaged in great affairs, rich and business-like in his habits, his outlook was the practical commonsense philosophy of the successful man. It was not subtle or refined. It did not luxuriate in fine-spun distinctions. It was, as we shall see, full of a healthy respect for property. It was the outlook of the "honnête homme" at its best. It recognized the value of thrift, prudence, enterprise. It sought for a freedom that could be placed at the service of these qualities. Its enthusiasm, for instance, for those English liberties of speech, of religious tolerance, of person and property guaranteed by trial by jury, were the liberties they sought also. "In England", he had written, "the Stock Exchange applies the term 'infidel' only to those who go bankrupt."[15] That was the secular morality the epoch required; and when it could not find its principles in the ancient books, it turned, not unnaturally, to the new for their discovery.

I do not mean by this that the eighteenth century went Voltairean in any fundamental way. The middle class took from Voltaire what it wanted—which was essentially a gospel of civil liberty. It joined to this, as in the writings of Necker, a real devotion to religion, on the understanding that it was kept in its proper place. By that it meant two things. It did not, firstly, propose to allow religion to interfere with the solid business of making a fortune; and it wanted, secondly, enough sanction to remain with its principles to keep the working classes in their proper place. It was, that is, acutely conscious that men who are deprived of property need consolation of some kind; and it saw every reason why the hope of future salvation should be promised them on condition that they were orderly, hardworking, and well-behaved in this one. With Voltaire himself, the prescription of religion as a way of keeping the masses in order is part of the cynical outlook of the worldling he always was; with men like Barbier it is something more. The eighteenth century achieved a separation between religion and morals which made their substance different for different social classes. For those with security, religion became a private matter between the citizen and his God or church; for the poor, it became an institution with the social context of necessity for public order. From this angle, it became permeated by utilitarian standards which had a different relevance according to the class to which they were applied. And this, of course, is not confined to France. It obtains equally with England and America, even with Germany. Hannah More and Bishop Watson, Jonathan Edwards, even Kant, would have fully understood Voltaire. In their various ways, it was for the same kind of society that they were seeking.

But when the business men found in the philosophers' works the new morality for which they were seeking, it was not that alone they discovered there. The atmosphere of the social literature of the time is exactly that combination of positivism and scepticism which represented their own attitude. There is the positive belief that a natural form of government can be discovered corresponding, in the social sphere, to Newton's great laws in the physical. And that natural form, by a singular coincidence, will give them the principles commercial prosperity demands. It will discover that the environment of freedom, which made England rich, is the natural environment. A man's property should be free; arbitrary taxation, arbitrary interference of any kind, is undesirable. A man should be free to comment upon public affairs. Not, indeed, to say anything he likes; there is a healthy fear of those whom Voltaire called the "canaille" and Burke the "swinish multitude". But he ought to be free to say the kind of thing a stout bourgeois, whether in business or, like Voltaire, in letters, is accustomed to want to say. He ought to be free in religious matters; the time has passed when a sensible man will accept the idea that persecution does anyone any good in affairs of conscience. He ought to live under law, rather than discretion; and that will mean, as most writers will say with enthusiasm after Montesquieu, some kind of constitutional system. They will find men like Darigrand arguing that the aristocrat who holds aloof from commerce does sorry service to the state.[16] They will hear from Boncerf of the inconvenience of feudal privilege.[17] They can read in the economists how much society suffers from an outworn fiscal system; and, if they are told there of the primacy of agriculture over commerce, the gibes of Voltaire and Galiani will reassure them. Grave lawyers will dig into ancient documents to prove, in Madame de Stael's famous phrase, that in France it is despotism that is new; liberty itself is of the ancient tradition. A shy girl, Mademoiselle de Lezardière, will show this in eight stout volumes;[18] and even the King will condescend to accept a copy of her work, it is true in an abbreviated edition. The danger of industrial combinations, the desirability of a uniform code of law, the reform of the savage punishments of the time, a modernized system of weights and measures, the value of governments which do not govern too much, the insistence that reform produces security, they can find all these. Men like Brissot will tell them of an America in which the social stratification of old Europe is without meaning;[19] and they will feel in Mr. Franklin, for whom French society is so enthusiastic, the embodiment of their own good bourgeois virtues. When they go to war on behalf of Mr. Franklin's America how is it not possible that they should dream of its freedom for themselves?

And the very scepticisms of the philosophers help them to emancipation. They throw doubt on the authority of the church, the utility of aristocratic privilege, even, though with caution, the case for a despotic monarchy. And the background of these scepticisms is always rational utility. Voltaire shows them how costly is the monastic system of the church, how expensive to industry are its feasts and fasts, how wise it is to live in the kind of society where a man can cultivate his own garden. The church tells them of the glories of other worldliness; but the six editions of the encyclopædia record, with an enthusiasm they can appreciate, the progress of science and trade, their intimate connection with material well-being. They learn from it the happy consequences of the progress of reason; and they learn also that the objectives of its editor are very much their own. They see a new proportion in things when they find a hardly more than casual treatment of famous confessional controversies; and can compare the enthusiastic detail of the articles on machinery with the perfunctory dismissal of religious principles. They find there a remarkable freedom from the thraldom of the past. Feudalism is attacked in a thorough-going fashion. The truths of the new political economy are assumed everywhere. Intolerance is dismissed as "a hateful injustice in the eyes alike of God and man".[20]

No doubt the influence of all this is indirect rather than immediate in character. Its point derived less from the impact of the argument itself than from the environment in which it was made. Intolerance, bankruptcy, corruption and despotism have a way in themselves of making men feel that novelty is called for. The fact that between 1715 and 1789 the foreign trade of France was quadrupled[21] was probably less important than the widespread feeling that the institutions and habits of the system stood in the way of even greater expansion. Control from the centre, as in the mining industry, interfered substantially with the possibilities of progress. They could see in the work of Turgot, both on its practical and its theoretical side, how the privileges of a landowning nobility stood in the way of their ambitions. If it be true, as the author of *La Theorie de l'Interet de l'Argent* tells us,[22] that "among the capitalists of the kingdom probably about a third do not dare to use their capital and direct it into the channels of trade" we have obviously an important interest which saw in the union of throne and altar a real barrier to their well-being. What the philosopher said of freedom of conscience and the mind, it was easy to transfer to the idea of property. Out of that transfer the bourgeois can build a social ethic with sanctions that do not interfere with his objective. He seeks wealth; he sees that a functionless aristocracy and a well-endowed church are not less avid than he in their pursuit. More, he perceives that the morality they enforce is built upon postulates which, while they do not interfere with them, are at every point an encouragement to their enterprise. He learns from Voltaire that persecution has merely enriched neighbouring countries at the expense of his own. A new ethos is offered to him in which he can find all the promise of the old, with much that the old has forbidden to him. Confronted with the choice between a philosophy of constraint, and a philosophy of emancipation, it is not difficult to see why he should have made the choice he did.

## II

I have already noted the drift towards *laissez-faire* in the England of the Restoration. The tendency becomes a movement in the eighteenth century. Parliament became increasingly unwilling to interfere by way of industrial regulation. Its attitude was very much that which Dean Tucker expressed in some emphatic words.

175

"The Statutes for regulating wages and the price of labour", he wrote,[23] "are another absurdity and a very great hurt to trade. Absurd and preposterous it must surely appear for a third person to attempt to fix the price between buyer and seller without their own consents. For if either the journeyman will not sell his labour at the fixed or statutable price, or the master will not give it, of what use are a thousand regulating laws? Nay, how indeed can any stated regulations be so contrived as to make due and reasonable allowance for plenty or scarcity of work, cheapness or dearness of provisions, difference of living in town or country, firing, house-rent, etc.; also for the goodness or badness of the work-manship, the different degrees of skill or despatch of the workman, the unequal goodness of materials to work upon, state of the manufacture, and the demand or stagnation at home or abroad? . . . And yet, were even this possible, a great difficulty still recurs, viz. who shall, or how can you, force the journeyman to work, or the master to give him work, unless they themselves shall mutually agree about it? And if they agree, why should you or I or anyone else interfere?"

Here is a plea for freedom of contract between master and man in amplitude indeed, and that from an Anglican Dean. It is the attitude of the masters themselves. They told the House of Commons that regulation of wages met technical difficulties incapable of resolution. They wanted individual settlement. It is impossible, they say, "or at the very least inequitable, by any positive law to put an equal value on every man's labour". The system takes no account of individual differences in the capacity of the worker. It seeks to give the poor worker more than he deserves as a craftsman. It **is** bound to send up prices. Wages must be left to the uncontrolled action of the law of supply and demand. And Parliament took the same view of the laws of apprenticeship. "The most useful and beneficial manufactures are principally carried on," a House of Commons committee reported in 1751,[24] "and trade most flourishing in such towns and places as are under no such local disabilities" as the Elizabethan statute; and the century is littered with particular Acts exempting trade after trade from its operation. Blackstone explains that the spirit of legal decisions is hostile to restriction, a temper they had increasingly displayed since the time of Coke. The antagonism to the settlement system is largely based upon the same ground; and a writer pointed out in 1779 that the towns where trade most flourished were those in which it was most neglected.[25] The wiser minds of the day, Tucker, Burke, Adam Smith, had no difficulty in applying the same attitude to fiscal relations with the colonies; "a great empire", Burke told his constituents in Bristol, "cannot at this time be supported upon a narrow and restrictive scheme either of commerce or of government."[26]

It is in the atmosphere of this outlook that Adam Smith wrote his great work. To grasp its significance, we must realize that the *Wealth of Nations* is but a part of an incomplete philosophic system of society. "The science of the connecting principles of nature" is to "render the theatre of nature a more coherent and therefore more magnificent spectacle".[27] He seeks to introduce order into chaos, to make the principles of wealth-getting apparent to the educated man. What are the keynotes of the book? It is secular in tone, rationalist in method, and individualist in outlook. It starts from the assumption that each man is best fitted to be the judge of his own actions; as he had written in the *Moral Sentiments*, "every man is by nature first and principally recommended to his own care".[28] That is his real task, and it is his good fortune that, as he attends to his own wants, he is "led by an invisible hand to promote an end which was no part of his intention".[29] For Adam Smith the myriad spontaneous actions of individuals, made for their own private benefit, results, by a mysterious alchemy, in social good. We do better for society by this "simple system of natural liberty" than if we consciously contrived its advantage. Underlying the structure of the universe is sympathy which compels the good of others to be involved in my good. Out of it is born justice "the main pillar" of the state. It is implanted in men's nature, giving him a consciousness of good and ill, a fear of punishment where he does wrong. He is bound by moral rules, and, in the long run, he can only attain his end by obedience to them. This enables him to be optimistic in outlook. There is less than we imagine in the difference between rich and poor. If man is left alone, he will work out his own salvation. Whatever disturbs the order of nature makes for evil and not for benefit.

Hence emerges Adam Smith's dislike of state-action. Supreme coercive power is mainly of use to protect us against injustice and violence, especially violence to property. It may act for education, or for those public works in the making of which the individual cannot find profit. But, beyond a narrow ambit, his supreme purpose is to protect the spontaneous activity of the individual. When that "insidious and crafty animal vulgarly called the statesman or politician",[30] has given us external peace and internal order, his main work is done. We can, apart from this, do better with "the natural rules of justice, independent of all positive institutions" than with his interference. Given security, he seems to say, there is hardly need of more political action. That is contrived, unnatural; it is contrary to the "simple system". It invades a man's natural rights, it usually so acts as to deprive him of the fruits of his labour. Most of us who "affect to trade for the public good" do very little by it. Let every man be free to seek his self-interest as he pleases, and maximum social good will be realized by his attention to his own concerns.

What is the effective result? With one or two notable exceptions, the Navigation Laws, for example, Adam Smith is the determined critic of most of the industrial regulations in vogue in his time. He is against protective tariffs, trade combinations, whether of capital or labour, bounties, labour legislation, monopolies. He sees industry as a mass of interrelated actions by individuals who will do well enough so long as promises are kept and violence prohibited; and the fuller the competition between them the greater will be the public advantage. Where the system of liberty obtains, each man has the maximum inducement to labour, since he has then the certainty of reaping the maximum reward from it. He makes little of differences between men in natural endowments. A bountiful Providence has created an order of Nature in which the individual owner of property is compelled in following his own objectives

179

to labour for the common good. For he has to produce in order to exchange. To live, he must satisfy the wants of others. There is a reciprocity of inherent benefit in the relations of men which interference can only destroy. For any interference, as he was at pains to show with a wealth of historical detail, will only aid a privileged few, who cheat the nation by representing a coincidence between their private advantage and the public well-being.

In a sense, perhaps, it is true to say that Adam Smith completes an evolution that had been continuous from the Reformation. The latter substituted the prince for the church as the source of the rules which regulate social behaviour. Locke and his school substituted Parliament for the prince as better fitted to pervade them with social purpose. Adam Smith went a stage further and added that, with minor exceptions, there was no need for Parliament to interfere at all. Granted, he said, in effect, that Nature has implanted in men the six motives of sympathy, self-interest, propriety, the propensity to truck and barter, a habit of labour so schooled as normally to prevent over-production, and a propensity to be free, and human wants can be satisfied so long as fraud and violence are punished and the nation safeguarded against external aggression. The real purpose of government, in a word, is the blessing of security. Granted that, there is no plausible ground for mistrusting the habits of individuals save when they act collectively, or press for special privilege. There is an identity of interest between classes in society which is the more fully realized the more they are left alone.

The appeal this doctrine made to its generation hardly requires any emphasis. It told the business man that he was a public benefactor; and it urged that the less he was restrained in the pursuit of his wealth, the greater the benefit he could confer upon his fellows. There was so much practical sagacity in the work, so magistral a summary of facts within the experience of every cultivated man, that it seemed difficult to reject its conclusions without denying the voice of reason itself. Every reader knew that he strove to better his own condition. Every reader, also, knew from daily experience that in his effort at betterment he was constantly hampered by governmental interference. Most of his readers knew only too well the corruption and inefficiency of those politicians he so contemptuously described. To have their own longings elevated to the dignity of natural law was to provide them with a driving force that had never before been so powerful. *Sic vos non vobis* is no unfair summary of the *Wealth of Nations*. If it displayed a caution about the habits of the mercantile community, a real dislike for the silent shareholder, a real affection for the sober working man, an uneasy sense that the limits of state interference were less easy to define in concrete than in abstract terms, the general impact of the book was overwhelmingly towards *laissez-faire*; and it gave to that policy the authority of nature and reason as its support. Nature, for the eighteenth century, indeed, for Smith himself, was that body of regular phenomena subdued by science to law; and reason was the weapon with which man had wrested new truths from the immense errors of the past. With Adam Smith, the business man is given his letters of credit. Liberalism has now a fully analysed economic mission. Let the business man but free himself, and, thereby, he frees mankind. But to free himself he must possess himself of the state; this he has already done in large measure. And now he finds that to employ it for the largest end he has no other task than to compel it to take the narrowest possible view of its functions. The workman may complain, or later, that spoiled monopolist the farmer. Neither has seen the meaning of that majestic law of progress which tells us that the least of government is the best of government. With Adam Smith the practical maxims of business enterprise achieved the status of a theology; and the state became the instrument by which, in the next seventy years, they were applied to the practice of its daily life.

Adam Smith, of course, does not stand alone; as always in the history of social thought the great man is what Emerson called a representative man, a summary of a doctrine being beaten out of the needs of his time by many predecessors. Less amply, indeed, but with an insight rarely less sure, Hume was pointing in the same direction; and Dean Tucker, while he lacked the range and imagination of Adam Smith, had the same message to deliver with an emphasis more logical and as constant.[31] That Burke had arrived at a similar standpoint we know from Smith himself; though, as we shall see, there were elements in Burke's thought to which he was a stranger. But nothing brings out more clearly the universal character of Adam Smith than an analysis of physiocratic doctrine.[32] The affiliation is the more remarkable for two reasons. There is no doubt, in the first place, that their ideas originated in complete

independence of one another; and the practical remedies each had to propose were very different. Yet, at
bottom, the basis of their outlook was the same. Each
was the proponent of economic liberalism. Each was
seeking to make the state no more than the interpreter
of a natural law which it could, indeed, deform, but
could not improve. Each, therefore, strove to free the
owner of property from the burden of regulation. The
insight of the Physiocrat was inferior to that of Smith,
above all in his view of the significance of commerce.
But the revolution he helped to effect was similar in
kind. Like Smith's, it was born of the errors, the in-
capacities, the corruption, of the eighteenth century
state; but, unlike his, it built for purposes far different
from those it set out to achieve.

The Physiocrats were innovators, but innovators
with a tradition behind them. Just as Adam Smith was
descended directly from Locke and the Tory free
traders of the seventeenth century and, indirectly, from
the natural law school of that epoch as it was shaped by
philosophy and science, so the Physiocrats can trace
back their pedigree directly to the neo-mercantilists of
the latter part of Louis XIV's reign, and, indirectly,
to the Cartesians who gave so different a meaning to
the idea of law than their medieval predecessors. They
have often been compared to a religious sect, and there
is real justification for the comparison. They had their
prophet in Quesnay, their creed in the *Table Oeconomi-
que*, their inspired apostles in Mirabeau and Mercier de
la Rivière, their *Summa* in the latter's *Ordre Essentiel*,
their missionaries in men like Baudeau, their journal of
the faith in the *Ephémérides*, their organs of propaganda

in the agricultural societies and provincial academies, even their affiliated statesmen in men like Turgot.

I am here less concerned with the technical aspects of their doctrine than with its general implications. Here they, like Adam Smith, start from the notion of a natural order of which the kinship to the "simple system of natural liberty" is profound. They assume, like him, an inherent impulse in man to pursue happiness, and an order in the scheme of things which provides the rules for its achievement. Their concern was to separate this scheme from the entanglements through which it had been concealed by the artificial contrivances of men. If, they thought, government could be so organized as to put the force of law behind the principles of this scheme the happiness of men would be assured. For obedience to these principles, whether in government or subjects, was necessary to right living. It was obedience to the law of man's nature given to him by the character of the universe in which he was involved. They did not doubt that these principles were as eternal and imprescriptible as those of physics. They conceived themselves, indeed, as doing for matters of social constitution what the great scientists of the seventeenth century had done for the physical universe. They were offering to statesmen a code of conduct which they evaded at their peril. "To recognize the primary and unique laws founded on nature itself", said Turgot in his Éloge de Gournay,[33] "by which all values in commerce are balanced with each other and fixed at a definite value . . . to perceive the reciprocal dependence of trade and agriculture . . . their near connection with laws, morals, and all the business of government . . . this is to look at the matter with the eye of a statesman and a philosopher". The ruler, in fact, is less to make law than to declare it. He is to discern certain inherent and permanent connections between phenomena. He is to deduce from them rules under the empire of which men necessarily live. By imposing those rules upon his subjects he assures their happiness. To go outside the boundaries of the action they trace is to bring misfortune upon his people.

The Physiocrats, as we know, were the protagonists of enlightened despotism. But it is important to realize that, for them, the despot is not an arbitrary master who can act as his fancy takes him. He is the subject of laws which impose themselves upon him by the sanction of nature itself. All good government, in fact, is constitutional government, not in the arbitrary sense that its precepts arise from the possibly mistaken whims of a legislative assembly, but in the much profounder sense that they are the necessary outcome of nature's plan which, when revealed, is binding upon all. Sovereignty, in a word, belongs to the plan; and we escape its consequences only by diminishing the happiness its acceptance enables us to secure.

What was the object of the Physiocrats? They offered, said Dupont de Nemours,[34] "a corps of doctrine defined and complete, which clearly lays down the natural rights of man, the natural order of society, and the natural laws most advantageous to men united in a society". Its purpose, as Quesnay said,[35] was "to obtain the greatest possible increase of enjoyments by the greatest possible diminution of expenses"; this is "the perfection of economy". Let us note at once the material

and utilitarian aim of the scheme. It is concerned with
an immediate and earthly recompense for labour. Its
foundation is the eulogy of the typical bourgeois virtues
of thrift and prudence. Its major premise is self-interest,
the right of a man to do what is most advantageous to
him, his right to those things which secure his satisfaction. These rights derive from the "imperious
necessity" of the law of self-preservation. We have to
obey that law under the sanction of misery or even
death. To obey it we must know its commands, and
these we learn by the research of reason and self-
interest into the nature of things. This research enables
us to use our faculties so as to know what is for our
advantage. We must follow its discoveries in the realm of
society just as we have to follow them in the physical
world. From the insight so gained we learn of the need
for free trade, for that scheme of taxation which places
the expense of government upon the shoulders of landlords, for the need (not wholly logical) for the absolute
security of the right to property. They will have nothing
to do with theories of equality; the unequal capacities
of men being in nature, unequal appropriation is merely
obedience to its command. They were prepared for
state-intervention on behalf of education, and the poor;
even for a kind of council of proprietors who shall
advise the government. But the essence of their scheme
is their demand for freedom of contract. It was this
which led them to support the programme of Turgot,
and to remove the internal restrictions on the French
corn trade. It was this also which led them to support
so strongly the Anglo-French commercial treaty of
1786.[36] The major premise of their thinking was the

argument that mercantilism meant an artificial scarcity. Government regulation ruined agriculture in the inter-est of privileged classes who contributed nothing to the national wealth. Abolish, they said in effect, the policy of regulation, and abundance is bound to be the out-come.

With the Physiocrats, in short, sovereignty and private property in land become identified. Let the proprietor and the farmer be free, and they will achieve social harmony by being allowed to follow their own advantage. We need not discuss the fallacies of this view. It is more important to emphasize the fact that they are concerned to draw up a programme of which the effect is to condemn the social policy of Louis XV as contrary to natural law. It is, of course, a philosophy for landlords, where Adam Smith may be said to have constructed a philosophy for merchants. It seeks to show that if the landlord is free to follow his self-interest he will, of necessity, work for the common good. It seeks to minimize the ambit of positive law as corrupt, capricious and mistaken, where the law of nature, that is, the pursuit by a rational landlord of his self-interest, is benevolent and bountiful. It argues, accordingly, that the more free from restriction the landlord is, the greater will be the abundance he produces; and since he works for the nation by devoting himself to his self-interest, his abundance will be its prosperity also. Even their lack of enthusiasm for commerce was more than atoned for by their emphasis on the harm done to commerce by regulation. They saw in it the endowment of privi-lege, an interference with abundance for the sake of scarcity, out of which a few men will make a special profit detrimental to true prosperity. As for the poorer classes, it is not unfair to say that, save as they worked on a farm, the Physiocrats did not think of them at all. If they were handworkers, they merely transformed materials provided for them by the agricultural producer; if they were servants, their interest was included in that of their masters. But the whole class of working men does not enter into the consideration of Quesnay and his disciples as a conscious and active element in the state. Its provisions were regulated by rules their views could not alter, rules, also, which benefited them even though they did not add to the common stock. They were the larger part of the "sterile" class.

It is easy to see that the general Physiocratic picture is an idealized portrait of eighteenth century France, as it would have been if every landowner had possessed a high sense of social obligation, and every farmer had known the latest developments of scientific agriculture. It emphasizes the interest of the land rather than the interest of industry and commerce simply because France was still a semi-feudal state in which the importance of the former bulked much more largely than in England. It was born of the sense that mercantilism was conducting to ruin a system that might easily be made to flourish. It is hostile to democracy for a number of reasons. Partly, the enthusiasm of its proponents; as so often with the missionaries of a gospel, they were anxious rather to impose their faith than to risk its rejection after debate. Partly, also, its thesis of property as sovereign was well fitted to the feudal climate out of which it arose. Partly, also, it was born of a real fear of commerce and finance as the source of inflation, the nurse of corruption and privilege, the begetter of those habits in the administration of which the results were so devastating to the agrarian interest. They offered the governing class of their day an opportunity of reform upon the basis that liberty is the law of life. They asked it to exchange privilege for opportunity. They argued that to make them rich was necessarily to elevate the standard of life of the whole people. They failed in their immediate objective; but they were an essential element in making the principles of economic liberalism a part of the intellectual stock-in-trade of their generation.

Their failure was their inability to see what both Adam Smith and Turgot had already perceived—that feudalism was becoming capitalism, and that economic theory could not, accordingly, confine its attention to the land. The insight of Turgot is, on any showing, remarkable. He understood with unsurpassed clarity the nature of interest in a capitalist society.[37] He saw the function of supply and demand as the determinant of price. He saw the vital difference between the fund of capital and the flow of capital goods, and this enabled him to understand the distinction between saving and investment. Upon this basis he was able to attack the whole foundation of the scholastic attitude to money. "Money considered as a physical substance, as a mass of metal," he wrote,[38] "does not produce anything; but money employed as advances for enterprises in Agriculture, Manufacture, and Commerce, produces a definite profit. With money one can purchase an estate, and thereby procure a revenue. The person, therefore, who lends his money does not merely give up the barren possession of that money; he deprives himself of the profit of the revenue which he would have been able to procure by it; and the interest which indemnifies him for this privation cannot be regarded as unjust." His concept of marginal productivity enabled him to show how the capitalist helps society by increasing the supply of savings and thus reducing the rate of interest. From the consideration of the effect of these rules, he concludes that "there exists no truly disposable revenue in a state except the net produce of lands".[39] From this, his inference is the obligation in the state to remove all burdens and restrictions, especially those of taxation, from industry and commerce, from money-lending and agriculture. Their proper place is on the landowner to whom all other classes in the community pay rent. The landowners are "the class of proprietors, the only one which, not being bound by the need of subsistence to a particular labour, can be employed for the general needs of the society".[40] In his view, the other classes receive a payment which is the proportionate recompense of their services; the landowner as landowner has an income that arises from ownership of resources to which he adds nothing. The impact of his theory, as it was the effort of his practice, was thus to throw the burden of taxation upon the aristocracy of his day. In a wider sense than that of the Physiocrats, he was seeking to free the cultivator and the industrialist from regulation and privilege. Nor is it without significance that in his explanation of the services rendered to society by each class the labourer should be adjudged in terms which foreshadow the Industrial Revolution. "The wages of the labourer," he wrote,[41] "who has nothing but his toil to sell, are fixed by contract with the cultivator who pays him as little as he can; and as he has the choice among a great number of workmen, he prefers the one who works cheapest. The workmen are therefore obliged to lower the price in competition with one another. In every kind of work, it cannot fail to happen, and, as a matter of fact, it does happen, that the wages of the workman are limited to what is necessary to procure him his subsistence."

"It was the object of the Physiocrats," said James Mill,[42] "to transform society without a revolution by taking their stand upon a small number of simple theoretic principles". That is no bad description of their aim. Let us note how its foundation is the idea of liberty. "It is of the essence of order," wrote Mercier de la Rivière,[43] "that the particular interest of one man should never be capable of separation from the common interest of all; we find a very convincing proof of this in the results naturally and necessarily produced by the fullness of freedom which must prevail in commerce in order not to injure property." The nation, therefore, can only prosper, as Adam Smith said, "under the exact régime of perfect liberty and perfect justice".[44] Since the interests of all classes are equal and identical, the case against intervention is final. A government, runs the new creed, can do best when it withholds its hand. Maybe there is evil in the world, yet the power of government to correct it is small compared to the sovereign influence of nature. Let each man look after himself. He knows better than any government can do what is best for his own advantage. Let him, therefore, make the rules of his own behaviour, especially in all matters of commercial intercourse. With the principle of the identity of interests, nothing matters but order, the enforcement of contracts voluntarily made, and a parsimonious government. With these achieved, we get the best of both worlds. We have the providential rules of the state of nature, and we have the benefits, also, of a progressive civilization. We have passed, as Turgot insisted, the religious and the metaphysical ages; we are now in that of science. Granted freedom, we may assume that moral and intellectual progress will follow naturally upon the development of science.

The outlook I have been summarizing is fittingly concluded by a reference to Bentham's *Defence of Usury*. Published in 1787, two years before the summons of the States-General, its major premises complete the evolution we have been discussing. That freedom of commerce in general is desirable Bentham assumes at once. He is concerned to show that its principles should be extended to trade in money also, that "no man of ripe years and of sound mind, acting freely, and with his eyes open, ought to be hindered, with a view to his advantage, from making such bargain, in the way of obtaining money, as he thinks best; nor (what is a necessary consequence) anybody hindered from supplying him upon any terms he thinks proper to accede to".[45] Bentham makes short work of the case against his argument. Either it is the outcome of the theological prejudice against wealth as such; or it is born of Aristotle's mistaken view that money is barren. The first is merely ancient superstition; the second is wrong because money represents the use of fertile natural forces. He proceeds

192

to show the harm done by the usury laws. They force the individual to sell under disadvantageous conditions. They conduce to evasion and therefore breed contempt for the law. They violate the maxim that every man is the best judge of his own interests. By a mistaken use of language they attach an evil repute to a valuable public service. They are simply the condemnation of a "perfectly innocent and even meritorious class of men"[46] who, as much for the benefit of others as for their own, have postponed present use to future consumption. They are condemned just as projectors are condemned, through the unfavourable connotation of the words used to describe them. In fact, exactly as the regraters and forestallers of the middle ages played, as Adam Smith had shown, a useful part as middlemen, so the usurer and the projector make possible developments of value to society. The more free they are to ply their trade the more profit will society secure from their exertions.[47]

It is all summarized with precision in a letter from Morellet to Shelburne, himself, let us remember, the patron of Bentham. "Because liberty", he wrote,[48] "is the natural condition, and restrictions, on the contrary, are a state of compulsion, by giving back liberty everything retakes its proper place, and everything is at peace, provided only that thieves and murderers continue to be caught." *Beati possidentes*; it is the function of the state to create the conditions of security for those who have property. All the rest can be left to individuals. All other intervention is the outcome, like the laws against witchcraft, of popular ignorance of sinister interest. We need, as Morellet happily put it, "freedom of conscience in trade".[49] With identity of interests we are entitled to optimism about the outcome. Men will realize their natural rights since each, in a condition of freedom, will get the fruits of his own labour. Enterprise and initiative will be encouraged; the power of corruption and ignorance to control virtue and knowledge will be put down. Society, as Paine was to say, is the outcome of our virtues, government of our wickedness. By keeping the functions of government within the narrowest limits, we give the virtues of men their widest opportunity.

It is difficult to see how a creed could have been devised more suited to the mental climate of the age. All its experience, at least so far as successful men expressed it, pointed in the economists' direction. The restrictive legislation was undoubtedly an inhibition on the production of wealth; the more it was removed or allowed to go by default, the more the nation prospered as a consequence. Even those who were horrified at the breakdown of the colonial system with the loss of America, soon learned the truth of Dean Tucker's remark that the colonies after emancipation would be as ready as before to buy in the cheapest and sell in the dearest market; Bentham's advice to the French legislature to emancipate its colonies seemed not less the fruit of practical experience than of theoretic doctrine. Every reform which moved to the acceptance of *laissez-faire* seemed, in this period, a liberation of productive power. The increase of population which followed seemed, at least until the age of Malthus, an additional proof that economic liberalism was well founded. Every exception to it came to be looked upon as an offering to that "prejudice of the people" which, as Adam Smith remarked, is part of the price government must pay "in order to preserve the public tranquillity".[50] Given that preservation, the business man could hardly doubt that the economists were right. In the next years they were to give the doctrine the status of a religious orthodoxy.

At a century and a half's distance, it is easy for us to see its flaws. Its conception of citizenship is, in fact, more limited than it is aware, for all its postulates assume that the individual for whom regard is to be had is a person with a stake in the country. The liberty of contract it eulogizes takes no account of equality of bargaining power. Its fusion of self-interest with social good ignores altogether the level at which men start, the price they have to pay if they occupy the lower levels. The degree to which the "public tranquillity" is regarded, as even Adam Smith knew, as simply the protection of property from the performance of public obligation, naturally affected the middle class less than any other portion of the population. The fact is that, granted its assumptions, economic liberalism was a doctrine limited to the service of a narrow section of the community. The price for its operation was paid by the factory operative and the landless worker who, forbidden to combine, largely deprived of the franchise, subject to courts of law which regarded the preservation of bourgeois ownership as the chief end of life,[51] were largely helpless before the new dispensation. We need not doubt either the sincerity of the economists in their enthusiasm for freedom, or the good faith of the men, whether in business or in politics, who gave effect to their conclusions. We need not doubt either,

195

that in the period of capitalist expansion, liberty gave better results than those attained by the system of regulation. The fact remains that the benefits of the system were not fairly distributed. The true comment upon its inadequacies is not merely the rise of socialism. It is also the need, so soon after emancipation was achieved, for a new interventionism in the name of obvious humanity. The business men themselves revolted against the implications of their own doctrines when they saw the results of child-labour, the mean and insanitary towns they involved, that conception of freedom, which, as T. H. Green said, gave the underfed denizen of the streets the choice between one gin-shop and another. What the new freedom meant when the bourgeoisie was master of the state we can find, not only in Shelley and Byron and Hood, in Dickens and Kingsley and Mrs. Gaskell, but in a hundred government documents compiled by men who depicted what they saw with relentless impartiality.[52] It is true enough that economic liberalism lifted the chains of state-servitude from the middle class; but it is not less true that it was a necessary outcome of its acceptance that the men so freed riveted those chains upon the workers who had helped them to their freedom.

### III

The great watershed of English political philosophy is Edmund Burke; for it was he, more than any other thinker, who gave to the metaphysical outline of Locke's theory of the state that substantial content it has possessed down to our own time. If the fundamental

196

emphasis of Burke is conservative, the utilitarian basis of his creed contained elements susceptible of a liberal interpretation. What is vital in his outlook is as living to-day as when he first uttered it. He is, as has been well pointed out, the true founder of the third British empire; for he legislated for posterity when he defended the American colonies from taxation and the Indian empire from tyranny. He was the first person to give the party system in Great Britain its full letters of credit; from that day to our own time the realization that party government is the essential principle of a representative constitutional system has not been challenged save by those who desire to desert its foundation. His criticism of the French Revolution—in substance still the soundest we have—is the basis upon which men have challenged the Russian experiment in our own day. His view of the relation of natural right to expediency; his theory of government as a trust; his insistence on the danger of sacrificing life to logic; his emphasis upon prescription and property as defining the effective contours of the state; his "disposition to preserve and ability to improve" as the criteria of statesmanship; these have entered into the thoughts of Englishmen to a degree it is difficult to over-estimate. Until our own time, at least, there is little political philosophy in this country that does not bear upon its face the mark, conscious or unconscious, of his mind.[53]

The essential Burke is, no doubt, a great and generous man, the springs of whose compassion were as wide as they were deep. Yet fully to understand his approach to his problems, we have in some sort to measure what he did with the inheritance he received. To do so, we have to remember that the essence of that inheritance was the ideas of Locke. It was the conception of England as a society in which men had property they were concerned to safeguard. It was a conception fantastically untrue when Locke made it. But it fitted a long tradition. In the reign of Elizabeth Sir Thomas Smith had written that of the labouring sort no account is to be taken;[54] they are made only to be ruled. Under the Commonwealth, Harrington, who had seen that political power goes with economic power, had divided the state into two classes; and of the servant or dependent class he had written that their condition was "inconsistent with freedom or participation of government in a commonwealth".[55] That had been the view, also, of the anonymous author of the *Standard of Equality*;[56] the poor are, he wrote, "necessitous persons, uninterested in the state, as obliged thereto by no considerable fortune". That also was the position taken by Ireton in the debates of the Army. Labourers, tradesmen, tenants, had, for him, no stake in the country. They had no more than the interest of breathing. They were like aliens who settled in the country. They had the right to live and work there. But they must, like aliens also, leave the making of the laws to those whose property gave them a real interest in their content.[57] So, also, in the same tradition, Adam Smith could write that the main function of justice is the protection of property. "The affluence of the rich", he said,[58] "excites the indignation of the poor, who are often both driven by want and prompted by envy to invade their possessions. It is only under the shelter of the civil magistrate that the owner of that valuable property, acquired by the labour of many years, or perhaps many successive generations, can sleep a single night in security."

This is the tradition to which Burke gave the whole weight of his influence. For him, the right of property, and especially landed property, to an exceptional position in the state was beyond discussion. The mass of the people, for him, had no place in the state. They were the "swinish multitude". They were "virtually represented" in the House of Commons, and he thought "such a representation . . . in many cases to be even better than the actual".[59] The people's business, for him, was simply to accept the rule of their superiors. They were "miserable sheep"; they exhibited "the fury of an enraged rabble" whose ignorant passions often seemed, when unrestrained by law, to justify the harshest despotism.[60] His famous separation of "moral" from "geographical" France enables him to insist that the real will of the French people is not with the National Assembly but with the émigrés at Coblentz. He has nothing but contempt for "the obscure provincial advocates . . . stewards of petty local jurisdictions . . . the fomenters and conductors of the petty war of village vexation" who ventured, out of their inexperience, to legislate for the world.[61] For him the right of property to rule was the "inarticulate major premise" of all his thinking. He might write that "in all disputes between the people and their rulers, the presumption is at least upon a par in favour of the people"; and he might even insist, with Sully, that popular violence is the outcome of popular suffering. But, at bottom, he assumed the unfitness of the masses for self-government. He assumed that they were unworthy of confidence. He might admit the power of public opinion; he might even recognize the corrupt character of the government under which he lived. But he was prepared for no considerable changes which might jeopardize its authority.

What is the ground for this view? In part, no doubt, it is due to his distrust of reason, his profound sense of the "wisdom of our ancestors". In part also, it is the outcome of his religious interpretation of politics. He thinks, too, of order as the condition of social well-being, and prescription as the only effective guarantee of order. But it is not, I think, a mistaken view to find the central clue to Burke's attitude in those *Thoughts on Scarcity* which so exactly suited the temper of his time. They are remarkable in many ways. Obviously born of Adam Smith's influence, they no less definitely foreshadow the coming of Malthus. They reflect, on the one hand, that optimism of the eighteenth century which believed that all would be well if "the simple system of natural liberty" were given its head, and, on the other, that settled pessimism about the future which arose between Malthus' blow at Godwin and the universal acceptance of the classical political economy.

What is their doctrine? It assumes, in the first place, the relative impotence of government. "To provide for us in our necessities", Burke wrote,[62] "is not in the power of government. It would be a vain presumption in statesmen to think they can do it . . . It is in the power of government to prevent much evil; it can do very little positive good in this, or perhaps in anything else." The poor will do themselves no good by antagonism to the rich. The latter are "trustees for those who labour"; their "hoards are the banking-houses" of the poor. What should be recommended to them are "patience, labour, sobriety, frugality and religion"; to urge any other course upon them is "downright fraud". Nothing can be done by state-action to help the economic condition of the working classes. "Labour is a commodity like every other, and rises or falls according to the demand." Wages, indeed, "bear a full proportion to the result of their labour". To attempt to interfere with the wage-relation by any sort of state-action cannot only do no good, but is a violation of the rights of the employer. For, Burke argued, "there is an implied contract, much stronger than any instrument or article of agreement between the labourer in any occupation and his employer—that the labour, so far as that labour is concerned, shall be sufficient to pay to the employer a profit on his capital and a compensation for his risk; in a word, that the labour shall produce an advantage equal to the payment. Whatever is above that, is a direct tax; and if the amount of that tax be left to the will and pleasure of another, it is an arbitrary tax".

But Burke goes farther. It is not only unwise for an ignorant legislature to intervene between master and servant. By a happy conjuncture of circumstances their interests are always identical. "In the case of the farmer and the labourer", Burke insisted, "their interests are always the same, and it is absolutely impossible that their free contracts should be onerous to either party. It is the interest of the farmer that his work should be done with effect and celerity; and that cannot be, unless the labourer is well fed, and otherwise found with such necessaries of animal life, according to his habitudes, as may keep the body in full force, and the mind gay and cheerful." From this he draws momentous conclusions. The whole of agriculture, he thinks, "is in a natural and just order". To interfere with it is reckless folly, for it injures the labourer himself. "It is therefore the first and fundamental interest of the labourer", he thinks, "that the farmer should have a full incoming profit on the product of his labour. The proposition is self-evident, and nothing but the malignity, perverseness and ill-governed passions of mankind, and particularly the envy they bear to each other's prosperity could prevent their seeing and acknowledging it, with thankfulness to the benign and wise Disposer of all things, who obliges men, whether they will or not, in pursuing their own selfish interests, to connect the general good with their own individual success." It follows that things should be left to take their own case. Political power is not, Burke thinks, like economic power. "Without question, the monopoly of authority is, in every instance and in every degree, an evil; but the monopoly of capital is the contrary. It is a great benefit, and a benefit particularly to the poor." Where, from the operation of this scheme of things, misfortune occurs, our business, therefore, is clear. We ought "manfully to resist the very first idea, speculative or practical, that it is within the competence of government, taken as government, or even of the rich, as rich, to supply to the poor those necessaries which it has pleased the Divine Providence for a while to withhold from them. We, the people, ought to be made sensible that it is not in breaking the laws of commerce, which are the laws of nature, and consequently the laws of God, that we are to place our hope of softening the Divine displeasure to remove any calamity under which we suffer, or which hangs over us".

From this view Burke is able, with some confidence, to prescribe the limits of state-action, though he admits, as he always admitted, that his principles will admit of exceptions, "many permanent, some occasional". "The state", he wrote, "ought to confine itself to what regards the state, or the creatures of the state, namely, the exterior establishment of its religion; its magistracy; its revenue; its military force by land and sea; the corporations that owe their existence to its feat; in a word, to everything that is *truly and properly* public, to the public peace, to the public safety, to the public order, to the public prosperity. In its preventive police, it ought to be sparing of its efforts, and to employ means, rather few, unfrequent and strong, than many and frequent, and, of course, as they multiply their puny, politic race, and dwindle, small and feeble." Burke, it should be added, does not deny the need to help those who can "claim nothing according to the rules of commerce and the principles of justice". But this has nothing to do with the state; it belongs to "the jurisdiction of mercy". "In that province", Burke thinks, "the magistrate has nothing at all to do; his interference is a violation of the property it is his office to protect." He does not doubt that Christians have the obligation of charity to the poor, but this is a private matter with which the state is unconcerned. Even the clamour of want does not involve political attention. "The cry of the people in cities and towns, though unfortunately (from a fear of their multitude and combination) the most regarded, ought, in *fact*, to be the *least* attended to upon this subject; for citizens are in a state of utter ignorance of the means by which they are to be fed, and they contribute little or nothing, except in an infinitely circuitous manner, to their own maintenance. They are truly *fruges consumere nati*."

This, in broad outline, is the "simple system of natural liberty" as it commended itself to the predominant political thinkers of the eighteenth century. It explains why Brown of the *Estimate* thought the people insignificant in the shaping of the life of a society. "The manners and principles of those who lead," he wrote,[63] ". . . not of those who are governed . . . will ever determine the strength or weakness, and, therefore, the continuance or dissolution of a state." It explains, also, why de Lolme should assume that the only right of the humble man was the right to be governed. "A passive share", he thought,[64] "was the only one that could, with safety to the state, be trusted" to him; for "the greater part of those who compose this multitude, taken up with the care of providing for their subsistence, have neither sufficient leisure, nor even, in consequence of their imperfect education, that degree of information, requisite for functions of this kind". It explains also why Blackstone should assume that the estates of the realm are coincident with the owners of property. The House of Lords exists as a separate chamber to prevent the people from encroaching upon the privilege of the nobility; the "Commons consist of all such men of property as have not seats in the House of Lords".[65] It explains, above all, Paley's amazing *Reasons for contentment addressed to the Labouring Part of the British Public* in which that eminent churchman is able to prove, at least to his own satisfaction, that not only are the "necessities which poverty (if the condition of the labouring part of mankind must be so called) imposes not hardships but (they are) pleasures"; and he dwells with pathos on the miseries of the rich with their "worn and tired" sensibilities, their "languid satiated existence". The road from Burke to Paley was more direct than it is comfortable to admit.

No doubt, of course, the eighteenth century contains also an alien tradition. After the middle of the century, the influence of French ideas combined with the attack of George III on the Constitution to awaken a deeper radicalism.[66] To this, also, the American Revolution made a profound contribution. But the true effect of it all was, for the time, superficial rather than profound. Price and Priestley, Cartwright and Jebb, who were its main exponents, were, after all, concerned rather with political forms than with the social substance the latter implied. The two former objected to the exclusion of Nonconformists from a full share in citizenship. They were led by their hostility to the narrow basis upon which Parliament then rested to insist upon the theory of popular sovereignty, with the inference, particularly emphasized in 1776 and 1789, upon the right of the people to cashier their rulers for misgovernment. But there is no evidence to suggest that their radicalism had any social content. Nothing they said indicated any realization of the relation between property and power. On the contrary, it was rather their sense that an important property-interest was governed without its own consent which led them into the camp of the reformers. One can read the works of both without any sense at all of the existence of a social problem. Liberty for them means political and civil liberty; by which, effectively, they mean the right to be elected and a full scheme of religious toleration. Both would have accepted the general principles of Adam Smith without any sense that they left the basic problems unsolved. Both differ from Burke less in the basis of their political thought than in the inferences they drew, in the light of their special religious interest, from that basis.

What, indeed, is singular in the English political thought of this period is the absence of any sense, at least in a notable expression, of what the social problem implied. A barely noticed pamphlet of William Ogilvie,[67] some scattered reflections of Dr. Wallace, the satirical comments of Mandeville in his *Essay on Charity Schools*, these are the main comments of the age upon the problem. It is, indeed, remarkable that the most explicit statement of the issue which the period was to see came in that *Vindication of Natural Society* in which Burke sought to overthrow attacks on social order by a *reductio ad absurdum* of the case against it. "In a state of artificial society", he had written,[68] "it is a law as constant and invariable that those who labour most, enjoy the fewest things; and that those who labour not at all, have the greatest number of enjoyments. A constitution of things this, strange and ridiculous beyond expression." But the whole of Burke's life was passed in defending exactly that "strange and ridiculous" constitution on the ground he himself noted that "the politician will tell you gravely that their life of servitude disqualifies the greater part of the race of man for a search of truth, and supplies them with no other than mean and insufficient ideas. This is but too true; and this is one of the reasons why I blame such institutions". But in his active political life he exemplified exactly the politician whom he here attacks.

The truth is that until the French Revolution the problem of the power of property in the state did not enter into English political speculation. It was, of course, known as a problem; journalists like Gordon, poets like Goldsmith, James Thomson and Crabbe, novelists like Fielding, caught glimpses of its significance. But there is nothing like the extraordinary discussion which took place in France. There is no English Linguet, no English Meslier, no English Mably or Morelly. The relative freedom of Englishmen compared to their continental neighbours, the great imperial triumphs of the age, the rising standard of comfort, all meant that the nation as a whole was contented with its lot and, save in detail, undisposed to reopen the conditions of the contract Locke had defined. When, after 1789, the working class began to be conscious of their rights, they had to discuss them in the atmosphere of insecurity and war engendered by the French Revolution. Its impact was fatal to all generosity of temper. The men of property were willing, as Canning told Lord George Bentinck,[69] to pay the costs of the poor law as a safeguard against rebellion; further than that they were not prepared for nearly forty years to go. And in those years, the worst features of the "simple system of natural liberty" were, so to say, congealed into a code. Burke's flashes of compassionate insight degenerated into the unctuous complacency of Bishop Watson and Hannah More. The prevailing outlook was that of Eldon and Sidmouth, of Braxfield and of Ellenborough. When, after Waterloo, England began to awaken from its long fit of reaction, the principles of economic liberalism had become a rule for the owners of property; and the well-being of the masses was unrelated to its application. For, by then, the coming of the factory system had created the urban proletariat; the agricultural labourer had largely been driven off the land; and these, as they sought their freedom, had to develop a new social philosophy upon which to base their demands.

A doctrine, that is, that started as a method of emancipating the middle class changed, after 1789, into a method of disciplining the working class. The liberty of contract it sought emancipated the owners of property from their chains; but in their achievement of this freedom was involved the enslavement of those who had nothing but their labour-power to sell. The conquerors justified their victory by the simplest of doctrinal devices. They declared that their freedom was the nation's also; they insisted that they could not pursue their own self-interest without, at the same time, achieving that of those who were dependent upon them. That outlook, as I have sought to show, was implicit in the teaching of practically all who sought to speculate upon matters of social constitution. When they were confronted by the fruits of their philosophy, they had little difficulty in reconciling themselves to its consequences. Either, like the authors of the Evangelical revival, they preached to the poor a doctrine

which made resistance to social misery an attack upon
the providence of God, or, like Pitt and his successors,
they terrorized their critics into submission by a relentless
application of the coercive power of the state. The
justification which satisfied them was put in a concise
form by Patrick Colquhoun in 1806.[70] "Without a
large proportion of poverty", he wrote, "there could be
no riches, since riches are the offspring of labour, while
labour can result only from a state of poverty. Poverty
is that state and condition in society where the individual has no surplus labour in store, or, in other words,
no property or means of subsistence but what is derived
from the constant exercise of industry in the various
occupations of life. Poverty, therefore, is a most necessary and indispensable ingredient in society, without
which nations and communities could not exist in a
state of civilization."

It was a comforting view, at least to those who had
somehow escaped the burden of poverty. And it was one
which, at least from the time of Mandeville, was characteristic of the age. For its results the most varied
explanations could be offered, all of which served as a
school to discipline the poor to their fate. The most
simple, perhaps, was Dr. Johnson's characteristic conclusion that subordination is necessary in society, the
most ugly the Methodist promise, so ceaselessly urged
by Wesley and his colleagues, of salvation in the next
world in exchange for passive obedience in this life.[71]
But no one put the motive of the new outlook so well or
so succinctly as Arthur Young. A careful observer, a
man of humane and liberal temper, willing to experiment, able, as in his account of France, to see that, at

some point, revolution is the necessary outcome of misgovernment, he had surveyed the English scene more
thoroughly than any other writer of his time. "Everyone
but an idiot", he wrote in 1771,[72] "knows that the
lower classes must be kept poor, or they will never be
industrious." That is an aspect of English liberalism
which explains not a little of its history in the next
hundred years.


IV

The outstanding feature of English political thought
in the eighteenth century is the absence of any original
note. Men were too satisfied with their achievements to
go outside the well-worn lines of tradition; even the
radicals go back directly to the mainstream of seventeenth century liberalism. In France, the reverse is the
case. We have a political philosophy so luxuriant in
its range of variation that no single generalization can
do it adequate justice. There is a liberal conservatism,
as with Montesquieu. There is a Utopian communism,
built upon an ethical defence of equality, of which
Mably and Morellet are the best-known, but by no
means the only, representatives.[73] Meslier stands alone
as a convinced and relentless revolutionist; but there is
a curious link between the foundations of his ideas and
that economic determinism the pessimist character of
which made Linguet a reactionary because he did not
dare to hope. Rousseau stands apart from them all.
Radical in theory, with even a proletarian nuance to
his thinking, in positive recommendations he added

little to his time. It was his special genius less to determine what men thought in matters of social constitution than to disturb their minds so profoundly as to
provide new foundations for their thinking. He incar-
nated in himself all the dissatisfaction and discontent of
his time. He taught men to see their wrongs with new
intensity. But it is not easy to say whether his influence,
as a whole, was radical or conservative. If Marat and
Robespierre were his pupils in one generation, Hegel
and Savigny were among the greatest of his disciples in·
the next, and the link between him and the romantic
reaction is, of course, direct and profound. Here, as
invariably in history, the search for any simple formula
is bound to do violence to the facts.

Yet the most characteristic representative of French
political thought in the age is Voltaire.[74] Here, as so
often, he invented nothing; but here, as so often also,
he typified the mind of his time with remarkable accuracy. He was typical of its temper in his sense that
great events were impending. He was typical, also, in
his passion less for the foundations of politics than for
the concrete remedy of concrete wrong. Voltaire is the
social reformer *par excellence*, careless about consistency
and system-making, eager to achieve immediate
practical results. He is the broker of ideas, and not the
architect of a system. Aware though he is of the importance of general ideas, he shrank from the price of their
applications. Tolerant, invincibly liberal, eclectic, there
was something in him which warned him always that
politics is a philosophy of the second best. At the back
of his mind was always the sense that too high a price
might be paid for the logic of justice. He was a man of

property, to whom the preservation of order was nature's first law. He was anxious for those improvements which might take place without risk to the foundations of the state. He recognized, with that sensitivity to the atmosphere which is not the least of his great qualities, that the foundations about him were undermined. That is why he was unready for any social philosophy which might add to the dangers he perceived.

It is, of course, true that, in an essential sense, politics proper was a secondary matter to Voltaire. The changes he recommended were always urged in the background of his own insistence that " je n'entre point dans la politique . . . la politique n'est pas mon affaire, je me suis toujours borné a faire mes petits efforts pour rendre les hommes moins sots et plus honnêtes".[75] That is of the inner reality of Voltaire. He is concerned not with the making of an ideology but the achievement of possible improvements. He had almost Burke's contempt for men who make political systems from the armchair of their study. To attack fanaticism and superstition, to fight for reforms which stand some chance of realization, this is how he conceived his task. If he did not refrain, on occasion, from theorizing, that was never the side of his work in which he took the greatest interest; it is even plain that it is in their preoccupation with general ideas that he found the main weakness of Montesquieu and Rousseau. Voltaire represents, at its best, the normal outlook of the good and humane bourgeois of his generation who recognizes the existence of profound wrong and is eager for improvement consistently with safety to his own well-being. But at the back of his mind there is always a fear of going too far in the direction of change, a dread that, once the floodgates are opened, nothing may be left standing as the tide sweeps through. He seeks accordingly, for terms of accommodation that will fit the immediate necessities. He shuts his mind to profounder issues he is too fearful to face.

He sees no case against republicanism or democracy, though he thinks men rarely worthy to govern themselves. He knows that the French system degrades the stature of man; "a citizen of Amsterdam", he wrote,[76] "is a man; a citizen a few miles distant therefrom is no more than a beast of burden". But he is profoundly monarchist so far as France is concerned, and he feared the tyranny of the lawyer more than he feared the tyranny of the King. "I would rather", he told St. Lambert,[77] "obey a fine lion which is born far stronger than I than two hundred rats of my own species." He wants, of course, civil liberty on the English model; he never confounds monarchy with despotism. A constitutional system like that of England, "royalist republican" as he termed it, would have satisfied his main political aspirations.[78]

But if Voltaire cares passionately for civil liberty under a constitutional system, he is also the great proprietor with a scrupulous regard to his rights as such. He hates religious fanaticism; but he is certain that religion is necessary for the people if the rich are not to be murdered in their beds. We need the conception of a God who rewards the good and punishes the evil for social purposes. "Je veux," he wrote in the *A.B.C.*,[79] "que mon procureur, mon tailleur, ma femme même croient en Dieu, et je m'imagine que j'en serai moins volé et moins cocu." The god of Voltaire is a social necessity for the maintenance of order; without him there would be no restraint upon the behaviour of men. "Quel autre frein", he wrote,[80] "pouvait-on mettre à la cupidité, aux transgressions secrètes et impunies, que l'idée d'un maître éternel qui nous voit et qui jugera jusqu'a nos plus secrèts pensées." It was for the same reason that he preached both freedom of the will and the immortality of the soul. As metaphysical principles he accepted neither; but, as he told Helvetius,[81] social considerations made it urgent that both should be defended as though they were in fact true.

In any essential sense, Voltaire has no use for equality. Equal property is a mere chimaera; it could only be attained by unjust spoliation.[82] "It is impossible", he wrote, "in our unhappy world for men living in society not to be divided into the two classes of rich and poor."[83] Without the poor, indeed, there could be no civilization; it is because men have to work that society can survive. We are not equally talented, and property, in general, is a return to talent. To pretend that men are equally members of society, that, as Jean Jacques said, a sovereign should be willing to marry his son to the executioner's daughter is simply the charlatanry of a savage.[84] Subordination is a social necessity; and the rich repay society by the opportunities they open to the poor. In any case, the relation of riches to happiness is greatly exaggerated, for a shepherd is often happier than a king.[85] We ought to give the poor the chance of growing rich; but more than this is unnecessary.

For the common people, indeed, he has profound contempt; they are the source of all fanaticism and superstition.[86] If sometimes he writes with enthusiasm about the possibilities of national education, for the most part he does not think it worth while. The "canaille"—the "swinish multitude" of Burke—is not "worthy" of enlightenment.[87] He congratulated La Chalotais in prohibiting educational studies to the working man.[88] "On my land", he wrote, "I want labourers and not tonsured clerics." He told Damilaville that the perpetuation of the uninstructed masses was essential and that anyone who owned property and needed servants would think the same;[89] and he wrote to d'Alembert that any effort spent on instructing the servant and the shoemaker was simply a waste of time.[90] So long as men like the philosophers were free to speculate, it did not matter if the tailor and the grocer remained under the domination of the church. He was, indeed, afraid of the social consequences of popular enlightenment; "when the people meddles with argument", he wrote,[91] "everything is lost". It is true that he wants, little by little, the power of reason to extend from important citizens to the poorer classes, and that, in a letter to Linguet, he seems to believe that the skilled artisan is capable of instruction. But the essence of Voltaire is a profound respect for the established order whose principles he is not willing to jeopardise by too drastic or too wide a scrutiny.

And this is the more apparent the more closely his programme of reform is examined. The changes he demanded were broadly those of the prosperous bourgeoisie. He wanted liberty; but he wanted, also, a liberty compatible with the fullest opportunities for men of property. Under the influence of Mandeville, he wrote an ardent defence of luxury.[92] He saw in the growth of commerce a social benefit indifferently to the distribution of its results. He objected to sumptuary legislation as a violation of the rights of property. His case against the church is largely founded on the incompatibility between its discipline and national prosperity. His interest in the poor does not extend far beyond a compassionate desire for the more obvious ameliorations of their lot. There is nothing in him of that passionate indignation against an unjust social order which is the clue to all Rousseau's thinking; he never, even, had those moments Diderot knew in which he was prepared to doubt whether a man of feeling could ever approve the irrationalism of social life. The world he wanted to build was, of course, an infinitely better world than the one he inherited. But the improvements would have been limited in their benefit very much to the propertied class. His liberalism, as an active and consistent principle, did not penetrate beyond their needs.

And this is true of the main body of thinkers associated with the movement he led. There is, no doubt, a profound radical in Diderot; but this is, with him, an inconstant and emotional outbreak rather than a considered intellectual principle. He attacked Helvetius' proposals for the diminution of inequality; they would, he said, injure property and destroy all industry. He had contempt for the common man. "L'homme peuple", he wrote,[93] "est le plus sot et le plus méchant de tous les hommes; se dépopulariser ou se rendre meilleur, c'est la même chose." He makes the rights of property almost as absolute as may well be imagined.

"Men in society who have property", he wrote,[94] "have a portion of the general wealth of which he is absolute master, over which he has the powers of a king to use or abuse at his discretion. A private citizen may cultivate his land or not as he pleases without the government having any right to interfere in the matter. For if the government deals with abuses of property, it will not be slow to deal with its uses as well. When that happens, there is an end to any true notion of property or liberty." His enthusiasm for Mercier de la Rivière is well known; and his general respect for the Physiocrats was undeviating. He differs, indeed, from Voltaire in his dislike of luxury and his refusal to believe that poverty and happiness were easily compatible. There are even bitter attacks on the injustice of the contemporary social order which almost reflect the spirit of Rousseau. But, in general, the economic outlook of Diderot was very much that of the Physiocrats. He felt sentimentally for the poor; but he had no criticism to make of the general contours of liberal economic doctrine.[95]

This conclusion must, I think, remain unaffected by the import of such essays as the *Entretien de l'aumonier et d'Orou* or the more famous *Supplément au voyage de Bougainville*[96] in which Diderot seems to outdistance Rousseau in his attack upon the foundations of civilized society. For even when they are read in conjunction with some of his more radical articles in the *Encyclopedia* they amount to little more than a pious hope that things will be better. Progressive taxation, a more equitable distribution of wealth, less luxury, a greater tenderness for the poor, a wider attention to education, it is difficult to see in Diderot's programme very much more than this. The sage in the Supplément does not ask for any fundamental change. "We shall attack bad laws", says Diderot,[97] "until they are reformed; meanwhile let us obey them. He who of his own private authority infringes a bad law authorizes everyone to infringe the good. There is less inconvenience in being mad with madmen than being alone in one's wisdom."

What, indeed, has been called the socialism of Diderot is, at bottom, nothing more than the feeling of doubt every sensitive and generous mind must have at the grim contrasts with which society presents us. It leads Diderot to make a gesture of moral protest against their result; it does not lead him to more. Much the same may fairly be said of Helvetius. Though his remark that work in moderation is no more difficult for the poor to support than is ennui for the rich suggests that the social problem was, for Helvetius,[98] an intellectual problem felt in a superficial way—the kindly compassion of a *grand seigneur*—he is uneasy about the conditions he confronts. He dislikes luxury and a too great inequality of economic condition; he argues that they lead to the ruin of states. But he has no remedy to suggest save an extension of proprietorship, and he has no method whereby to achieve this end save by hoping that wise legislation will secure it. He thinks it would be just to redistribute the ownership of the land; but such a scheme "is inconvenient because it violates the right to property which is the most sacred of all laws". Property, he writes, is "the moral god of empires". It makes possible the unity of a state. It is one of those laws without which society cannot be preserved. What, therefore, we should aim at is equality of happiness, and in a well-governed country this is fortunately attainable without any basic change in the nature of economic arrangements.

Helvetius is a liberal unprepared to confront the price of change; the Baron d'Holbach is, in essential political principle, conservative in outlook.[99] He may admit, like so many of his generation, that the system of government is wholly evil, so evil that it makes men criminals despite themselves. He agrees that luxury should be restrained. True wealth in a state, he says, consists in the comfort of the many, not the opulence of the few. It is more important that the people should have bread than that a monarch should have his gorgeously furnished palaces. There is always a tendency in every society for the rich to grasp at all they can. He wants more charity, and workshops in which the laborious poor may find the means to live. But he favours inequality. He thinks that division between rich and poor is inevitable. He is afraid of any measures that may attack or endanger the sacred principle of private property. At bottom, it is not unfair to say that while the spectacle of social misery causes him discomfort, he has no more than a moral gesture to make about its consequences. Like most thinkers of his time, he has been profoundly affected by Rousseau's assault upon the adequacy of social foundations. But his response to Rousseau's challenge occupies a very limited place in his work, and it is enough for him to signalize the existence of the evil without attempting any profound or systematic search for the remedies.

And this attitude, it may be said, is broadly character-istic of the time. It is no doubt true that there is immense preoccupation with social problems; on the problem of the poor alone there exists a vast literature full of deep feeling and no little inventive ingenuity. But any analysis of this literature reveals no desire to grapple with the central issue of private property. There are eulogies and to spare of the spirit of equality and of the duty of the rich to be generous to the poor; it is notable, for instance, that the Archbishop of Paris had to rebuke some of his clergy for excessive radicalism in this regard. There is even a number of plans, some worked out in great detail, for the construction of national workshops in which the unemployed poor could find a living; but these are always, even with the most radical, built upon the principle that the wages paid in them must never be at such a level as to interfere with the demands of private enterprise. The poor, in a word, are to pay the price of their poverty. The liberal thinkers of the time are anxious to mitigate their poverty; but that is the limit of their effort. Even where, as with Mably, they defend a communist framework of social organization, this is always in the background of a virtual admission that they are outlining an impossible dream. Even, again, when Linguet depicts with relentless clarity the roots of the *malaise* from which civilization is suffering and predicts that, from the misery of the poor, a new Spartacus will arise, he has no remedies to suggest. He praises the despotism of the Orient because, secur-ing as it does a blind obedience from the people, it preserves the safety of the state. He told Voltaire that in his view a knowledge of arts and letters is dangerous for the working class. "The condition of society", he wrote to the latter,[100] "condemns him to the use of his physical strength alone. Everything would be lost once he knew that he had a mind." Linguet, in a word, foresaw that social injustice implied inevitable catastrophe; but he did not know how to prevent it, and he was convinced that no good could come of the destruction of the old order. He tears aside the veil which conceals its monstrosities more vigorously and more relentlessly than any Frenchman save Meslier before the Revolution. But when his analysis is done, he can do no more than throw up his hands.[101]

The French critics of the *ancien régime*, in short, sought to accomplish two things. France needed a constitution which would redress the balance between an outworn political system, and a new distribution of economic power; they sought, with unsurpassed energy, to trace the outlines of what that system should be. They sought, also, in building the new system to release its cultural foundations from the prison in which organized religion still sought to confine them. They were hostile to the church and the aristocracy; they were critical of those who lived on society without labouring on its behalf; they were sympathetic, often generous, to the sufferings of the poor. But they were not seriously prepared to confront the problem of the poor except in terms of charity. They were unable to discern behind the Third Estate a Fourth with claims as wide as, and interests different from, those of the bourgeoisie. They assumed that their own emancipation implied also advantages to the workers, and they were content with that. They saw no way in which the problem of poverty could be solved and, charity apart, they averted their eyes from it. Voltaire summarized their effective attitude with his usual precision. "It is inevitable", he wrote in the *Philosophic Dictionary*,[102] "that mankind should be divided into two classes with many sub-divisions—the oppressors and the oppressed. Fortunately, use and wont and the lack of leisure prevent most of the oppressed from realizing their condition. When they do feel it, civil war follows which can end only in the enslavement of the people, since the sovereign power in the state is money." Another passage in the *Siècle de Louis XIV* emphasizes the same attitude. "The labourer and the artisan", Voltaire wrote,[103] "must be cut down to necessaries, if they are to work: this is human nature. It is inevitable that the majority should be poor; it is only not necessary that it should be wretched."

An eminent critic has remarked that no one can read Voltaire's discussion of the economic problem without the sense that he is uncomfortable at his own conclusions. That explains both his evasions and his cynicism, the absence from his analysis of that noble indignation he displays whenever it is intolerance he has to attack. The remark is a just one ; though it should be added that its application is not limited to Voltaire. All French liberalism of the eighteenth century is permeated by a similar temper. Its exponents were demanding in effect the emancipation of the whole nation; but when they applied themselves to the details of their programme their imagination limited its range to the freedoms sought by men of property. Farther than this they were not prepared to go. Their justification is a complicated one. In part, as they would have explained, if they avoided the issue of justice, they confronted the obligation to be generous; provision for the poor by the state plays a large part in all their discussions. In part, again, they were overwhelmingly individualist in temper. The state they knew was arbitrary, corrupt, incompetent. They sought to free themselves from its control, to trace out limits to its activities, not to fall again under its domination in a new form. In part, also, they feared and distrusted the working class. They feared its ignorance and its savagery; they distrusted its ability to make a contribution of value to the state. They themselves, from nothing, had become everything; it seemed to them that their obligation to society was above all the translation of their moral claims into legal rights. They set out their case in universal terms, because they needed, like the English reformers of 1832, the support of the working class if they were to triumph. But they no more conceived that their victory could mean the emancipation of that class than did the English reformers half a century later. Their view was intelligible enough when we bear in mind that not until the middle of the nineteenth century were the workers organically conscious of their claims. A class enters into history only when it is a plaintiff in its court. In the eighteenth century, the bourgeoisie alone was in this position; and the thinkers were rare who could see that the conquest of its revolutionary demands would be a stage only, and not the term, of human development. French liberalism, with great power and insight, formulated the demands of the new claimant to human rights without seeing that when they had been satisfied, they would merely set the conditions of a new conflict. But it is the way of history to blind men's vision to the destiny of man's effort. Perhaps he travels a longer distance because he has no foreknowledge of the end of his journey.

V

Nothing bears out more conclusively the argument here put forward than the Revolution itself. Whether we take the composition of the National Assembly, the character of the *Cahiers de Doléances*, the legislation which marks the course of the Revolution until the advent of Napoleon, the great mass of pamphlets and journals which poured forth unendingly in its course, we are watching throughout the affirmation of its own essence by the middle class; in that affirmation the wants of the workers find no effective place. The chevalier de Moret, who wrote in 1789, has a phrase which accurately describes the position. "We are wrong", he said,[104] "in thinking of the Third Estate as a single class; it is composed of two classes whose interests are different, and even opposed."

The working classes, practically speaking, were excluded from the electoral assemblies which chose the deputies; these were confined to the taxpayers. There is no evidence of working-class meetings, or the exploration of working-class needs. The men elected, as in Paris, for example, were mainly small professional men, lawyers and doctors. If the industrialists complained, in the name of the working class, at their under-representation, their attitude assumes, as Jaurès has pointed out,[105] an identity of interest between employer and worker. We find nothing in the cahiers which look to the latter's special concern; and all their proposals about the poor remain on that plane of philanthropy which is concerned, above all, for measures of relief which will not injure the sacred rights of property. The attitude to working-class organizations, later summarized in the loi le Chapelier, is essentially a continuance of the hostility to them characteristic of the parliaments of the old régime. It is symptomatic of their temper that in Languedoc, for example, the employers demand that any workers who want work shall be compelled to address themselves to employers' organization. And no one can read in the cahiers the insistent defence of bourgeois property-right, as against feudal and aristocratic privilege, without seeing the limited experience and need that they embody. They fear bankruptcy, since this would injure many middle-class people with a stake in the funds. They want a constitution which shall end arbitrary rule and privilege, especially in fiscal matters. They desire that the nation shall, through its own representatives, control the system of taxation. They ask for civil and political liberty, as the philosophers had taught them to understand these things. But the end in view is the liberation of agriculture and commerce from hampering restrictions which limit the rights of ownership. Whenever questions relating to the protection of labour appear it is invariably from the angle of the problem of public assistance; it is never from a view which assumes a labouring class with rights in the state as a class. It is assumed throughout that the well-being of employer and farmer includes that of those who are dependent upon them.[106]

The reason, of course, is clear. The workers had as yet no sense of an identity of interest; so far as they appear in the preliminary literature of the Revolution it is as isolated groups, posing their special problems, and with no sense of common issues that they confront. They were content, until the old régime had been broken, to see the triumph of ideals which could have meaning for them in an indirect way only. It was not until war and counter-revolution exacerbated their misery that they developed a consciousness of separate aims which the victorious revolution would not promote. There then arose, in the *Enragés* and the Babouvistes, men who realized, like the Levellers and the Agrarian Communists under Cromwell, that the victory that had been won, however important, was not their victory, that the legislation which had been enacted had not touched the problems with which they were concerned. They had the same sense as their English precursors that they had won a campaign, the fruits of which other men had garnered; but it was then either too late, or, perhaps, too early.

There are many criteria by which to test the truth of this hypothesis. The simplest, I think, are to analyse the attitudes of the Civil Code, as the legislative deposit of revolutionary experience, and the attitude of Barnave to the Revolution in which he played so eminent a part. For the first, like so much of the Revolutionary reconstruction, is the ultimate deposit of a slow effort fragments of which go back to the search, by men like Guy Coquille, Loisel and Pothier, for a body of common principles amid the luxuriant diversity of ancient legal tradition. Lamoignon under Louis XIV, d'Aguesseau under his successor, all added to the labour of unification; and as early as August 1790, the Constituent Assembly voted for the construction of "a general code, with simple laws which shall be both clear and appropriate to the Constitution".[107] The effort to realize this purpose in a final way lasted some eleven years; and it is no doubt true that only an energetic administrator of Napoleon's genius could have insisted on giving so massive a project instant actuality. The code, which its makers thought of as nothing less than "universal morality",[108] which Napoleon himself said at St. Helena "nothing can efface",[109] lays down with a clarity that is almost startling the effective principles of that French liberalism which triumphed in 1789. By analysing some of its major aspects we gain an unmistakable insight into its nature and limitations.

It has been the argument of these lectures that the liberty of liberalism is set in the context of property; and it is this juxtaposition that above all marks the Civil Code. It registers the victory of merchant and peasant proprietor against feudal privilege; it embodies, in a word, the principles of the Revolution. Its temper was that of the men who, in 1793, made the proponents of an agrarian law liable to the death penalty, of that Commune of Paris which, in 1791, warned the working class to do nothing which might "alarm citizens and persuade the rich to emigrate from the city".[110] Just as each of the revolutionary constitutions declared the right of property to be "inviolable and sacred",[111] so the Code may be regarded as giving to this principle its full procedural guarantees. It transformed the vague, if urgent, declamation of fifty years into an organic

227

system of safeguards which still, in its essential outlines, resists the onslaught of time.

Its authors were aware of what they were doing. "Its grand and principal object", said Louvet,[112] "is to regulate the principles and the rights of property." "Respect for property", said Jaubert in the Napoleonic legislature,[113] "is displayed on every page of the Code." "Its most precious maxim", wrote the judge, Lahary,[114] "is that which consecrates the right of property; everything else is but the logical consequence of this fact." Within the law, it gives an absolute right to the enjoyment and disposal of property. There is no obligation to dispose of it in a useful way. An owner is even safeguarded against having to recompense his tenant for improvements. In dealing with minors, and with marriage, the main preoccupation is the protection of property. In dealing with contract little is regulated which involves the use of property as capital, and a contract of service barely receives protection at all. If usury in loans is prohibited, nothing is said of that usury which extracts excessive rents, or pays impossible wages. In forming the jury, membership is limited to persons with property. In more technical procedure, its substance is explained at length by Faure as "in a word the guarantee of property".

The regulation of labour conditions occupies a very modest place. Contracts of service for life are prohibited. Where disputes arise between master and man, the master's word, given on oath, "suffices for the amount of wages, their payment during the past year, and all accounting due during the current year".[115]

Domestic servants may bring action against their employers within a twelvemonth of its origin; but workers in industry are limited to a six-months' period. Where a lessee brings an action on a verbal lease for real property, the lessor is believed in any statement he makes upon oath, unless the lessee demand—what no poor person could afford—investigation by an expert. All strikes and trade unions are forbidden, the promoters of the former being liable to imprisonment for from two to five years; on the other hand, employers are permitted their chambers of commerce, and common action by employers to lock-out their men is punishable by six days' imprisonment or a fine which may range from two hundred to three thousand francs. It should be added that certain rights were accorded to building workers in rights of action for work done; though the procedural difficulties which surrounded the right made it, in fact, inoperative. The motive of this protection is shown in the remark of another clause of the Code that such a benefit legitimately comes to "those who augment the patrimony of the entrepreneur".[116]

"To tell the truth", wrote the French historian Glasson,[117] "the worker was pretty completely forgotten in the Code." That is, in fact, to do it a grave injustice. The worker was not forgotten; both in substance and in procedure his rights were deliberately subordinated to those of his master. He is forbidden to organize; he cannot strike; but no such prohibition upon the employer (as in the British Combination Acts of 1749-1800) is effectively organized. In all the material conditions of his work, his employer's word has a greater evidential value than his. His rights of action are more limited;

229

and where he is a tenant, all the weight of favour rests with his landlord. We are watching, in fact, the construction of a bourgeois code for a bourgeois society. It must be said that no attempt was made to conceal this fact. Boulay de la Meurthe said frankly that so long as the law was known to those who had the chief interest in maintaining it, they would see that the masses became aware of it in the measure of their need; "it suffices", he said,[118] "for this section (of the population) to have the time and the proper means to be assured that laws exist and are promulgated." For the authors of the Code, in a word, the remarkable speech of Boissy d'Anglas, when, as reporter, he introduced the Constitution of the Year III to the Convention, explains the whole matter. "We ought", he told its members,[119] "to be governed by the best men; and these are they who are most instructed, and most interested in the maintenance of the law. Now, with very few exceptions, such men will only be found among the owners of property who, thereby, are attached to their country, to the laws which protect their property, and the social peace which preserves it. . . . A country governed by property-owners is a true civil society (est dans l'ordre civil); one where men without property govern is in a state of nature." Certainly that was akin to the condition to which the authors of the Civil Code reduced the mass of the working-class. But it is important to note that, in doing so, they did not doubt they were fulfilling the revolutionary ideal.

The same conceptions as those of the Civil Code are to be found in the unduly neglected *Introduction à la Revolution Française* published posthumously from the manuscripts of Barnave in 1845. He had been one of the leaders of the liberals in the National Assembly;[120] and the ideals for which he fought may be fairly identified with those which, in a broad way, became the settled principles of the social constitution of France after the defeat of the Jacobins. More than this: the careful student of Barnave's speeches will find in their substance affiliations of ideas with what became, with Royer-Collard and Benjamin Constant, the essence of French liberalism after the Restoration. The *Introduction* is the more important since much of it was written without a view to public influence; we are watching, as it were, Barnave's own explanation to himself of the events in which he had played an eminent part. Since he was not eligible, as a member of the National, for election to the Constituent Assembly, he used his enforced leisure in Dauphiné to penetrate the meaning of those first three passionate years. We catch him thinking aloud, and, as the document itself shows, so to say in undress uniform; for what Berenger published are clearly rather the notes for a book than the considered and polished sentences which alone Barnave would have passed for publication.

He distinguishes between the occasions and the profound historical causes of great events; it is with the latter only that, in the context of the Revolution, he proposes to concern himself. These, he has no doubt, are rooted in the immense economic changes which preceded the Revolution. Like a good eighteenth century *philosophe*, he traces the evolution of property from a primitive communism to a landed system in which superior knowledge has given to aristocracy an immense superiority of economic wealth.[121] With this individual ownership, there goes a new distribution, which grows greater as population grows, of economic power, and this is reflected in the character of institutions. "It is", he writes,[122] "a fixed principle that where all income is derived from the land, the great properties will, little by little, engulf the small." In such conditions the small proprietor will become dependent on, and ultimately absorbed by, the rich; he cannot maintain his independence in the face of his needs. "Power", he writes,[123] "remains where riches are, and the reign of an aristocracy lasts so long as an agricultural people continues either to be ignorant of, or to neglect the arts, and the ownership of land continues the sole source of wealth."

But a change comes, however retarded by institutions suited to the needs of a landed aristocracy, when industry begins to develop. "As soon", argues Barnave,[124] "as the arts and commerce succeed in penetrating the life of the society, and of opening up a new source of wealth for the labouring class, a revolution is prepared in political laws; a new distribution of wealth produces a new distribution of power. Just as the possession of land created aristocracy, so industrial property gives rise to the power of the people. It acquires liberty; it grows in numbers, it begins to influence affairs." In the small state, Barnave remarks,[125] this new wealth creates a "new aristocracy, a kind of bourgeois and merchant aristocracy", whose wealth makes it "the master of the government". In the great state, "all its parts are linked together by reciprocal communication. There is formed a large class of citizens who, owning the great wealth of industry, have the most powerful interest in maintaining internal order and, through taxation, give to the state (*puissance publique*) the force necessary to impose the laws. A great volume of taxation, moving ceaselessly from centre to circumference and back again, a disciplined army, a great capital, a mass of government departments, become so many links giving a great nation the unity and intimate cohesion which assure its life".

The relation of this view to the Revolution is clear. Barnave is arguing, like Harrington, a century and a half before him, that a new distribution of economic involves a new distribution of political power. The coming of a commercial economy meant the unified and centralized state in which a bourgeois democracy takes the place of an agrarian aristocracy. "In the governments of Europe", he writes,[126] "the basis of an aristocracy is the ownership of land, the basis of monarchy is public power, the basis of democracy is movable capital." More than this. "In the degree", he says,[127] "that industry and commerce enrich the working class, and, impoverishing the great landed proprietors, tend to make classes equal in wealth, the progress of education makes them equal also in knowledge and revives, after a long forgetfulness, primitive ideas of equality." The great Revolution, he suggests, has passed through three great phases in its influence on European institutions. In the first the communes, growing rich by labour, bought first their liberty, and then their lands, so that the aristocracy, losing successively its empire and its wealth, found the feudal régime, as a form of civil state, deprived of validity. It was this cause, secondly,

233

strengthened by the growing significance of industry, which freed all Europe from the temporal power of the Pope, and wrested from him the half of his spiritual supremacy.[128]

The third phase is the most significant of all; and it is well that I should describe it in Barnave's own remarkable words. "The same cause," he writes,[129] "that is, the progress of movable property is the cause, in Europe, of democracy, and the cement which binds together the unity of states; it has modified successively all the governments of Europe. As geographical position has been more or less favourable to it, so the systems of government it has established have been various. In one place, where the people have been very strong in a small state, it has established a republic; in another, where the territory is extensive, it has had strength only to maintain, by the power of taxation, the monarchical power against that aristocracy which is the common enemy of kings and peoples; it has established, that is, absolute monarchies. Where it has been able to go farther, after having been, for a long period, the support of the throne against the great nobles, it has become revolutionary (a fait explosion) and, taking its place in the system of government, has established limited monarchy. Only where its evolution has been feeble have the aristocratic and federal forms of feudal government been able to survive. . . . It is this evolution, common to all European governments, which has prepared in France a democratic revolution, and caused it to break out at the end of the eighteenth century."

I do not need to emphasize the superb insight of this analysis. Sixty years before Marx, Barnave has seen the whole character of the French Revolution. He has traced its ideology to its economic foundations. He has seen this in its full perspective, not as some parochial fact, but in its proper place as part of a vaster European movement. He has realized that a change in the character of property-relations requires a change in the character of political institutions and that a revolution is essential to effect the necessary adaptation. The French Revolution, for him, is not a local phenomenon, but the expression of a universal and secular tendency. Property-relations, he says in effect, are sovereign, and they are bound, in the long run, to capture their political empire.

For Barnave, therefore, clearly, the Revolution may be described as the apogee of the historic process. An economic power born of the travail of men at long last asserts its title to political dominance. It establishes democracy by dissolving at once the power of kings and that feudal system which enslaved peasant and merchant alike to the authority of the landed proprietor. The new democracy, for him, is the reign of liberty and equality; he assumes that with its triumph, there is no horizon beyond for him to scan. For industrial capital, born of human effort, is opposed to landed property, the fruit of violence. It is vital to his outlook that he does not in any degree realize either that industrial capital may be born of privilege, or that it may give birth, in its turn, to a system of privilege not less deadly than that which it replaced. In the whole of his analysis, as Jaurès has well pointed out, there is no discussion of the wage-earner, not a word to suggest that he realizes his existence. With all his remarkable insight, Barnave cannot conceive a revolution which goes beyond that in which he participated with such distinction. For him there is no proletariat. The Revolution ends with the triumph of the owner of industrial capital. He sees the class of industrial proprietors conscious of their strength. He realizes that they will not be satisfied until their strength is expressed in the conquest of the state-power. That, beyond them, there was a new class, preparing also to enter into history, he does not suspect. That it will come to feel an antagonism to the owners of industrial capital as profound as the latter came to feel to the owners of landed property is beyond his imagination. That this new class will, in similar fashion to the old, become revolutionary also, does not enter into his calculations. His liberalism, so to say, is limited by the horizon of that bourgeoisie of Dauphiné to which he belonged. It is their wants and their claims that he translates into a political system; when he has done that, his work is complete. But the new class, in similar fashion, and as it becomes conscious of its destiny, will require on its behalf a new exponent to trace the outline of a new philosophy. It remained for Babeuf and St. Simon to plant the seeds from which Marx and Engels gathered so rich a harvest.

# Conclusion: The Aftermath

THE nineteenth century is the epoch of liberal triumph; from Waterloo until the outbreak of the Great War no other doctrine spoke with the same authority or exercised the same widespread influence. Its triumph, no doubt, was a complex phenomenon; complex if only because, as in its rise, many of those who rendered it the most profound service conceived themselves to be worshipping at a different altar. Its conquests are so vast that the world it created in those hundred years would have seemed well-nigh unthinkable even to men who, like Adam Smith, were the principal doctrinal architects of its advent. It was the prophet of industrialism; and it transformed Great Britain into the workshop of the world. It was the exponent of free trade; and it created a world-market which has broken down the isolation even of the most distant peoples. It was the advocate of religious toleration; and it both broke the temporal power of Rome and ended the right of religion to define the boundaries of citizenship. It insisted that statehood should be in general coterminous with the boundaries of states; and, under its ægis, Italy and Greece, Hungary and Bulgaria, realized a new consciousness of self. It established universal suffrage and parliamentarianism almost as principles of natural law; and those who, in Western Europe opposed their advent, were always on the defensive. There is a sense, indeed, in which American civilization of the last hundred years may not illegitimately be regarded as the fulfilment of the liberal ideal. America, and the awakening of the ancient East are nothing so much as a tribute to its world-wide empire.

Nor, indeed, that either as fact or as doctrine the victory of liberalism was an easy one. After the first enthusiasm for the French Revolution had faded, it fought, for nearly half a century, an unending battle on two fronts. On the one hand, it confronted a renovated conservatism which, in the hands of men like de Maistre and Hegel, sought to set limits to individualism in the name of an authority which, whether as church or state, should prevent the drift to social anarchy which they believed to be inherent in the liberal idea.[1] On the other, from St. Simon onwards, that release of the individual which expressed itself as the *laissez-faire* state was attacked on the ground that a liberty which was confined, in grim reality, to the owners of property, was not liberty at all unless it was set in the context of an equality attained by the deliberate and purposive intervention of the state. This view had advocates as varied as any in the history of political philosophy. There was the school of which the most moving representative, perhaps, was Lamennais, which sought to limit the power of the individual by subduing it to a framework of Christian principle directly related to medieval ideas.[2] There was a school, brilliantly represented by Sismondi and Buret,[3] which was so horrified by the social results of *laissez-faire* as to envisage a state bound to the service of the disinherited. Comte and his disciples rejected the liberal idea in the name of a science which, in their view, made it incumbent upon the state

238

to undertake the regulation of social life in the interest of an organic community superior in its claims to any part of its membership.[4] In England, Coleridge and Carlyle, Southey and Disraeli, developed with remarkable insight the idea of a state which passed beyond the relation of a cash-nexus to the conscious mitigation of the results of inequality.[5]

But the essential attack on the liberal idea in the nineteenth century was that of socialism. It is not a movement the summary of which is simple. There go to its making ideas derived from the most disparate sources. But it is not, I think, an inaccurate emphasis to say that the essence of its attack derived from the realization that the liberal ideal secured to the middle-class its full share of privilege, while it left the proletariat in their chains. The effort of socialism was towards the correction of this inadequacy. In its vital formulation by Marx and Engels, it was an insistence that the bourgeois revolution merely transferred effective political power from the owners of land to the owners of industrial property. The state, in their view, was not a neutral organ seeking as best it could the well-being of the whole community, but a coercive power enforcing upon the working class that social discipline required by the owners of property in their search for profit. They denied that a just society was attainable in these terms. They argued that precisely as the middle class had overthrown the feudal aristocracy, so the working class would be compelled to overthrow its masters in order to obtain possession of the state for its own benefit. For them, the effective revolution lay not in the past but in the future. The *laissez-faire* state, of which Marx drew an imperishable picture in the first volume of *Capital*, was for them simply the organized subjection of the masses to claims on profit made legal by that coercive power which always relates itself directly to the possession of economic power. Only as economic power was transferred, through the revolutionary action of the working class, to society as a whole could men, in any full sense, enter upon their heritage.

The socialists rejected the liberal idea because they saw in it simply one more particular of history seeking to masquerade as a universal. They argued that it was not, in fact, a final doctrine, but a fitful and temporary phase in man's endless struggle with his environment. For the first half of the century it looked, at least superficially, as though they were right. Until 1849, Europe was never free from the shadow of conspiracy and revolution; and the *annus mirabilis* of 1848 made it evident that, behind formal political claims, a social ideology was always struggling for expression. After 1848, for something like half a century again, the liberal idea seemed to have entered amply into its kingdom. The immense wealth it produced made possible concessions to the masses which, if they did not arrest the progress of socialism, at least blunted the edge of its revolutionary fervour in most states in which political democracy had obtained an effective foothold. Liberalism did not abandon its belief in the validity of the private ownership of the means of production; its conquests were too spectacular, not least in the United States, for that to be practicable. But it was at least taught by the pressure of trade unions, on the one hand, and by thinkers like

Green and Matthew Arnold,[6] in England, by Tocqueville in France,[7] by the socialists of the chair in Germany, that it must adopt a positive conception of the state. The conception of progressive taxation in the interest of the masses then became an essential part of the liberal idea. The revolutionary challenge was to be evaded by the gospel, as Mr. Chamberlain termed it, of "ransom", a gospel which, in essence, was the notion that wealth must justify its possessors by paying for reasonable amenities for the poor. Hence the emergence after, roughly, the 'seventies of the last century of the social service state. Its fundamental principle was twofold. While it affirmed that, as a general rule, the private ownership of the means of production was to be maintained, it was prepared to regulate the consequences of that ownership in the interest of those who could not afford, out of their wages, to purchase those amenities which had come to be regarded as part of a reasonable standard of life.

Until, at least, the war of 1914 this phase of the liberal idea dominated the mind of all Europe save those who were infected by the Marxian philosophy. How dominating it was can be seen, above all, by the failure of Marxism in this period to obtain any serious hold of the English mind. The typical English socialism was Fabian, a body of doctrine upon which the emphasis of John Stuart Mill's ideas was far more profound than that of Marx. Fabianism assumed that revolution as a method of social change was outworn, and it did so for two reasons. Born in the serene self-confidence of Victorian England, it was profoundly rationalist in temper; and it therefore believed that the straightforward capture

241

of Parliament by the conversion of an electoral majority to socialism would enable the machinery of constitutional democracy to be used for the peaceful transformation of a capitalist, into a socialist, state.[8] Accepting, in the second place, the fundamental economic postulates of liberal capitalism, it saw no reason to anticipate that collapse of the post-war years which would not only set definite limits to taxable capacity under a system based upon the predominant motive of profit-making, but would also, once the making of profits was in jeopardy, persuade, as in Italy and Germany, the owners of economic power to overthrow the democratic foundations of society in the interest of their right to make profit. Neither Fabians nor advanced liberals had seen that the success of parliamentary government was dependent upon two conditions. It required, first, the sense of security that came from the ability to go on making profit, that enabled it, from its surplus wealth, to continue the distribution of amenities of the masses. It required, in the second place, an agreement among parties in politics to all matters of fundamental social constitution in order that each might succeed the other as the government of the day without a sense of outrage. Without the ability to operate these conditions, parliamentary government was powerless to settle differences in terms of reason. The political forms of liberalism, in a word, were dependent upon a conjuncture of economic circumstances the permanence of which could alone guarantee their effective functioning.[9]

That had been seen by St. Simon at the beginning of the nineteenth century. "The law", he wrote,[10] "which

242

constitutes the powers and the form of government is less important and has less influence on the happiness of nations than that which constitutes property and decides its use." He thought parliamentary government preferable to all others; but, at bottom, it was still only a form, and the "law which constitutes property is the thing which gives it its true character".[11] That was the seminal truth that liberalism was never able to see. It did not realize that the political democracy it brought into being was established on the unstated assumption that it would leave untouched the private ownership of the means of production. It might plead for terms with the owners; and in a period when the results of the profit-making system were satisfactory, it might secure concessions which perhaps surprised those who made them even more than those for whose benefit they were made. But political democracy, and the liberal ideology which expressed its inner purposes, could no more pass beyond the framework within which it was confined than feudal society could pass beyond its own constitutive principle. A fundamental change in class-relations requires now, as it required at the end of the fifteenth century, a revolution in the idea of property, of, therefore, the state that is its guardian, if it is to be effective in altering the character of the forces of production.

## II

This it is which explains the declining authority of liberal doctrine in our epoch. It was so preoccupied with the political forms it had created that it failed adequately to take account of their dependence upon the economic foundation they expressed. They taught the citizens of the democracy they established that they were the sovereign people; and they insisted that the state must serve their wishes as sovereign. They did not tell the people that their sovereignty was in fact conditioned by the obligation to accept the bourgeois revolution as, broadly, a final term in the evolution of the idea of property and its relations. The people had been schooled by their nineteenth-century experience to see in the state an organ from which, under sufficient pressure, they might expect a continuous flow of material benefit. And as science made possible an ever greater productivity, its magic seemed to them to confer upon them a title to an ever greater benefit. They accepted the idea of increasing material well-being as a law of nature from whose operations they might exact their full share. With growing emphasis, they used the political power that universal suffrage conferred upon them to secure this share.

What had been forgotten as this evolution took place was the flaw in the economic system. The class-relations it established made it impossible for the power to distribute to keep pace with the power to produce; the forces of production were in contradiction with the relations of production. To make profit, the whole motive-power of the economic system, the owners of the instruments of production were driven into an ever intensifying struggle for markets. Out of that struggle there emerged the search for colonies, the clash of competing imperialisms, the economic nationalism which made the political configuration of the world deny the plainest implications of its economic configuration. In the period of capitalism's expansion, the economic system had been, with all its deficiencies, largely self-regulating. There had been crises; there had been unemployment; there had been wars largely motivated by the greed to acquire new wealth. But in the period of capitalism's contraction, discernible to an acute observer as long ago as the 'eighties of the last century, though, in its catastrophic proportions, obvious only since the war, the capacity of self-regulation, and, therefore, of recovery, increasingly disappeared.

With its disappearance there went, also, the power to confer increasing material benefit upon the masses. A halt had to be called to social legislation, to the advance, also, of the workers' standard of life, because, on the assumptions of capitalism, these interfered with that access to profit which was the rationale of the whole economic adventure. The owners of property in the liberal state were no more prepared to forgo the privileges of ownership than were their predecessors in feudal society. They might seek to persuade the working classes to sacrifices which, as they insisted, were temporary in character; this, plainly, as Tocqueville had seen nearly a century ago,[12] was an argument of passing validity only. It was inherent in the liberal idea that men should use their political power for the improvement of their material position. Capitalism, increasingly, found itself in the dilemma that if it pursued the liberal experiment, it would co-operate in its own destruction; while, on the other hand, if it destroyed liberalism, it still set sail upon an uncharted sea the voyage upon which could be justified only by an economic success which was doubtful. In that dilemma, all its self-confidence and security disappeared. Confronted by the challenge of socialism, dramatically reinforced by the advent of Soviet Russia, it fell into that mood of panic by which it was obsessed during the French Revolution. Rightly enough, it realized that the new mental climate had thrown all its traditional values into the melting pot. Rightly enough, also, it began to understand that the challenge it confronted went to the foundations of its claims. It did what every economic system does when challenged at its foundations. It armed itself for the defence of what, naturally enough, it regarded as its rights.

For, in a legal sense, they were indeed its rights; increasingly, for over four centuries, it had used the supreme coercive power of the state to write them into every nook and cranny of the society it controlled. The law, education, religion, the family, all of these bore upon their face the mark of its influence. Not only its beneficiaries had done what has been the habit of men throughout history; they confounded the institutions to which they had grown accustomed with the necessary foundations of society. They assumed, with full sincerity, that an assault upon the privileges by which they lived was, in fact, to attack the basis of civilization. They no more doubted the moral rightness of their attitude than those who fought the French Revolution, or the Russian bourgeoisie when it sought to hurl Lenin from power. They became an armed idea, defending a traditional conception of society; and when ideas fly to arms there is no room in society for liberal doctrine.

To understand our own epoch, in short, we must

think ourselves back either to the epoch of the Reformation or to the period of the French Revolution. When a system is fighting for its life, it has no time for the habits of a debating society. The passion of conflict makes reason its slave. Those dominate the political scene who are prepared to use the means which will accomplish the end. In such a period there is rarely the prospect of either tolerance or rationalism. The men who assume control are, above all, determined that their purposes shall conquer; and they are not prepared to brook either criticism of, or opposition to, those purposes. Clearly, in this atmosphere, the liberal theory of constitutional government can have no meaning; for its inherent idea is the right of the citizen to call into question the ultimate principles of the system under which he lives. That is impossible under the dictatorships which have rejected the liberal philosophy for the simple reason that, were it permitted, the dictatorships would be unlikely to survive. No régime, so far in history, has deliberately connived at its own overthrow; and even liberal régimes have only permitted discussion in the periods when they did not feel themselves to be in jeopardy.

The proof of all this is not far to seek. In part, it is most plainly shown in the meaning of European Fascism; but, in part also, its meaning is being not less clearly displayed by the attitude of the Supreme Court of the United States to the Roosevelt experiment. Fascism, in its essentials, is the destruction of liberal ideas and institutions in the interest of those who own the instruments of economic power. The causes of its rise are, no doubt, complicated; but the purpose of its operation is unmistakable. What it has done, wherever it has gained power is, above all, to destroy the characteristic defences of the working class—their political parties, their trade unions, their co-operative societies. Parallel with this has been the suppression of all political parties save the Fascist party, of free discussion, and of the right to strike. Before their advent to power, Fascists, often enough, have proclaimed objectives with a socialistic flavour. But it is notable, first, that they have always attained power in concert with the army and big business, and that, after its attainment, they have left effectively unchanged the ownership of the means of production. Fascism, in short, emerges as the institutional technique of capitalism in its phase of contraction. It destroys the liberalism permitted by the experience of expansion in order to impose upon the masses that social discipline which creates the conditions under which, as it is hoped, the making of profit may be resumed. It is this which explains why, in Fascist countries, working-class standards have continuously declined since the suppression of liberal ideas and institutions.[13]

The American position, if more subtly complicated, points in a similar direction. Mr. Roosevelt took office in 1933 amid circumstances of crisis such as the United States had hardly known since its foundation. He was driven to large experiments in federal regulation by the very nature of the situation he inherited. The measures he proposed passed through both Houses of Congress by triumphant majorities; and among them, those, at least, which sought to aid the farmer were widely popular in the country as a whole. His two main measures, the National Industrial Recovery Act, and the Agricultural Processing Tax, have, nevertheless, been declared unconstitutional by the Supreme Court on grounds which are wide enough, in their nature, to make it doubtful whether the Federal Government is, on the present interpretation of the Constitution, charged with authority wide enough to permit it to undertake the functions with which the modern industrial state is driven by its very nature to charge itself.[14]

Superficially, no doubt, the decisions of the Supreme Court are purely legal interpretations of whether certain Acts of Congress fall, or do not fall, within the ambit of the Constitution. It is decided, as in *U.S.* v. *Schecter*,[15] that what is in effect legislative power cannot be delegated to a President who is to be conceived as vested with an executive function without violating that dogma of the separation of powers upon which the constitution is based; or, as in the agricultural processing tax, it is held that, under the constitution, the welfare of a farming population of nearly fifty million persons is a matter only of state concern with which, whatever the emergency, the Federal Government may not interfere. And these decisions must be read in the context of earlier judgments prohibiting legislation which sought, for example, to compel railways to pay pensions to their employees,[16] or to prevent the employment of child labour.[17] But the basis upon which all such decisions rest are really much more matters of social philosophy than of pure law. They depend upon the meaning which the Court, or its majority, attaches to words like "reasonable", or phrases like "liberty of contract" or "due process of law".[18] They are, in effect, the substitution of the Court's view of what these words or phrases shall mean for the view that, after the usual discussion, the legislature either of a state or of the Federal Commonwealth has chosen to give them.[19]

In essence, that is to say, and subject of course, to the power of federal amendment, the true source of legislative authority in the United States is in a majority of the Supreme Court. It will not, as it has explained,[20] suffer what it takes to be the sovereign purposes of the Constitution to be controlled by an emergency; and this, therefore, means that the elected government of the United States can enact only those measures which the Court is prepared to approve. Since what it approves is, at base, essentially a conception of the limits within which government may interfere with the rights of individual property, in effect the result of the Court's attitude is to subject the opinion of Congress to a theory of the state upon which Mr. Justice Holmes commented, many years ago, with some emphasis when, in a dissenting opinion, he reminded the Court that the Fourteenth Amendment did not enact Mr. Herbert Spencer's *Social Statics*. What emerges from the decisions is, broadly, that the major part of the social legislation enacted in this country since 1906 is held to be beyond the power of the Federal Government; and, if enacted by the separate states, its validity would depend upon its conformity with canons of "reasonableness", the control of which is in the discretion of the Court alone.

In the United States, therefore, the political right of the President and Congress to enact liberal, much less socialist, measures is limited, as it is limited in no other country of the world, by a judicial view of the rights of

250

property which only the haphazard exercise of the appointing power can control. The limitation is a grave one. For it entrusts the interpretation of the claims of property to a legal class whose distinction is mainly won by defending the claims it is appointed to examine. Within the framework of a constitutional system, there is no more striking example on record of the subjection of political to economic power. But the system raises the grave issue of how far, and for how long, a political democracy can survive which is denied the opportunity of affirming its own essence. What, for example, would happen to the American system if dissatisfaction with the existing social order among the masses were to result in the election of a socialist President and a socialist majority in Congress? Could it even attempt the fulfilment of its programme? And if, within the Constitution as the Supreme Court now interprets it, that fulfilment is legally impossible, would not a socialist majority, perhaps, even, a liberal majority, be driven to attempt drastic constitutional revision? And would such drastic revision be peacefully accepted by an economic oligarchy habituated by the Supreme Court to believe in the "unreasonableness" of the new canons it was sought to impose?[21]

American capitalism, as it seems, has entered upon the same phase of critical contraction as European capitalism, with results upon its liberal ideology that are not dissimilar in character. The attempt to satisfy the established expectations of the masses is in contradiction with the claims upon the national dividend made by those who own the instruments of economic power. The authority of democracy to enforce its will, at least so far as its elected representatives express its will, is, at present, thwarted by the Supreme Court; in Europe the same end has been served, more brutally, by the advent of men like Hitler and Mussolini. In each case, what is at stake is essentially a social philosophy, a view of the way in which the national income should be distributed. The President and Congress seek to use the supreme coercive power of the state for their view; but the Constitution stands in their way. In such a dilemma, the stage is set for one of those fundamental conflicts of which no one can predict the outcome.

It is urgent to remember that his dilemma was fully grasped in the making of the American Constitution a hundred and fifty years ago. "The diversity in the faculties of men," wrote Madison in the *Federalist*,[22] "from which the rights of property originate, is not less an insuperable obstacle to a uniformity of interests. The protection of these faculties is the first object of government. From the protection of different and unequal faculties of acquiring property, the possession of different degrees and kinds of property immediately results; and from the influence of these on the sentiments and views of the respective proprietors ensues a division of society into different interests and parties. . . . The most common and durable source of factions has been the various and unequal distribution of property. Those who hold and those who are without property have ever formed distinct interests in society. Those who are creditors, and those who are debtors, fall under a like discrimination. A landed interest, a manufacturing interest, a mercantile interest, a moneyed interest, with many lesser interests, grow up of necessity in civilized nations, and divide them into different classes, actuated by different sentiments and views. The regulation of these various and interfering interests forms the principal task of modern legislation, and involves the spirit of party and faction in the necessary and ordinary operations of the government."

The view taken by Madison was fully shared by such contemporaries as Jefferson, Marshall, and Alexander Hamilton. It was responsible for that interpretation of the Constitution which, under the masterful Chief Justiceship of Marshall, gave to the claims of property its special place in the American system. Their whole purpose was to prevent the invasion of those claims by the masses, and they were successful in that effort. So long as America was expanding, the vast opportunities made possible by the exploitation of its resources, largely concealed the results of the process. To-day, its implications are clear. America is involved in the same difficulties as the economic systems of the old world. The contradictions of the one imperil the liberal ideology in the same way as the contradictions of the other. The period has arrived in American economic evolution when the postulates of its system of ownership are incompatible with political democracy. Either the class-relations of America must be changed, or it will be compelled to change the democratic basis of society in order to realize its fundamental objective of profit.

This incompatibility is not a special insight of our own age. The fear of democracy in the early nineteenth century was, above all, the fear that its extension would destroy the safety of the owning class. It is implied in Macaulay's warning to the House of Commons against the consequences of universal suffrage.[23] It is a central thesis, later, in the analysis of democracy by Bagehot and Sir Henry Maine.[24] In France, it underlies the social philosophy of men like Royer-Collard and Guizot;[25] and its implications were the object of perhaps the most striking and most prophetic of Tocqueville's warnings. It was the reason why Bismarck sought to stay the progress of socialism in Germany by measures like his scheme of social insurance. The existence, in fact, of a small owning class, and a vast body of workers who could live only by the sale of their labour-power was felt to create a disharmony in the state which it would take the utmost ingenuity of governments to overcome. The hatred of the trade unions, the fear, in the 'sixties and 'seventies of the last century, of the First International, the long delay in the postponement of the working-class franchise are all traceable to the realization of this incompatibility. For the greater part of the nineteenth century, and over the greater part of Western Europe, government presented itself to the owning classes as nothing so much as the defensive rampart by which their privileges were protected from invasion by the poor. For them, until the advent of what Dicey calls the "collectivist" age the main function of the state was essentially what Adam Smith, in a possibly incautious moment, had proclaimed it to be. It enabled the rich to sleep peacefully in their beds.

This attitude, it is worth observing, explains the peculiar form that Ricardo gave to classical economics in the nineteenth century. His approach was essentially a simple one, even if his statements gave birth to the most diverse consequences in application. He assumed two fundamental constitutional principles. Private property in land and capital was to be beyond hazard; and free contracts between individuals were to be enforced as sacred. Granted the assumptions, he showed that the class of proprietors would provide a subsistence-wage for the rest of the community if they worked with energy and continuity. The proprietors would themselves invest their surplus income as capital, and this would maintain the nation as a going concern. Ricardo concealed neither from himself nor his contemporaries the immense contrast his principles would produce between rich and poor; nor did he doubt that the contrast would give rise to grave popular discontent. But, living as he did in the age of profound disillusion with the results of the French Revolution, any other prospect would have seemed to him Utopian. Like Austin, like Nassau Senior, like MacCulloch, like Malthus, society seemed to him imprisoned within the postulates he laid down so as to leave it with no practicable alternative.

Why, it may be asked, did not Ricardo's generation recognize the possibilities of the positive state? The answer, I think, is a simple one. It was too near the period of its own victory over the state to see its intervention as other than uncreative. It looked upon state-activity, which meant for it its noxious regulation in industry, persecution, more or less serious, in politics and religion, as an enemy to be defeated rather than as an ally to be invoked. It was still, over two-thirds of Europe, fighting the decaying remnants of feudalism; and, to its eyes, the state was a power which sought to protect the obsolete from the new ideas. There was no civil service, in the modern sense of the term, to show

the capacities of administrative technique. Sir Robert
Peel had not, in Ricardo's day, renovated the police
force. The state seemed the organ which safeguarded
the vast corruption of municipal life, on the one hand,
and such "sinister interests" as the Speenhameland
system, on the other. What passed for socialism in
Ricardo's time—the name itself had not yet been
invented[26]—was rather a *cri de cœur* than a coherent
social doctrine; and, even in the generation after him,
it was too mixed with that romantic utopianism of which
Fourier and the St. Simonians were so amply capable
as to seem worthy of admiration from sober and practical men. It is worth remembering that it was not until
the latest years of his life that John Stuart Mill sufficiently freed himself from the Ricardian prepossessions
of his youth as to find in socialism the only alternative
to a spectacle of misery he no longer found endurable.[27]

The result was that, in the formative years of the
nineteenth century, liberal ideology maximized the
splendour of freedom of contract—by which, in grim
truth, it meant absence of any effective check on capitalist enterprise—and refused, in any profound or coherent
way, to consider the state as a potential source of social
good. No doubt there were protests, from men like
Oastler and Shaftesbury in politics, from men of letters
like Southey and Coleridge and Carlyle. But, harnessed
to scientific discovery, freedom of contract made victories so spectacular that the price of the victory was
forgotten or unconsidered. Nothing shows more clearly
the buoyant attitude of the post-Ricardian economics
that there was, in fact, no practicable alternative to its
postulates than the complete ignoration of socialism

by its votaries until the last third of the nineteenth century. When it could no longer be neglected, it was too late. For the capitalism which had then domesticated itself into every nook and cranny of the social fabric had developed vested interests it could not, in any ultimate sense, venture to sacrifice. It had become, as Mr. Keynes has written,[28] "absolutely irreligious, without internal union, without much public spirit, often, though not always, a mere congeries of possessors and pursuers". As he foresaw during the making of the Peace of Versailles, its basis was built upon a principle (which) "depended on unstable psychological conditions it may be impossible to recreate. It was not natural for a population, of whom so few enjoyed the comforts of life, to accumulate so hugely. The war has disclosed the possibility of consumption to all and the vanity of abstinence to many. Thus the bluff is discovered; the labouring classes may be no longer willing to forgo so largely, and the capitalist classes, no longer confident of the future, may seek to enjoy more fully their liberties of consumption so long as they last, and thus precipitate the hour of their confiscation".[29]

The picture, it may be added, is even more grim than Mr. Keynes has painted it; for, prophetic as was his insight, there were elements in the post-war years of which even he could not foresee the full impact. That the world would treat the Russian Revolution with the same lack of understanding as it displayed to France after 1790; that economic nationalism would re-discover, under the conditions of a world-market, all the oldest fallacies of mercantilist doctrine and then intensify them; that the relation of debtor and creditor states

257

part, it set itself out to break up the great estates without seeing that, thereby, it was calling into existence a class of peasant proprietors without the means of effective economic independence, and without the coherence or the leisure to take an elevated view of public questions. Its whole philosophy was so much the outcome of its concentration upon the powers and the possibilities of the free entrepreneur with whom its rise is associated, that his needs exercised an altogether excessive influence in the making of its principles. Its purposes, no doubt, were always expressed in universal terms; but they were, in practical operation, so much the servant of a single class in the community that it was his wants which predominated in the making of the liberal state.

That state, in fact, by reason of the interests which went to its making, had purposes more limited than the general well-being of the community. Its fundamental aim was to serve the owners of property. It extended, no doubt, the idea of ownership in such fashion as to confer rights in law upon all who exercised effective demand. It destroyed the claim of births to specialize rights to itself. It prevented the owners of land from claiming any special privilege in the state. But its fundamental horizons did not extend beyond that achievement. That is shown by its attitude to the poor. It is shown by its attitude to the rise of trade unionism. It is shown by the long struggle which was necessary—a struggle still far from ended—to establish decent standards of education, of health, of housing and labour protection. For, given the nature of the liberal state, all questions had ultimately to be referred to the essential motive upon

260

which the liberal state was built—the motive of profit-making.

It was in the interest of profit-making that it had broken the discipline of the medieval *Respublica Christiana*. It was to prevent infringement of its opportunities that it established constitutional government. It was for the same end that it accepted, after a century and a half of bitter struggle, the economic necessity of religious toleration. Even when, as with utilitarianism, its votaries accepted a criterion which, at least in theory, would have made possible wider horizons, their employment of its criteria always assumed that the business man is what Macaulay called the middle class—"the natural representative of the human race". As an organized society, the liberal state, at bottom, had no defined objective save the making of wealth, no measurable criterion of function and status save ability to acquire it. If in England, for example, it sent an occasional poet, a rare man of science, an infrequent doctor, to the House of Lords, after the middle of the nineteenth century it doubled the size of that chamber by its elevations of business men to the peerage. And just as it reduced the medieval craftsman to the status of a factory "hand" or a tender of machines, so it assumed that a "successful" man was simply and literally one who had made a fortune. So obsessed had it become by its material achievements that it was unable to think of success in any other terms.

Because it assumed that profit-making was the essential social motive, it was compelled to mould human relationships to its service. That implied the need for a class-state whose supreme coercive power was used to enforce upon all ranks the conditions under which

261

nineteenth century; but, for the most part, they had refused to take those steps by which its acerbities might have been assuaged.

So that when the conflict did come, they were unprepared for its advent. Like their predecessors, they fell into angry panic, and felt with conviction that no price was too high to pay for the retention of their privilege. Even when the price exacted was the destruction of the liberal spirit, they did not hesitate to justify that sacrifice. They called it the common well-being, the maintenance of order, the preservation of civilized life. They refused to admit that the energizing principle of their society was exhausted. They could not believe— even with the evidence dramatically before their eyes— that mankind was ready for a new social order based upon a new relation of man to man. They had in their hands the choice between peace and war. But so completely were they in thrall to the profit-making motive that, in the name of humanity, they blindly chose war, without the vision to perceive that the thing they called humanity was no other than the greed they served. So, as in the sixteenth century, mankind seemed to enter upon a long period of winter. We can comfort ourselves only with the hope that a later generation will detect in its rigours the grim prelude to a brighter spring.

# NOTES

## CHAPTER ONE

[1] On St. Godric. Cf. H. Pirenne, *Les Villes du Moyen Age*, p. 105.

[2] On Jacques Coeur. Cf. R. Bouvier, *Jacques Coeur* (1928).

[3] Max Weber's famous book is the *Protestant Ethic and the Rise of Capitalism*. It has given birth to a vast literature among which the works of Sombart, Troeltsch, Hauser, and Tawney are the most notable. The last-named's *Religion and the Rise of Capitalism* (1928) may fairly be said to be the best general discussion of the subject. Cf. also his introduction to the English translation of Max Weber's essays.

[4] Tawney, *op. cit.*, p. 232.

[5] On Luther's economic ideas. Cf. especially *Werke* (Erlangen edition), Vol. 22, p. 201 and Vol. 23, p. 306. On his economic ideas there are good discussions in Grisar, *Luther* (1912), Vol. III, 579f and Troeltsch, *Social Teaching of the Christian Churches* (1933), Vol. I, Chap. III, Sec. 2.

[6] On Calvin at Geneva, see E. Choisy *L'État Chrétien Calviniste* (1902) ; on Calvin's economic ideas the best discussion is in H. Hauser, *Les Débuts du Capitalisme* (1925), Chapter II.

[7] The letter is printed in his *Epistolae et Responsa* (1575), p. 355 ; and see Sermon XXVIII on usury.

[8] Cf. the remarks of Professor Tawney, *op. cit.*, p. 107.

[9] For St. Antonino, cf. *Opera* (1745), Vol. III, p. 25 and, on his views, C. Hegner, *Die Volkswirtschaftlichen Anschauung Antoninus von Florenz* (1904).

[10] Biel, Sententiae, IV, 15 ; XII, S.

[11] Robert Crowley, *Select Works* (1872), especially *The Way to Wealth* and *Epigrams*.

[12] Lever, *Sermons* (ed. Arber, 1895).

[13] Hugh Latimer, *Sermons* (Everyman's Library).

[14] Seebohm, *Oxford Reformers* (ed. of 1914), pp. 230-47.

[15] *The Praise of Folly* (Holbein ed.), pp. 258-70.

[16] Simon Fish, *A Supplication for the Beggars* (ed. Arber, 1878).

[17] For the King's attitude to Fish's pamphlet cf. Foxe, *Acts and Monuments* (1846), IV, p. 657.

[18] More's answer is his *Supplicacyon of Soulys*.

[19] Strype, *Ecclesiastical Memorials* (1822), Vol. I, pp. 75, 112.

[20] *Calendar of State Papers*, etc. Henry VIII, Vol. VI, No. 1164. Cf. Bayne, *Life of Fisher* (1921), p. 78.

[21] Hall, *History of Henry VIII* (ed. of 1901), II, p. 210.

[58] See Professor A. Wolf's massive *History of Science and Technology in the 16th, 17th and 18th Centuries* (1935) on the succeeding paragraphs. I owe much to this invaluable guide.

[59] This subject has been attractively presented by the Russian savant B. Hessen in his *Economic Roots of Newton's Principa* (1931).

[60] On Giordano Bruno, see G. Gentile, *Giordano Bruno* (1920) ; L. Kuhlenbeck, Giordano Bruno (1913) ; and V. Spampanato, *Sulla Soglia del Secento* (1926).

[61] The strength and weaknesses of Bacon are brought out with great incisiveness by C. D. Broad in his *Philosophy of F. Bacon* (1926).

[62] Cf. R. H. Tawney, *op. cit.* for an account of this literature. There is much interesting material also in A. V. Judges, *The Elizabethan Underworld* (1930) with a valuable introduction ; and in L. B. Wright, *Middleclass Culture in Elizabethan England* (1934) which has an invaluable bibliography.

[63] P. Boissonade, *Le Socialisme d'État* (1927), p. 205.


## CHAPTER TWO

[1] Cf. Charles Davenant's insistence on the value of merchants to the community. *Works* (ed. cf. 1771), I p. 31.

[2] *The Spectator*, No. 1.

[3] *Notes and Observations to the Emperor of Morocco* (1674).

[4] Locke's views on education are conveniently brought together in J. W. Adamson, *The Educational Writings of John Locke* (1922).

[5] *Histoire des Variations* (1688), v, p. 31.

[6] Tawney, *op. cit.*, esp. p. 198f.

[7] The best picture of persecution in this period is still Elie Benoist's *Histoire de la Revocation de l'Edit de Nantes* (1695). On England H. F. Russell Smith, *Religious Liberty under Charles II and James II* (1911) and A. A. Seaton, *Toleration under the later Stuarts* (1911) effectively summarize the literature; but they fail to bring out adequately its relation to economic change. There is some useful material on this in R. L. Poole, *The Huguenots of the Dispersion* (1887).

[8] For Bossuet's realization of Molière's secular outlook cf. *Correspondence* (ed. Levesque and Urbain), vi, p. 256.

[9] On La Bruyère and his world, M. Lange, *La Bruyère, Critique Social* (1909) is indispensable.

[10] *Correspondence*, III, p. 370.

[11] *Projet du Gouvernement* in *Écrits inédits* (ed. Faugére), Vol. IV, p. 191f.

[12] On Claude Joly there is a monograph by J. Brissaud, *Un libéral du XVIIme Siècle* (1896), and a succinct account of the Mazarinades in H. Sée, *Histoire des Idiés Politiques en France au XVIIme Siècle* (1923). Ch. But a much fuller treatment is required.

[13] On the Levellers, the best book is T. C. Pease, *The Leveller Movement* (1916), on the Agrarian Communists that of L. H. Berens, *The Digger Movement* (1906), though his account is vitiated by his own enthusiasm for the single tax; on Baptists and Fifth Monarchy men there is a competent monograph by Louise F. Brown, *Baptists and Fifth Monarchy Men* (1912). But the best introduction to the study of all these movements is Margaret James, *Social Policy and Problems during the Puritan Revolution* (1930). A good account of Leveller disappointment with Cromwell will be found in an unpublished London thesis of A. S. H. Hill, *Moderate Royalist Doctrines in the Seventeenth Century* (1932). Dr. Gooch's *English Democratic Ideas in the Seventeenth Century* (1898) contains a general sketch of the whole movement.

[14] On the attempts to effect this compromise, in which the adaptation of Bodin to an English climate played a large part, see Hoe, *op. cit.* and Hill, *op. cit.*

[15] The debate can be followed in the *Clarke Papers* (ed. Firth), 4 vols. (1894).

[16] On this summary account see Hoe, *op. cit.*, especially for his treatment of Hunton.

[17] *History of Independency* (1661), p. 216.

[18] James, *op. cit.*, p. 3.

[19] Laud, *Works* (1847), I, pp. 28-9.

[20] Cf. R. R. Reid, *The King's Council in the North* (1921), esp. pp. 408f., 412.

[21] Cf. W. R. Scott, *Joint Stock Companies* (1912), I, p. 216f.

[22] Quoted by James, *op. cit.*, p. 80.

[23] Scott, *op. cit.*, I, p. 119f. The quotation is from a speech of Sandys in Parliament.

[24] Lewis Roberts, *The Treasure of Traffic* (1641).

[25] *A letter from the Gentry of Norfolk and Norwich* (1660).

[26] *Good work for a good magistrate* (1660). *The Vanity and Mischief of making earthly Treasures our chief Treasure* (1655).

[27] *The Nobleman's Pattern* (1653).

[28] Cf. Gooch, *op. cit.*, p. 230.

[29] Cf. his *The Parliament's Reformation* (1646); *London's Charity Enlarged* (1650).

[30] *A character of England* (1659) in Harleian Miscellany (1813), X, p. 189.

[59] A pleasant English account of Bayle is in *Howard Robinson, Bayle the Sceptic* (1931), but the work of Delvolvé, *Pierre Bayle* (1906) still remains the best analysis of his ideas.

[60] B. Bekker, *The Significance of Comets* (1683); Góngora, who was a professor in the University of Mexico wrote a warning to the same effect. Within a generation, the fear of comets was dead.

[61] *Wealth of Nations*, Book IV, Introduction.

[62] *England's Interest and Improvement* (1663), p. 18.

[63] Cf. E. Ginzberg, *The House of Adam Smith* (1934), p. 11f. for a useful, and amusing, summary of Adam Smith's suspicion of the business interest.

[64] Cf. Lipson, *op. cit.*, III, p. 25f.

[65] *Ibid.*, p. 328.

[66] *Ibid.*, p. 265.

[67] *Ibid.*, p. 374f.

[68] *Essays*, Of Usury.

[69] *Table-Talk* (ed. Pollock), p. 135.

[70] *Works* (ed. of 1801), V, p. 36.

[71] *Works* (1771), I, pp. 98-9.

[72] *England's Safety in Trades Encrease* (1641).

[73] *A Treatise*, etc. (1671-5).

[74] *A New Discourse of Trade*, p. 157.

[75] *A Discourse of Trade* (1621), p. 54. The quotation in the text is from *England's Treasure by Foreign Trade* (1664), p. 87.

[76] *A Discourse of the Poor*, p. 64 (ed. of 1753).

[77] Unwin, *Industrial Organization*, Appendix A.

[78] *Journals of the House of Commons*, XIII, p. 783.

[79] *A New Discourse of Trade*, p. 3.

[80] *Ibid.*, p. 159.

[81] *A Treatise*, etc. (1671), I, p. 70.

[82] *Britannia Languens* (1680), p. 97.

[83] *A New Discourse of Trade*, p. 182.

[84] Cf. Blackstone's remarks, *Commentaries*, I, p. 415f.

[85] *A Treatise*, etc. (1671), I, p. 74.

[86] *A Discourse of the Poor*, p. 62.

[87] *Works* (1771), II, p. 226.

[88] *Ibid.*, p. 205.

[89] Tawney, *op. cit.*, p. 228f.

[90] *The Tradesman's Calling* (1684), p. 35.

⁹¹ *A Vindication of a Regulated Enclosure* (1656), p. 9.

⁹² On French political thought in the last years of Louis XIV, see, generally, Kingsley Martin, *The French Liberal Tradition in the XVIIIth Century* (1929). On Vauban, the best technical study is F. K. Mann, *Dei Marschall Vauban* (1914), and on Boisguillebert, that of Hazel Roberts, *Boisguillebert* (1935). The latter, though a valuable summary, makes excessive claims for its hero.

⁹³ *Le Parfait Négociant* (1675), Introduction.

⁹⁴ *The Tradesman's Calling* (1684), p. 22. Cf. *The Grand Concern of England* (1673), p. 60; Davenant, *op. cit.*, I, p. 100 ; T. E. Gregory, *The Economics of Employment in England*—I, *Economica*, p. 37f., where the whole subject is brilliantly analysed.

⁹⁵ *Clarke Papers* (1891-4), II, p. 217f.

⁹⁶ *An Arrow against all Tyrants* (1646), p. 4.

⁹⁷ Richard Hardley, *Faults on Both Sides* (1710) in *Somers Tracts*, Vol. XII, p. 679. Nothing is known of the writer. Is his name a pseudonym for Defoe?

⁹⁸ *A True and Impartial Narrative* (1659) in *Somers Tracts*, Vol. VI, p. 477.

⁹⁹ Edward Chamberlayne, *Angliae Notitia* (1669), p. 447.

¹⁰⁰ *England's Monarch*, etc. (1644).

¹⁰¹ *Civil Government*, II, XI, p. 138.

¹⁰² *A Collection for Improvement of Husbandry and Trade*, April 16, 1698.

¹⁰³ *Spectator*, No. 294.

¹⁰⁴ *Absalom and Achitophel* (1681) in *Select Poems* (1901), ed. Christie, p. 104.

¹⁰⁵ *Ibid.*, p. 101.

¹⁰⁶ II, V, p. 50, *Civil Government*.

¹⁰⁷ *Op. cit.*, pp. 682-3.


## CHAPTER THREE

¹ Priestley, indeed, did deny the right of anyone to use property in an anti-social way. His phrase is emphatic. "Every society has a right to apply whatever property is found, or required, within itself to any purposes which the good of society at large really requires." *An Account of a Society for encouraging the Industrious Poor* (1787), p. 13. But this is hardly the general tenour of Priestley's doctrines, and he did not develop its implications beyond an emphasis upon society's duty to the poor.

[54] *De Republica Anglorum* (1583), Book I, Chap. 24, ed. Alston (1906), p. 46.

[55] *Oceana* (1656), p. 147. Cf. Russell Smith, *Harrington and his Oceana* (1914), pp. 46-7.

[56] *The Standard of Equality* (1647). *Harleian Miscellany*, IX, p. 114.

[57] *Clarke Papers*, I, pp. 299-345.

[58] *Wealth of Nations*, Book V, pp. i, ii.

[59] *Works* (Bohn ed.), III, pp. 334-5.

[60] *Annual Register* (1781). Cf. *Select Letters* (World's Classics ed.), p. 213.

[61] *Reflections* in *Works* (1815), Vol. V, p. 93.

[62] This, and the quotations which follow, are all from the *Thoughts on Scarcity*.

[63] *Estimate of the Manners*, etc. (1757), p. 86.

[64] *The Constitution of England* (ed. cf. 1817), p. 243.

[65] *Commentaries* (1765), I, p. 171.

[66] Cf. the standard work of Professor G. S. Veitch, *The Genesis of Parliamentary Reform* (1913).

[67] On Ogilvie and Wallace, cf. my *Locke to Bentham* (1920), Chapter V.

[68] *Works* (1813), Vol. I, pp. 69-70.

[69] B. Disraeli, *Life of Lord G. Bentinck* (ed. Whibley, 1905), p. 127.

[70] *A Treatise on Indigence* (1806), p. 7.

[71] Dr. W. J. Warner has stated the case against this view in his *Wesleyanism in the Industrial Revolution* (1930). Cf., however, J. L. and B. Hammond, *The Town Labourer* (1918), Chapter XIII.

[72] *Eastern Tour* (1771), IV, p. 361.

[73] On French socialism in the eighteenth century, the standard work is that of A. Lichtenberger, *Le Socialisme Français au XVIIIme Siècle* (1895). The reader, however, should note that a good deal of what M. Lichtenberger calls "socialism" is, as with Rousseau or Diderot, little more than deep indignation against injustice and is unrooted in any serious economic analysis.

[74] On Voltaire's social ideas the best discussion in English is Mr. H. N. Brailsford's remarkable *Voltaire* (1935). There is an able French work by G. Pellissier, *Voltaire Philosophe* (1908) which takes a different view from that in the text.

[75] Letter to Frederic the Great, November, 1769. *Oeuvres* (ed. Beuchot), LXVI, p. 76.

[76] *Pensées sur le gouvernement*. *Ibid.*, XXXIX, p. 427.

[77] *Lettre à St. Lambert*, April 7, 1771.

[78] *Siècle de Louis XIV. Oeuvres*, XIX, p. 461.

[79] *Oeuvres*, XL, p. 134.

[80] *Dieu et les Hommes. Oeuvres*, XLVI, p. 102.

[81] Letter of Sept. 11th, 1738.

[82] *Diction. Philos.*, s.v. *Egalite*, XXIX, p. 10.

[83] *Ibid.*, p. 8.

[84] *Siècle de Louis XV*, XXI, p. 431.

[85] *Premier Discours sur l'Homme*, XII, p. 45f.

[86] Cf. his letter to d'Argental, April 27, 1765.

[87] Cf. his letters to d'Alembert, February 4, 1757, and to Frederick, January 5, 1757.

[88] Letter of February 28, 1763.

[89] Letter of April 1, 1766.

[90] Letter to d'Alembert, September 2, 1768.

[91] Letter to Damilaville, April 1, 1766.

[92] *Le Mondain* (1736). On this, and the controversy to which it belongs, see the critical edition by A. Morize, *L'Apologie de Luxe* (1909) and the valuable remarks of Dr. F. B. Kaye in his edition of Mandeville's *Fable of the Bees* (1925).

[93] *Oeuvres* (ed. Assézat et Tourneux 1875-7), III, p. 263 (*Essai sur les règnes de Claude et de Neron*).

[94] *Ibid.*, VI, p. 449 and cf. *Ibid.*, V, p. 298. (*Fragments du portefeuille; Entretien d'un père avec ses enfants*).

[95] Cf. *Oeuvres*, II, p. 419.

[96] *Ibid.*, II, p. 225.

[97] *Ibid.*, II, p. 249.

[98] On Helvetius, cf. Lichtenberger, *Le Socialisme au XVIIIme Siècle*, p. 261f. (1895).

[99] On Holbach, cf. W. H. Wickwar, *The Baron d'Holbach* (1935) for a admirable account of his views.

[100] *Oeuvres de Voltaire* (ed. Beuchot), XLV, p. 123. There is no really adequate book on this remarkable man. The best is Jean Cruppi, *Un Avocat Journaliste* (1894). H. R. G. Greaves has summarized his political ideas. *Economica*, Vol. X, p. 40. See also Lichtenberger, *op. cit.*, pp. 288-305.

[101] On Meslier, cf. the study of his editor in the edition of the *Testament* (1864). There is a short summary of his ideas in Lichtenberger, *op. cit.*, p. 75f.

[102] *Oeuvres* (Beuchot), Vol. XVIII, p. 473.

[18] Cf. the famous dissent of Mr. Justice Holmes in *Lochner* v. *New York*, 198 U.S., 45, 74.

[19] Cf. Mr. Justice Holmes in *Noble State Bank* v. *Haskell*, 219 U.S., 104.

[20] *U.S.* v. *Schecter ut supra at* p. 503.

[21] On the Supreme Court and its functioning there is now a vast literature among which I venture especially to refer to the following : E. S. Corwin, *The Twilight of the Supreme Court* (1935); L. B. Boudin, *Government by Judiciary* (1932), and the remarkable essay of Brooks Adams, *The Theory of Social Revolutions* (1913).

[22] No. 10.

[23] Speech of May 3, 1842.

[24] Cf. his *Works*, Vol. III, p. 109f, and Maine, Popular Government (1885).

[25] Cf. my *Authority in the Modern State* (1919), Chapter IV for Roger-Collard. On Guizot, there is a brilliant essay by E. Faguet in his *Politiques et Moralistes* (1896), Vol. I, p. 307.

[26] It appears first to have been used in 1827 by *The Co-operative Magazine*, cf. M. Beer, *History of British Socialism* (1919), Vol. I, pp. 185-7.

[27] On Mill's conversion to socialism, cf. L. Stephen, *English Utilitarians*, III, pp. 224-37.

[28] *Essays in Persuasion* (1931), p. 306.

[29] *The Economic Consequences of the Peace* (1919), p. 165.

[30] *History of European Liberalism* (Trans. Collingwood, 1927), p. 417.

[31] G. O. Trevelyan, *Life and Letters of Lord Macaulay* (Nelson's ed.), Vol. II, p. 382.

[32] Joseph Dorfman, *Thorstein Veblen and his America* (1935), p. 122f., esp. pp. 133-4.

[33] Pease, *op. cit.*, p. 258.

# Index